IN LABOR

Women and Power

in the Birthplace

By Barbara Katz Rothman

In Labor:
  Women and Power in the Birthplace

Recreating Motherhood:
  Ideology and Technology in a Patriarchal Society

The Tentative Pregnancy:
  Prenatal Diagnosis and the Future of Motherhood

IN LABOR

Women and Power
in the Birthplace

Barbara Katz Rothman

W. W. Norton & Company

New York / London

Portions of the Prologue appeared in *Ms.* magazine, December 1976,
"The Way We Live Now: In Which a Sensible Woman Persuades Her
Doctor, Her Family and Her Friends to Help Her Give Birth at Home."
Portions of Chapter 6 appeared in *Symbolic Interaction* 1 (1978):
124–47, "Childbirth as Negotiated Reality."

Library of Congress Cataloging in Publication Data
Rothman, Barbara Katz.
  In labor. Women and power in the birthplace.
  Includes index.
  1. Maternal health services—United States.
  2. Childbirth—United States. 3. Midwives—United States.
  4. Obstetrics—Social Aspects—United States. I. Title.
RG960.R67 1982   362.1'982   81–19027
                                        AACR2

W. W. Norton & Company, Inc. 500 Fifth Avenue, New York, N.Y. 10110
W. W. Norton & Company Ltd 10 Coptic Street, London WC1A 1PU
2 3 4 5 6 7 8 9 0

IBSN 0–393–30798–0

To the midwives,

daughters of time

Acknowledgments

I have just come to realize that when authors write that "this book could never have been written without the assistance of . . . ," it's probably true. These are the people who have made this book possible:

—The members of my study group, who deciphered reams of rough drafts, criticized constructively and lovingly, and functioned as my toughest critics and staunchest supporters: Betty Leyerle, Meredith Gould, Jean Mussachio, and especially Eileen Moran, who sat down with me and explained what I was doing at a point where I'd lost sight of it;

—The members of my dissertation committee, Rochelle Kern, Irwin Goffman, Peter Conrad, and Edwin Schur; and my mentor and friend Judith Lorber, whose editing and organizing skills were invaluable;

—Rosalyn Weinman Schram, who will listen to any number of pages read over the phone at any time, and who understands perfectly the meaning and place of work in my life;

—Maren Lockwood Carden, Malcolm Spector, Kristen Luker, Karen Reed, and the several anonymous reviewers who have read parts of the manuscript;

—Mary Cunnane, my editor at Norton, who helped me translate from "sociologese" into English without losing the essence of what I want to say, and whose enthusiasm has made the work a pleasure;

—the Scholars Assistance Program of Baruch College of the City University of New York, which paid for typing expenses, and Leon Chazanow, who quickly and capably typed the final draft;

—my family—parents, siblings, and in-laws—who served as a clipping service, as typists, and as baby-sitters, when the occasion arose, and who have always provided loving support.

—And above all, I want to thank my husband, Herschel Rothman, for his typing and proofreading, for his faith in my ability to accomplish whatever I try, and for being the best possible midwife and father for our children.

Introduction to the 1991 Edition

In the decade since I wrote *In Labor,* American society has seen some extraordinary changes in maternity care and the experience of motherhood. The contradictions and puzzlements I describe in this book have grown. While the home-birth movement became more accepted—or at least more *known*—the cesarean epidemic grew so rapidly that even the most mainstream obstetrical caregivers became concerned. Some observers think we may have hit and passed the peak: with some hospitals reporting cesarean rates of upwards of one-third, there may be nowhere to go but down.

We experienced what is called a "malpractice crisis" in obstetrics—and so firmly has the perspective of the obstetricians, rather than that of the patients, dominated the discussion, that the crisis is understood to be one of insurance costs. The very word "malpractice" now conjures up an image not of bad-practice, inappropriate, or harmful medical care, but of overly large insurance payments. Faced with greater economic accountability and liability, many obstetricians held on to the gynecological surgery end of their practices, but gave up the less lucrative obstetrical work.

And in a perhaps not-unrelated phenomenon, midwives have become better known. While most people probably still don't understand just what it is they do, and how they do—or do not—fit into the medical system, more people seem aware that midwives are practicing in and out of American hospitals.

From the woman's perspective as child-bearer, the experience of pregnancy has also changed. The field of prenatal diagnosis has expanded dramatically. Amniocentesis (tests on amniotic fluid drawn from the woman's abdomen during early to mid-pregnancy) has gone from being a rare test for a few women at grave risk of bearing a child with a genetic disorder to being almost a standard part of the pregnancy experience in some circles. Chorionic villus sampling, a prenatal test that can be done earlier in the pregnancy than amniocentesis, has been introduced and met with some enthusiastic acceptance. Maternal blood tests, including Alpha Feta Protein testing (AFP), have become routine. All of this testing of the fetus, in the absence of any treatment possibilities for the conditions which can be diagnosed, has made the potential for abortion very much part of many wanted pregnancies—one of the greatest contradictions of all.

Along with the prenatal tests, fetal imaging techniques have grown; X rays have been replaced by sonograms, which have gone on to become another routine part of prenatal care. Ultrasound, with its surprising clarity of detail, shows us the fetus, but entirely outside of the context of pregnancy. Vulnerable-looking fetuses float in seeming solitude. The image of the fetus has very much entered public consciousness, used in everything from ad campaigns aimed at pregnant women to get them to stop drinking or smoking, to anti-abortion literature and placards picketing outside of clinics, to car ads, urging us to choose a safer car. And a sonogram is often pasted as the first picture in a baby's photo album.

There's an increasing fascination with the fetus, and an increasing fascination with babies. Babies became, in the 1980s, a hot-ticket item. The baby-boomers seem to have—a bit late—discovered parenthood. And we made it the center of the universe, just as we had done when we discovered childhood, adolescence, college, and adulthood. And once again, American marketing responded in every possible area. The fertility, and would-be fertility, of the baby-boomers has made for big business in infertility services, black and gray market adoptions, day care, the fashion industry, baby food, and baby toys. Even Hollywood discovered and packaged Parenthood.

The economic dislocations of the eighties have also hit motherhood in more distressing ways. More mothers of infants are employed outside the home than ever before, more in fact than not employed. Some are in jobs they value, care about, work at by choice. But most are faced with hard choices: leaving the baby all day in less-than-ideal settings, or not making the rent, the mortgage, the car payments. Day care has become big business, and big business discovered day care.

Infertility treatments have expanded in ways few would have guessed possible. From the first "test tube baby" through headline after headline on medical breakthroughs and "new hope for the childless," treatment after treatment has been developed, and sold. In vitro fertilization clinics have opened up all over the United States. Half of them have never produced a baby, and about 90 percent of the women going through IVF programs will never give birth to a live baby. But the image of high-tech baby making is very much with us. In fact, the "production" of babies came to be seen so much as just that, a "production" process, that "surrogacy" became a social reality.

It's been, all in all, quite a decade. Where the mother and baby imagery of earlier times may have been the Madonna and child, or even Lucy Ricardo and Little Ricky, the images the eighties brought us were Mother Hale of Harlem and her abandoned "crack babies," and Mary Beth Whitehead and her hotly contested Baby M.

So what does it mean, then, to turn to the arguments, the passions, the concerns of the home-birth movement of the 1970s with the world-weary wisdom of the 1990s? Some of the specific practices addressed in this book have been improved. Obstetricians are no longer ordering extreme weight-gain limitations; mothers and babies are now allowed more time together after birth; pediatricians are no longer prescribing the early introduction of solids. But the issues that we face are not so altogether different. Much more basic than any given practice is the underlying ideology, the approach. The control issues have not budged: doctors still see themselves as ordering, allowing, and prescribing the care of mothers and babies. Women still too often see themselves as subject to these orders, permissions, and prescriptions.

And at the larger level, the political issues too remain the same: midwives are still battling, state by state, for the right to practice—to practice not medicine, but *midwifery*. In some states they are losing ground and in some gaining. One of the more hopeful signs is their own coming together. The Midwives Alliance of North American (MANA) was organized in the early 1980s to represent ALL American midwives, those in and out of hopsitals, in and out of nursing. By coming together to represent themselves, midwives are doing the best thing to help birthing women.

This book was originally written in a spirit of cautious— very, very cautious—optimism. Things were bad and maybe getting worse, but there was hope. There was an active home-birth movement, an active women's health movement, an active feminist movement. We talked about re- claiming birth, taking our bodies back.

And now, in the 1990s, I offer it to you again, with both the caution and the optimism. Things are worse, and probably getting worse yet. But times of crisis—the crisis in health care, the crisis in the family, the crisis in the economy—can also be times of change for the better.

Motherhood can bring with it enormous energy. Mothers and midwives of the 1990s have the strength and the wisdom of the home-birth movement of the '70s and '80s to draw upon, just as we who made up that movement drew upon the women of the natural childbirth movement that preceded us.

As we grapple with the problems of the last decade, and consider the problems of the coming century, I rededicate this book to the midwives, and especially to the women of MANA.

Barbara Katz Rothman
April 1991

Contents

Part III/Beyond Obstetrics:

Midwives in Transition

Prologue

In 1973, when I became pregnant for the first time, I thought that the profession of medicine and its hospitals were geared to meeting the physical-health aspects of maternity care. I assumed that hospitals were the safest place for giving birth, but that there were attendant costs to having that safety: notably, a loss of personal autonomy for the birthing woman, and the absence of a loving and warm atmosphere. I divided maternity care into two categories: physical care, which I thought was best obtained in a hospital under careful medical supervision; and socio-emotional support, which was best provided in one's own home by family and friends. That left two choices for optimal care: bringing personal autonomy and social support into the hospital, or bringing safety home. As a sociologist, I thought the former was impossible. I set about researching the latter.

I learned that hospitals have never been demonstrated to

be the safest place for a woman to give birth. I learned that hospitals pose unique dangers for birthing women and their babies, including the overuse of medication, higher risk of infection, and numerous obstetrical interferences in the physiological process of birth. I began thinking about the medical management of maternity care in terms of its social and political history, its cultural context.

I think I first got the idea of giving birth at home in a college health course. I saw two childbirth films. One was a Lamaze film with everybody running around and carrying on in French at a woman all draped in white on a table. The other was a film of a down-South black midwife at work. The black woman giving birth did not know anything about exercises for tensing her left foot and relaxing her right hand at the same time, or panting in rhythm, or any of the other Lamaze techniques. And she was definitely feeling pain sometimes. But she was in her bedroom with one nice woman she knew, and sometimes they chatted and sometimes not, and the midwife dealt with her as an entire person: helping her get out of her nightgown when she was hot, wiping her face, and delivering her baby. Her husband came in sometimes, but it was clearly women's territory only. You could see the sun coming up through the windows, and hear the other children waking up—it was all of a piece.

I made dozens of phone calls to find one obstetrician who would even talk to me about a home birth. She wasn't about to commit herself to the idea and said if she were giving birth she'd go to the hospital. But at least she would discuss it with me.

My husband, Hesch, and I went to see her. She suggested that we consider using the nurse-midwives then in practice at the hospital where she was affiliated. No, I said, in words that will embarrass me forever: while it was very important to me to have a woman birth attendant, I had "nothing against education"—I thought a woman obstetrician, with her extra years of training, would be more qualified than a midwife. Forgive me, my midwife friends.

We continued talking in her office and found ourselves in a strange kind of bargaining position. She promised me a "relaxed hospital environment," no prep (enema and shave), and that I could go home as soon after the delivery as I wanted to—measured in hours, not days. All I had to do was go to the hospital. That took the wind out of my sails. I still didn't want to go to the hospital, but somehow had to think through more carefully why not.

First off, I couldn't imagine what a "relaxed hospital environment" was supposed to mean. It sounded like that George Carlin comedy routine about inherent contradictions: jumbo shrimp, military intelligence, and so on. Then I decided I needed to know more about birth. I picked up a book on maternity nursing written for nurses, not one of those pretty little things written for the mother-to-be. I went on to some obstetrical texts. I thought I'd read about all the things that can go wrong and scare myself out of the whole idea. But the more I read, the less I wanted to go to the hospital.

I did not want my consciousness raised on the delivery table. I was a feminist and I was pregnant. Those terms should not be mutually exclusive, but in 1973 it often felt as though they were. There had to be a way of having a baby with dignity and joy—as a feminist, not in spite of being a feminist.

I read about "natural childbirth." I started with the classic: *Thank You, Dr. Lamaze.* From other, more recent books, I gathered that if you were a very good girl and you showed how cooperative you were being, the nurses probably wouldn't strap your hands down. If you were very polite and rational with your doctor, then maybe you wouldn't be anesthetized when you didn't want to be. Terrific, I thought. A woman doesn't have enough to handle in labor—she has to be careful not to hurt the doctor's feelings! It seemed to me that she should be able to make decisions when at her best and be able to expect that nobody would double-cross her when she was defenseless.

Sound paranoid? I was starting to feel it. We've been raised to think of hospitals as not just the best but the only place for giving birth—and we have lost sight of the fact that hospitals are a fairly recent invention which, like all institutions, are run more for the convenience of the staff than for those they ostensibly service. But if I reminded friends or acquaintances of that, they told me, "We all have our hang-ups."

I found I was getting basically two kinds of responses to the idea of having the baby at home, once people began to believe I meant it. It was 1973 and New York, and *nobody* had births at home, it seemed, except maybe some people in communes in California—certainly not Ph.D. students married to computer programmers and living in Flatbush. But an astonishing number of women that I talked to, of all ages, said that they had thought of it and had been talked out of it. They'd been reasonable, and most expected me to be reasonable eventually also.

The second response was that it wasn't safe. When I, ingenuously, asked why, I got the strangest answers. Some women told me how they, or their mother or aunt or friend, would have died if she hadn't been in a hospital. And when I again asked why, it always turned out not to be so simple. Some were in labor for frighteningly long times, and needed medical assistance, even a cesarean. Long labors, by definition, are not sudden medical emergencies. There is lots of time, more than enough time to move to a hospital. Some had breech births or Rh problems—but those things you know about weeks ahead of time. When you have good reason to expect a problem, then, I figured, you *do* go to a hospital.

But the best story came from the friend who told me that her mother would have died without emergency care. Why? The hospital had given her the wrong drug and if she hadn't been in a hospital they couldn't have corrected the error!

Talking to others was not enough. I spent a lot of time soul searching. Perhaps it meant so much to me not to go to the hospital because my father had died in one when I was a child. But there was much more to it than that. That bit of my own biography did explain why for once in my life I had no mixed feelings at all on a subject. Friends who followed my intellectual home-birth argument point by point asked, "But wouldn't you just *feel* safer in a hospital?" Hell, no.

What were the other reasons? It had something very basic to do with control, power, and authority. At home, I would have them; in the hospital they would be handed over to the institution. I read arguments for home rather than hospital birth that spoke about privacy. For me it was less a question of privacy and more a question of authority. At home, nobody was coming in the door whom I did not choose to have come in. One doctor alone or a dozen assistants—they would all be there because I personally hired them, and I personally could tell any one of them to leave. I was willing to delegate control over my body to the doctor—more so then, in fact, than I ever would now—but it was only because I expected her to be making her decisions on the basis of what I thought of as "medical expertise," and not on the basis of "them's the rules," or of whatever is most convenient in an institution that's simultaneously processing umpty-seven baby-making women.

Besides the authority/control issue, there were other reasons. I was having a baby, after all, and not an appendectomy. It's a condition of healthiness, not of illness. At home I would be simply having a baby. At the hospital? You do not put someone in a hospital gown, place her on a hospital table under hospital lights, and affix little bracelets to her arm so that you can always tell whose baby is whose, and not create the image of "patient." A woman cannot view herself as healthy while all the external cues proclaim illness. At home I would go into labor and call the doctor, and eventually she would show up and eventually the baby would be born, and eventually the doctor would leave, and I'd be there, with the baby outside of me instead of inside. There would be a continuum, and I would always be me, my own self in charge of my own self. The hospital alternative meant that first I would go into labor and then we'd have to decide when it was "serious" enough for me to be driven to the hospital, to become a patient. From there on, I'd be processed through —in clearly demarcated stages—labor room, delivery room, wherever one goes there after, and then back home. So, it was partly a question of how the situation is defined, and again partly a question of control over self and situation.

But what about safety? How would I feel if something went wrong? There was something very interesting that I realized I had to deal with. Anything that went wrong was going to be my fault if I did it at home, or at least was going to be perceived as my fault. I had to take on that responsibility personally—I couldn't even share it with Hesch. It was my problem. If the child was born without arms or something, somehow it was going to be my fault for having had it at home. Logic or no, that was going to be in people's minds, and maybe even in the back of my mind.

It's a tricky question, maybe best dealt with through the sociology of knowledge, as to what we define as risk-taking behavior, and what as normal, acceptable behavior. One of the many doctors I talked to about home birth assured me that I would not have to go to the hospital until I was pretty far along in labor. And the one I was seeing had said that I could go home right after the birth if it was important to me.

Now, things *do* sometimes go wrong early in labor, babies *do* sometimes die when they're two days old, women *do* sometimes hemorrhage twelve hours later—but those were acceptable risks, risks the doctors were willing to take. So it was never a question of risk or no risk, but of *which* risks.

That was never so clear to me as when I saw women who would never subject their babies to the risk of home birth leaving the hospital to drive home, without seat belts, holding their babies loose in their arms in the front seats of Volkswagens. I, on the other hand, with fears of a baby smashed on the windshield in a sudden stop, went out and purchased the best infant car seat made and bolted it into place before the baby was even born, so that if we had to transfer it to a hospital we would have safe transportation.

There were some risks I knew I could take that were totally acceptable socially. I was not held responsible, for example, for how I chose a doctor. Had I taken just the local doctor because I hated traveling on subways, that would have been considered legitimate. And if he/she screwed up, that wouldn't have been my fault. Back in 1973 I could still ask to be drugged out of it completely, and would not have been held socially accountable for whatever risks that entailed. A friend of mine went to a doctor I know to be something of an idiot and asked that she be knocked out when she got to the hospital and not brought to until they had a clean, preferably diapered, baby to show her. And she got that. And that was socially acceptable. A friend's mother took diet pills all through her pregnancy twenty years ago because the doctor prescribed them. The pills have since been taken off the market for everybody, not just pregnant people. A friend of my mother's was given diethylstilbestrol (DES) to prevent miscarriages; her daughter by that pregnancy now waits to see if she will develop cancer. But none of these women are responsible, because they followed the doctor's orders. The moral was that the more control I gave up, the more responsibility I gave up for the consequences, and the more socially acceptable my behavior would be.

Appeals to the doctor about the beauty of the birth experience did not impress her. I'm not even sure that I myself was convinced on that level. But the issues of autonomy and control were good, solid, feminist issues she could relate to —it was, after all, the basic issue of a woman's right to control her body. She agreed because she was a good feminist. So, we were on.

Around three-thirty on a Tuesday morning, the week before my due date, I woke to find myself in labor. It must be awkward and make a person feel silly to go rushing off to the hospital on a "false alarm," but to bring the doctor to me if I wasn't really in labor was unthinkable. So I just stayed in bed, read the *Times,* polished my nails, made a list of things to get done, and sometimes tried to time the contractions. But I kept getting up to go to the bathroom and losing track.

By eight-thirty I decided it was time to get mobilized. I woke up Hesch and handed him the watch and the list (things like "make sure we have ice cubes, clean the bathroom, make the bed, sweep"—baby or no baby, we had company coming!). I left a message with the doctor's answering service that I was almost certainly in labor and called my mother and asked her to drop off the cushions she was recovering for my big platform rocker. She and my sister visited for a few minutes on their way to work.

I sat in my rocking chair while Hesch cleaned up. We found pretty music on the radio, and chatted and timed contractions. On Hesch's list (we are crackerjack list makers) he noted that at eleven o'clock I was looking happy and self-satisfied, beginning to feel an outward, downward thrust to the contractions. But by eleven-thirty he noted that I was looking decidedly uncomfortable.

The doctor had returned our call and told Hesch to remind me that it was really going to hurt. It helps us to understand what is going on anatomically when we speak of "contractions" rather than "pains"; but the contractions of labor are painful, and I guess it's easier to deal with them if your expectations are realistic. So I wasn't frightened or worried, and knew perfectly well what was happening, and started using the breathing techniques I had been taught. By then my mother had left work and was sitting in my room looking at me—compassionately. I didn't think I would be able to deal with it all in a grown-up, sensible way with her there, but would revert to being a little girl with a bellyache who wanted her mommy to make it all go away. So, my mother left me alone with Hesch.

If I had been going to the hospital, that is probably the point at which we'd have gone. Contractions were strong and occurring every three minutes. I was still sitting in my chair, with Hesch sitting opposite me and very gently rubbing my belly, when the doctor arrived, at around two o'-clock. By then we had given up timing, no longer able to sort out the pain into separate contractions. The doctor timed the contractions at two and a half minutes, with ten-second rests, and told me I could expect a "horrendous but short" labor. She also asked if I drank, and when I said yes, had my mother send up some gin. She examined me again about an hour later, and thought maybe it wasn't going to be such a short labor after all, and decided to go to the drugstore for Demerol. I never had to use it. By the time she got back I was making real progress.

All afternoon our family had been arriving, one by one. My mother sat tensed at the bottom of the stairs while Hesch's mother compulsively cooked chickens. Father and siblings sat around. When I cried out during a particularly painful examination, the doctor went out afterward to explain to them that I was okay—and came back with the message that they were all bearing up well.

Sometime after four o'clock, I entered the phase of labor called transition, in which the last few centimeters of dilatation takes place, the cervix opening up completely to let the baby come through. Birth-preparation classes warn that it is the most difficult stage, but for me it was an incredible relief. The contractions may have been more painful—I really don't know— but they started sorting themselves out into separate entities, maybe ninety seconds on and sixty off. Again, I'm not sure. But they did have peaks and, blessed be, valleys. Hesch (who never moved from his seat opposite me) suggested I deal with the contractions by using two pants and a blow. That was the smartest thing I've ever heard in my life. I was impressed by how clever and insightful he was—it sounds silly, but that's just the way I felt: how clever an idea. That, I gather, is what they mean when they say you need strong direction during labor.

I'd read that women get a "second wind" once they're fully dilated and ready to begin pushing the baby out, and it was certainly true for me. Pushing was the strangest, and in some ways the nicest, sensation I've ever had. I could actually feel the shape of the baby, feel myself sitting on the head as it moved down. The doctor said I looked comfortable enough on the chair, and I didn't have to get to the bed if I didn't want to. At the time, the thought of moving, especially from a good, comfortable, well-supported seated position, to flat-out on a bed, seemed ridiculous. So there I was, on my rocking chair, with my feet up on two little kitchen chairs, with Hesch on one side and the doctor on the other, and pushing like crazy. It was like moving a grand piano across a room: that hard, but that satisfying, to feel it moving along.

The doctor asked if there was a mirror around. I said "Skip

it," I didn't really want one. Hesch read my mind and said that there wasn't a lot of blood and that I looked fine, and sent down for a mirror.

Eventually the doctor said I could have the baby in two pushes with an episiotomy (the small incision to widen the birth outlet), or maybe ten pushes without. I said no thanks. I thought, hell, I still wasn't sure it was happening; maybe I could accept the reality of it given the few extra minutes. I really needed the time to prepare myself, as with the last-second cramming before the exam booklets are passed out.

Hesch said my mother wanted to come in. For a moment, I wanted to say no but realized that was just too selfish, that I was fine now. I said to send her in. My mother-in-law came in shortly afterward. It didn't take me ten pushes, just five. I heard noises coming out of my throat that I couldn't believe —like the soundtrack of a horror movie, but I had no time to laugh. And then I felt myself sitting on the head, felt myself opening, felt the head push through: a beautiful, total sense of opening and roundness. The shoulders seemed big, and the shape was less comfortable than the symmetry of the head. And then—slurp, wriggling, warmth, wetness, and there was a baby. He was up in the air, upside down, the doctor holding him over me. The longest few seconds in the world passed, and then this gray-blue thing became alive and pink and breathing. The doctor handed him to my mother. I kept reaching out for him, but my mother was too dazed to move. I watched the cord being clamped and cut, and my baby, my son, Danny, was suckling by the time the placenta was out.

After maybe five minutes I stood and spilled blood all over the floor, and my mother walked me to the shower. As much as I had needed Hesch's support before, I felt the need for mothering then. I got the shakes—part physical, part emotional reaction, I guess. She bundled me up so that I was warm and helped me put on a sanitary napkin—it was like the first time I got my period and was initiated into all the mysteries. Once I was changed and back into the rocker, and Hesch and his mother had cleaned up the blood that had spurted from the cord, the whole world was in my room. Brothers and sisters and parents; suddenly, aunts and uncles and grandparents. They brought with them champagne and flowers and a teddy bear and a silver spoon, and looks of wonderment and love. It was the best birthday party I had ever been to. I had another gin and tonic and a chocolate malted and champagne all at once, while everybody ate dinner. We'd been smelling my mother-in-law's garlicky chickens for hours.

As much as I had wanted it, I don't think even I had understood how good it can be to have a baby at home. I never really was a "patient." I wasn't in bed; I had my contact lenses in throughout (only the myopic can understand what it means to remain in touch with the world visually); I gave birth, freely and consciously—I was not *delivered.* And my baby and I were surrounded by love, not efficiency. Images pass through my mind—my mother-in-law helping me get my breast out of my nightgown and to Danny; my brother carrying a big plastic garbage bag down from the bedroom, singing "afterbirth" to the tune of "Over There"; my mother and Hesch trying to clean up the meconium (the baby's first bowel movement) in the middle of the night without waking me. I am sure there are more efficient ways to do these things —but who needs them?

The pediatrician came the next day to examine the baby. She kept telling us we were crazy. The baby looked big and healthy (he was eight pounds, five ounces, and had been a nine-plus on the Apgar newborn scale of ten), and I looked good, dressed and walking around, up and down stairs; but still we were crazy.

Once that was over, my sociological interest remained. I'd done what I did for ultimately personal reasons, to meet my own needs and because of who I was. But I was, and am, many things, including a sociologist. I am an academic, a social scientist, someone who is trained in the examination of data and the development of theory from data. In my personal research I had begun to uncover a fascinating lode of data. As a social scientist I was eager to go back and mine it. Some basic questions of sociology were involved, as I saw it: how do people know what they know; how do social groups —movements like the home-birth movement or established professions like obstetrics—arise, gain power, maintain themselves? I read extensively in the area of medical sociology. Specifically, I began thinking about, researching, and writing about women's health care, and the way medicine managed it. I began to look for alternative ways in which knowledge about women's health was being constructed, particularly knowledge about pregnancy, childbirth, and lactation. I looked into the beginning home-birth movement. By contrast with my original idea that home birth was for socio-emotional reasons, and hospitals for safety, I heard home-birth advocates offering arguments stressing safety and the physical health and well-being of mothers and babies. It was not just being more "humane" or more concerned with emotional needs that differentiated the home-birth movement from modern American obstetrics: these people were seeing things in really different ways. Both groups were taking the same objects—fetus, milk, placenta, term—and forming different ideas about them. They responded differently because they saw it all differently.

It seemed to me that there were two fundamentally different models being used. One was the medical model. Arising out of a male profession in a patriarchal society, that model reflected a man's-eye view of women's bodies. It also reflected the technological orientation of modern, industrial society. I read through the major American obstetrical textbooks and journals of the 1970s especially, and tried to piece together what their underlying beliefs, assumptions, and values were—how they saw pregnant, birthing, and lactating women. It became clear to me that within the medical model the body is seen as a machine, and the male body is taken as a norm. Pregnancy and birth are at best complications, stresses on the system. At worst, they are diseaselike states. In either case, in that model, they need treatment, medical management.

How else could we see it? What other model was available? I read the literature of the home-birth movement, went to conferences, talked to people like me who were "on the lunatic fringe"—who wanted not just prettier or more humane births but a whole different approach.

Finding that other approach was not like researching the medical model, where all the information is gathered in one library, and one has only to read and then to analyze. Here I had to piece together what was being said. I found similar ideas in the writings of eighteenth-century midwives, and being voiced by contemporary feminist activists, by conservative, often religious mothers of large families, and by lay midwives living on communes. The essence of what they were saying came across to me as very different from the medical model: they took women as their norm, and focused and centered on women; and they saw our reproductive processes in a holistic, naturalistic way. They believed that women's bodies are meant to bear children—not necessarily that we should, or have to, but that when we do it, we are no more "stressing" the system than we are when we are digesting a nutritious meal.

I thought about calling this approach the "alternative model," but that seemed unfair. It was buying in to the idea of the medical approach as the basic or standard. And this "alternative" was there first. I considered calling it a "home-birth model," but that was too restricting. Doctors can bring the medical model right into the home. I saw that for myself when my obstetrician handed my son to my mother, who was standing behind her, where a nurse would be, and not to me, right in front of her and reaching out. I saw it when she offered me Demerol and alcohol for pain relief, and when she quickly and efficiently clamped the cord and extracted the placenta almost at once. And a midwife can bring much of the alternative model into the hospital. One nurse-midwife described holding her foot against a labor-room door to keep it shut and give the mother five minutes of privacy in order to get the baby out herself before the residents took over.

I have decided to call this other, nonmedical approach the "midwifery model," out of respect for our foremothers who were midwives, and to honor the work of our sisters who are now midwives. These midwives, the daughters of time, have much to teach us about birth, babies, our bodies, and our lives.

In Part I of this book I will discuss the politics of maternity care: who controls birth and where that control came from. There are a number of interest groups involved in American maternity care, including the professionals: obstetricians, nurse-midwives, lay-midwives, neonatologists, and others; and consumer groups of all kinds. Part II will lay out the two models of maternity care in America as they work in practice —what pregnancy, birth, and early parenting mean within the medical model and within the midwifery model. Part III is about a group of women I admire enormously, women who are part of both worlds: medically trained certified nurse-midwives who have become active in the home-birth movement. They were trained in hospitals, as nurses, to see birth essentially as the medical model presents it; but they have moved, or are moving, beyond that, beyond obstetrics and into midwifery.

It is with respect and appreciation that I dedicate this book to them.

PART I

The Politics of
Maternity Care

1

Birthing Babies or Delivering Neonates: Two Perspectives on Childbirth

Jimmy Carter was the first president of the United States to have been born in a hospital. Your grandparents, whether or not they were born in the United States, were probably born at home. If you are young, you may have to go back to your great grandparents to find home births. If you are older, or from a poorer family, or from more recent immigrants, your parents or you yourself may have been born at home. The transition from almost all births taking place at home to almost all births taking place in the hospital took just over two generations. In those two generations, birth changed from being an event in the life of a family to being a medical procedure. New mothers became patients, and the care of newborns became a thriving medical specialty.

The early hospitalization and medicalization of childbirth was extreme. Pregnant women were indeed treated as sick, and childbirth became very much a surgical procedure. General anesthesia was the norm. The delivery room was an operating room and the obstetrician was a surgeon.

The first generation of women thus treated, those giving birth from the 1920s through the 1950s, seem to have welcomed some of the changes. In an era of large families the two weeks of hospitalization may have been a luxury, a relief from the demands of many small children and the running of a household. And the modern surgical competence of the doctor contrasted with the traditional skills of the midwife, just as the clinical, gleaming white porcelain kitchen of the 1930s contrasted with the traditional farm kitchen.

By the 1950s, women began to sense that something was amiss. In the era of the feminine mystique, when mothering was considered a woman's greatest skill, childbirth and proper baby care were turned over to male authorities. The feminine fulfillment women sought from motherhood was thwarted at every turn: by the drugs they were given; by the leather straps holding them down to labor beds and delivery tables; by the hours they spent sterilizing baby bottles while the baby cried, waiting for the medically prescribed feeding time.

The "natural" childbirth movement developed as a reform movement to do away with the excesses of medical management. The movement began in the United States over forty years ago with the publication of Grantly Dick-Read's *Childbirth without Fear,* but did not come of age until the 1950s and the introduction of the Lamaze technique of "childbirth without pain." Women were encouraged to remain awake and aware, working along with their doctors in the delivery of their babies. Doctors remained in charge (both Dick-Read and Lamaze were obstetricians), but women could watch, could help, could be part of their labors and deliveries. By the 1970s fathers, too, were allowed to be there in the labor and the delivery rooms, watching masked and gowned doctors holding up their newly born babies.

Far from being a novelty, the idea of a "natural" birth has become not only accepted but expected, certainly for middle-class, educated mothers. The Lamaze classes and breathing exercises have entered into the popular image of pregnancy and childbirth as surely as have the pickles and the boiling water of yesteryear.

Even as childbirth without fear, childbirth awake and aware, became a valued accomplishment, however, the technology of childbirth grew ever more complex. Today's pregnant woman faces, along with her natural-childbirth classes, amniocentesis, ultrasound diagnosis, ultrasound monitoring, and in many hospitals, upwards of a one-in-four chance of having a cesarean section. Her childbirth classes will in fact "prepare" her for those procedures and eventualities. The goal of a "natural" childbirth has been replaced by the goal of a "prepared" childbirth.

What we are seeing is more than the cooption of a reform. It is one of the several fundamental contradictions surrounding pregnancy and birth in America today. On the one hand, pregnancy and birth are increasingly coming under technological control: women who were unable to conceive are being made pregnant; genetic diseases are diagnosed prenatally; fetal monitoring samples the very blood of the unborn. But even as medical control of pregnancy increases, we are turning away from the idea of pregnancy as a disease. Pregnant women, we believe, are not to be "confined" or treated as sick. Childbirth is healthy and normal. Yet surgical intervention increases: a puzzlement.

There are other contradictions. A home-birth movement is growing in the United States today—more and more women are *choosing* to birth at home. Some are attended by midwives, some by physicians; and some choose or are forced to be unattended by any trained practitioner. Who belongs to this home-birth movement? Some of the women come from the feminist health movement, women who have been fighting for abortion rights and see birth as another issue in reproductive freedom. A very different group sees the husband/father as having a right to be with his wife, and birth as belonging in his territory. And still others, such as a home-birth group in Kansas, see birth as "bringing genuine fulfillment to husband and wife," concluding that "birth belongs in the bedroom." Feminists, traditionalists, spiritualists, and sensualists: a puzzlement.

Why all these strange coalitions and contradictions? Why the juxtaposition of the high technology of birth with a back-to-nature approach? Why does our society produce "family-centered cesarean birth experiences"; husbands wearing "coach" T-shirts as their wives labor; a Tennessee commune that trains midwives and will welcome any woman to come to them and leave her baby rather than abort; and feminists fighting for abortion and for home birth? Why do we have women being threatened with arrest for child abuse as they give birth at home? Why do we welcome the return of the midwife and at the same time rush to explain how the new midwife is different from the "granny"? Why do the same hospitals that have the highest cesarean-section rates open "birthing rooms"? Why do we talk about pregnancy as being *not* a disease, and then define all pregnancies as either "high risk" or "low risk"?

Understanding these situations requires placing them in the larger context in which they occur. When we try to unravel the puzzlements surrounding our society's management of maternity care, we must consider the meaning of pregnancy, of birth, and even of parenthood itself. And when we look at the use and misuse of technology in maternity care, we must consider the *meanings* we attach to the human body, as machine, as organism, and as the embodiment of personhood.

Pregnancy and birth have different meanings to different people. What, after all, is a pregnancy? Pregnancy is, sometimes, a contraceptive failure, a side effect of a not very reliable method of birth control. Pregnancy is also the effect of a successful treatment for infertility. Pregnancy is a condition of a woman's body, to be distinguished from ovulation, menstruation, and menopause. Pregnancy is the presence of a man's baby in a woman, as when a man wants a woman to bear him a son to carry on his name. The meaning of pregnancy it seems, like everything else, is in the eye of the beholder.

The foremost "beholder" of pregnancy in America today is the obstetrician. The obstetrical perspective on pregnancy and birth is held to be not just one way of looking at it, but to be the truth, the facts, science: other societies may have beliefs about pregnancy, but we believe our medicine has the *facts*. But obstetrical knowledge, like all knowledge, comes from *somewhere:* it has a social, historical, and political context. Medicine does not exist as "pure," free of culture or free of ideology. The context in which medical knowledge develops and is used shapes that knowledge. Doctors see pregnancy, childbirth, and the entire reproductive cycle from their perspective. This book examines that perspective and compares it with the perspective being developed by home-birth advocates and lay midwives. These two perspectives are very different: in some ways they are diametrically opposed. Pieces of both perspectives, or the models they use in managing maternity, have come into popular American culture. It is in the conflict between these two perspectives that the contradictions surrounding birth in America arise.

The "medical model" shows us pregnancy and birth through the perspective of technological society, and from

[33]

men's eyes. Birthing women are thus objects upon whom certain procedures must be done. The alternative model, curently being developed by the home-birth movement, which I will call the "midwifery model," combines elements of the holistic-health, back-to-nature movement. Equally important, it is a woman's perspective on birth, in which women are the subjects, the doers, the givers of birth. It is the medical model which is dominant in this society, and I begin by looking carefully at how that model is constructed, and how it affects birthing women and their children.

The primary characteristic of the modern medical model of health and illness in general is that it is based on the ideology of technology, that appropriate to the technological society, with its values of efficiency and rationality, practical organization, systematizing, and controlling. The application of a technological model to the human body can be traced back to René Descartes's concept of mind-body dualism. For Descartes, the body was a machine, the structure and operation of which fell within the province of human knowledge, as distinguished from the mind, which God alone could know. Even though the Hippocratic principles state that the mind and body should be considered together, most physicians, whatever their philosophical views on the nature of the mind, behave in practice as if they were still Cartesian dualists.[1] The Cartesian model of the body as a machine operates to make the physician a technician, or mechanic. The body breaks down and needs repair; it can be repaired in the hospital as a car is in the shop; once "fixed," a person can be returned to the community. The earliest models in medicine were largely mechanical; later models worked more with chemistry, and newer, more sophisticated medical writing describes computerlike programming, but the basic point remains the same. Problems in the body are technical problems requiring technical solutions, whether it is a mechanical repair, a chemical rebalancing, or a "debugging" of the system.

In contrast to the mind-body dualism of the medical model, the midwifery model presents an integrated or holistic approach. Consider this statement from the book *Spiritual Midwifery*, by midwife members of a commune in Tennessee:

> Since body and mind are one, sometimes you can fix the mind by working on the body, and you can fix the body by working on the mind.[2]

The book is filled with "amazing birthing tales," stories of births at which this belief is put into practice. Uterine contractions to these midwives are "rushes": "a whole lot of energy flowing up your neck and into your head. It leaves you feeling expansive and stoned if you don't fight it."[3] The entire chapter on labor in *Obstetric-Gynecologic Terminology*,[4] on the other hand, has not a word about what labor feels like, not a word to indicate that there is a mind connected to the pelvis.

This approach to the body as a machine, found in the medical model, both comes from technical/industrial society and reflects that society, shaping it and its members. This was a major theme of Ivan Illich's book *Medical Nemesis*, in which the author states that our entire life span is being medicalized.[5] Medicalization, or defining life's events and feelings in medical terms, as medical issues, is found as frequently in some socialist countries as in the capitalist West. Technological society dehumanizes people by encouraging a mechanical self-image—people viewing themselves as machines.[6] Capitalism adds that not only is the body a collection of parts; its parts become commodities. In the United States the essential fluids of life—blood, milk, and semen—are all for sale. To understand fully the way obstetrics conceptualizes the reproductive cycle, however, a second major ideological basis of the medical model must be considered: medicine is based not only on the ideology of technological society, but also on the ideology of patriarchal society. Medicine is androcentric and patriarchal, and its values are those of men as the dominant social power. Medicine treats all patients, male and female, as "machines," in conformance with the ideology of technological society. The treatment of women patients is further affected by the ideology of patriarchal society.

The first implication of this situation is that medicine has fared no better than any other discipline in arriving at a working model of women that does not take men as the comparative norm. Medicine has treated, and in many instances overtly defined, normal female reproductive processes as diseases. Certainly American medicine is disease oriented, and has been since its early formal organization. That is very true; and that particular critique of medicine, and medicine's management of women's reproductive functions especially, has been made over and over again. Yes, doctors are illness oriented, and yes, they did and sometimes do treat pregnancy, birth, menstruation, and menopause as diseases. But knowing that is not enough. We must go beyond that and ask *why.* Medicine does not, after all, treat all of our biological functions as diseases: the digestive system, for example, is usually considered well unless shown otherwise. Neither a full nor an empty colon is seen as a diseaselike state, and normal bowel movements are not medically monitored. Why are female reproductive processes singled out to make women "unwell," in a "delicate condition," constantly moving from one diseaselike state to another?

The source of the pathology orientation of medicine toward women's health and reproduction is a body-as-machine model (the ideology of technology) in which the male body is taken as the norm (the ideology of patriarchy). From that viewpoint, reproductive processes are stresses on the system, and thus diseaselike.

Contemporary physicians do not usually speak or write of the normal female reproductive functions as diseases, with the exception of menopause. The other specifically female reproductive functions—ovulation and menstruation, pregnancy, childbirth, and lactation—are regularly asserted in the latest texts to be normal and healthy phenomena. However, these statements are made within the context of teaching the medical "management," "care," "supervision," and "treatment" of each of these "conditions."

For example, while menstruation is no longer viewed as a disease, it is seen as a complication in the female system, by contrast to the reputed biologic stability of the supposedly noncycling male.[7] As recently as 1961 the *American Journal of Obstetrics and Gynecology* was still referring to women's "inherent disabilities" in explanations of menstruation:

Women are known to suffer at least some inconvenience during certain phases of the reproductive cycle, and often with considerable mental and physical distress. Woman's awareness of her inherent disabilities is thought to create added mental and in turn physical changes in the total body response, and there result problems that concern the physician who must deal with them.[8]

Research on contraception displays the same mechanistic biases. Doctors claim that contraceptive research has concentrated on the female rather than the male because of the sheer number of potentially vulnerable links in the female chain of reproductive events.[9] Reproduction is clearly a more complicated process for the female than the male.

While the laywoman's view has been that it is safer to interfere in a simpler process, medicine has tended to view the number of points in the female reproductive process as distinct entities. Reproduction is dealt with not as a complicated organic process but as a series of discrete points, like stations on an assembly line.

The alternative to taking the female system as a complication of the "basic" or "simpler" male system is, as found in the midwifery model, to take the female as the working norm. In this approach, a pregnant woman is compared only to pregnant women, a lactating breast compared only to other lactating breasts. Pregnancy, lactation, and so on, are accepted not only as nominally healthy variations, but as truly normal states. To take the example of pregnancy, women *are* pregnant; it is not something they "have" or "catch" or even "contain." Pregnancy involves physical changes: in the medical texts these changes are frequently called "symptoms" of pregnancy. In the alternative, midwifery model, pregnancy is not a disease; its changes are no more "symptoms" than the growth spurt or development of pubic hair are "symptomatic" of puberty. There may be diseases or complications of pregnancy, but the pregnancy itself is neither disease nor complication.

The working model of pregnancy that medicine has arrived at, in contrast, is that a pregnant woman is a woman with an insulated parasitic capsule growing inside her. The pregnancy, while physically located within the woman, is still seen as "external" to her, not a part of her. The pregnancy, in this medical model, is almost entirely a mechanical event in the mother. She differs from the nonpregnant only by virtue of the presence of this thing growing inside her. Differences other than the mechanical are accordingly seen as symptoms to be treated, so that the woman can be kept as "normal" as possible through the "stress" of pregnancy.

Pregnancy is not necessarily unhealthy in this model, but it is frequently associated with changes other than growth of the uterus and its contents, and these changes *are* seen as unhealthy and thus subject to medical treatment.

The medical conceptualization of pregnancy as a stress situation is compounded by the other aspect of the ideology of patriarchal society. Not only is the male body taken as the norm by which the female body is understood, but the female reproductive processes are also understood in terms of men's needs. Thus, in the medical model, the woman is pregnant with the man's child. The influences of these conceptualizations on the management of pregnancy are elaborated in Chapter 4.

Pregnancy is a condition or state of women, while childbirth may be viewed either as an activity that women engage in or as a service that medicine supplies. To medicalize childbirth is to move it from the former area to the latter. Applying the medical model to a physical phenomenon creates patients out of people and places them in the "sick" role. When someone is sick, there is no blame and there is no credit. The illness is something that happens to the person, not something the person is or does.[10] That is the basis of the sick role, and the essence of medicalization. The medical model is inappropriate for pregnancy, since "pregnant" is indeed something one *is,* not something one *has.* Childbirth on the other hand, may be better viewed as something one *does.*

The medical management of childbirth is firmly rooted in the model of the body as machine, from its earliest times right up to the present. An 1800s physician, even a noninterventionist physician as opposed to a "regular" physician, would give a laboring woman a catheter, some castor oil, or milk of magnesia, bleed her a pint or so, administer ergot, use poultices to blister her, and so on. These therapies would be administered simply to set the woman up for an easier and less painful labor, while the physician felt he was letting nature take its course.[11] In a similar way, current obstetrics has redefined "natural childbirth," in response to consumer demand for it, to include spinal or epidural anesthesia, inhalation anesthesia during the second stage of labor, forceps, episiotomies, and induced labor.[12] Under the title *Normal Delivery*, an obstetrical teaching film purports to show the "use of various drugs and procedures used to facilitate normal delivery." Another "normal delivery" film is "a demonstration of a normal spontaneous delivery, including a paracervical block, episiotomy."

These are the normal, noninterventionist techniques, the physician just helping things along. The analogy that comes to mind is of the person with a new color television, endlessly fiddling with the fine tuning, occasionally giving a whack on the side for good measure. The person's not really doing anything to the TV—not taking off the back panel or rewiring. Once the body is conceptualized as a machine, then it is going to be treated in much the same way as any other machine in our society—pushed to be more efficient, more economical, faster, neater, quieter. An infinite number of procedures and interventions are so readily normalized because that fits in with our view of the world: one is compelled to take action in order to get results. In medicine, as in much else in technological society, even action with very little chance of success is preferable to no action at all, on the spurious assumption that doing something is better than doing nothing.[13] In technological society, where the imposition of "man made" order is highly valued for its own sake, medicalization will mean intervention, active management, constant adjusting of the controls.

Childbirth is a highly managed event in modern obstetrics. By modern obstetrics I mean hospital obstetrics: the medical model of childbirth needed the hospital in order to develop to its logical conclusion. In the medically managed institutional setting, the medically managed birth becomes a reality.

What does a medically managed birth mean for women and babies today? Medicine would have us believe that it means above all a safer birth. The profession of medicine would have us believe that the decline in maternal and infant mortality that we have experienced in this century is a result not so much of women's hard-won control over their own fertility, or even of better nutrition and sanitation, but rather of medical management per se. Medical expansion into the area of childbirth began, however, *before* the development of any of what are now considered to be the contributions of modern obstetrics: before asepsis, surgical technique, anesthesia. Even at the time when physicians were taking over control of childbirth in the United States, the noninterventionist supportive techniques of the midwife were safer for both the birthing woman and her baby.

In Washington, as the percentage of births reported by midwives shrank from 50 percent in 1903 to 15 percent in 1912, infant mortality in the first day, first week, and first month of life all increased. New York's dwindling corps of midwives did significantly better than did New York doctors in preventing both stillborns and puerperal sepsis (postpartum infection). And in Newark a midwifery program in 1914–1916 achieved maternal mortality rates as low as 1.7 per thousand, while in Boston, in many ways a comparable city but where midwives were banned, the rates were 6.5 per thousand. Infant mortality rates in Newark were 8.5 per thousand, contrasted with 36.4 in Boston.[14] (The current United States infant mortality rate is 14 per thousand.) The situation was similar in England, where an analysis of the records of the Queen's Institute for Midwives for the years 1905–1925 found that the death rate rose in step with the proportion of cases to which midwives called the doctors.[15] At that point in its development, the medical model was not working.

Currently the United States ranks approximately fourteenth in infant mortality, with 14 deaths per 1,000 live births. Home-birth advocates like to point out that the countries that have the lowest mortality rates, notably Sweden and the Netherlands (10.8 and 11.4), rely on midwifery and home birth. Doris Haire, for example, the president of the American Foundation for Maternal and Child Health, has observed maternity hospitals throughout the world—in Great Britain, Western Europe, Russia, Asia, Australia, New Zealand, the South Pacific, the Americas, and Africa. She claims that those countries which have the lowest rates of infant mortality and birth trauma rely heavily on professionally trained midwives.[16]

Cross-cultural comparisons are of limited value: there are too many factors for which we cannot control. The same is true of historical studies. Of greater interest are contemporary home-birth statistics in the United States.

The home-birth statistics circulated by the American College of Obstetrics and Gynecology, which is strongly opposed to home birth, make home birth appear to be quite unsafe, with neonatal death rates double that of hospitals. However, those statistics rely on reported home births only and are collected from state registrations. Not all home births are reported: a 1975 study found that 75 percent of the home births in the Santa Cruz area in California were *not* reported.[17] Births are more likely to be reported when complications arise and medical services are used; this skews the reported data. Second, the state statistics make no distinction between planned home births and unplanned, rapid labors where the woman gives birth at home by accident. These rapid, or precipitous, labors usually involve premature babies. Thus, every seventh-month fetus that is born at home before the mother could get to a hospital may be included as a "home birth." What is needed is a matched-sample comparison between hospital and *planned* home births.

There exists such a study, by Lewis Mehl and his associates.[18] They matched 1,046 planned-home-birth women with 1,046 planned-hospital women for maternal age, parity, socioeconomic status, and risk factors. The home-birth group included all those women planning to deliver at home prior to the initiation of labor, rupture of membranes, or emergence of a complication necessitating immediate hospitalization and delivery. All cases transferred to the hospital during or after labor were included in the home-birth group. The births were then analyzed for length of labor, complications of labor, neonatal outcomes, and procedures utilized. In this study, the best we have so far, using matched samples, home births were found to be *safer* than hospital births for both mothers and babies. This flies in the face of so much accepted, conventional wisdom that I present the data in some detail.

The hospital births had a five times higher incidence of maternal high blood pressure, which may be indicative of the greater physical and emotional stress for mothers in the hospital, as may be the three-and-a-half times more meconium staining (fetal bowel movement expelled into the amniotic fluid, indicative of fetal distress). The hospital births had eight times the shoulder dystocia (the fetal shoulder getting caught after the head is born). Mehl and his associates state that this may be caused by the flat-on-the-back position, in which the fetus must rise upwards to be born, with a greater chance of the shoulder's catching on the mother's pelvic bone. Several midwives told them that they move the mother to a hands-and-knees position for shoulder distocia, and get the baby born that way, a procedure not used in American hospitals. Hospital births also had three times the rate of postpartum hemorrhage. Cutting the cord too early, or pulling on the cord to extract the placenta, or reaching in and manually removing the placenta, are practices found in hospital and not in home births which may contribute to postpartum hemorrhage. Medication during labor and delivery may also be a factor.

The infant death rates, both perinatal (during birth) and neonatal (after birth) were essentially the same for the two groups. The Apgar scores, measure of the status of the newborn at one and at five minutes, were better for the home-birth babies; but this measurement is not free of bias, since it is done by those present at births. We cannot be certain that home-birth attendants were not more lenient in their scoring practices than were hospital attendants—or vice versa. Three and seven-tenths times as many hospital babies required resuscitation, and four times as many hospital babies became infected. Thirty times as many hospital babies suffered birth injuries, a difference attributable to the use of forceps, which were twenty-two times more common in labors planned to be in the hospital. The birth injuries consisted of severe cephalhematoma (a collection of blood beneath the scalp, sufficient to cause anemia and to require phototherapy and/or exchange transfusion), fractured skull, fractured clavicle, facial-nerve paralysis, brachial-nerve injury, eye injury, and the like. Fewer than 5 percent of the home-birth mothers received analgesia or anesthesia, while such drugs were administered to over 75 percent of the women in the hospital group (even though almost all of the women in both groups had attended childbirth-preparation classes). Cesarean sections were three times more frequent in the hospital than in the planned-home-birth group. Finally, there were nine times as many episiotomies (which are supposed to prevent tearing) in the hospital group and nine times as many severe (third- and fourth-degree) tears in the hospital group. Although as many mothers and babies survived the hospital births as the home births, the home-birth group had appreciably better outcome.

The medical management of birth becomes more and more technologically advanced. There have been two significant changes in the management of labor and delivery in American hospitals in the past few years: the majority of hospital births are now being electronically monitored; and up to 25 percent of births are being done by cesarean section.

Fetal-monitoring equipment is similar to the monitoring equipment used in coronary-care units. Marcia Millman has pointed out that this kind of electronic equipment is produced by the same electronics industry that suffered some depression after cutbacks in military and defense spending, and attributes its recent growth to the diversification of the electronics industry into health care. Much of the monitoring equipment developed under the space program.[19] Electronic monitoring was widely accepted in medicine with almost no reservations because it fits so perfectly into the medical model of the body as a machine. Fetal monitoring provides, or is believed to provide, a wealth of information about the progress of labor and the status of the fetus, in three ways: externally, by ultrasound monitoring of the fetal heart rate and uterine contractions; internally, by fetal electrocardiogram obtained with electrodes attached to the baby's head and uterine monitoring by means of a catheter passed into the uterus through the cervix; and by direct sampling of fetal scalp blood, obtained from an electrode screwed into the baby's head.

But does all this information help? The National Center for Health Services Research announced in December of 1978, "electronic fetal monitoring may do more harm than good," and stated that fetal monitoring was not "medically evaluated" before it was introduced. That is, fetal monitoring was not scientifically evaluated, though it was medically accepted. The NCHSR report was based on an assessment of the technique's safety and cost effectiveness, and states that the uncertain benefits and the known costs and risks do not seem to justify the technique's widespread use. While the monitoring directly costs about $80 million, no small sum itself, the hazards could cost $300 million or more. Approximately $222 million of that pays for the 100,000 unnecessary cesarean sections that result from misinformation or misreading of information from the monitors. Risks to the mother of death and pelvic infections from the cesarean sections and from the monitoring itself could add up to another $58 million annually. An additional $50 million is spent on the hazards to the baby of hemorrhage and infection at the site of the electrode, and potential respiratory distress resulting from the unnecessary cesarean sections. A cost analysis barely hints at the human meanings of surgery, infection, hemorrhage, and death.

The fetal monitors were originally introduced as a diagnostic technique for high-risk pregnancies, but they rapidly spread to routine use. This is a fairly typical pattern in American medicine. In this instance, the effectiveness even for the high-risk situation has yet to be established. A study of fetal monitoring in high-risk pregnancy[20] compared electronic fetal monitoring with nurse auscultation (listening with a stethoscope). In that study, all women had membranes ruptured and monitors inserted, although the monitors were not used in the nurse auscultation group. Under those circumstances, fetal outcomes were equivalent in two groups, although the cesarean-section rate was 2.5 times higher in the machine-monitored group. One has to wonder whether the results in the nurse auscultation group might not have been even better without unnecessary rupturing of membranes, which increases both the risk of infection and the pressure on the fetal head. Machine monitoring requires membranes to be ruptured; nurse auscultation does not.

Monitoring, both archetypal and symbolic of medical management, is dangerous and expensive. But even for women and babies who are not physically compromised, who do not have unnecessary surgery, infections, or hemorrhage, the technique is not benign. Monitoring has profound effects on the quality of the birth experience. One of the nurse-midwives I interviewed responded as follows to the changes in the hospital service where she works that came with the introduction of electronic monitoring:

> We're going to have centralized everything, man. A woman comes in in labor, you put an electrode in her rectum to record temperature, you put an internal monitor on the [fetal] head, you put the other one in the uterus, you put the blood-pressure cuff on—that's it, baby—you don't have to go in there till the head's out.

Medicine has not, thanks to consumer pressure and the home-birth movement, completely ignored the emotional needs of women. To meet these needs, interior decorators have been called in. We have seen in recent years the rise of "interior-decorating obstetrics": photomurals and flowered sheets, wood, brass and wicker headboards, even a plant on the IV pole. Hospitals, to entice women in, offer liberal visiting hours for fathers, some visiting hours for siblings, even champagne-and-lobster postpartum dinners. These things are available for "low risk" women, often in a labor room set aside as a "birth room." In one major teaching hospital I observed labor rooms one through ten opening on a central corridor. Number five, end room on the right, was the birth room. It had flowered sheets; and low-risk mothers, who had asked and received permission ahead of time, could deliver in there, free of monitors, IVs, and certain other procedures standard in rooms one through four and six through ten. But relatively few births took place in the birthing room. Most women, it seems, were not "low risk" enough to earn the pretty surroundings.

Midwives have told me again and again that it is not the way the room looks that matters. What matters are the attitudes of the attendants—the beliefs, values, and ideas they hold about women, babies, and birth. The profession of medicine would have us see a dichotomy between safety and emotional needs. Specifically, we are told that home or homelike atmospheres may be of some emotional importance to the mother, but that the hospital and its efficient, rational, technological management are important for physical health, especially the physical health of the baby. Doctors accuse women who choose not to use the hospital of putting their own emotional needs before the physical needs of their babies. That is because the medical model dichotomizes not only mind and body, but also mother and infant. Mother/ fetus are seen in the medical model as a conflicting dyad rather than as an integral unit. In the midwifery model, mother and fetus are genuinely one, and that which meets the needs of the one meets the needs of the other. Emotional, physical, maternal, and infant needs are not, in the midwifery model, at odds.

Most of the attempts to reform the medical management of women's health care in general, and childbirth in particular, have not recognized the profound importance of the underlying ideologies in medicine. There have been attempts to make doctors more caring, more humanistic, more responsive to the emotional needs of women: important goals, all. But for the most part these reform movements, such as the natural-childbirth movement, and Leboyer's work with newborns, have not challenged the dichotomies established by medicine. Mind and body, emotional and physical needs, are still seen as separate, with emotional needs clearly secondary. And mother and baby are still seen as linked in a parasitic relationship, rather than as a unit. In the abortion-rights movement, the embryo/fetus is understood to be part of its mother's body, but that insight has not been systematically carried through to an analysis of pregnancy and the maternity experience.

Even within the attempts to reform maternity care, different organizations have evolved to handle different aspects of the experience: the Lamaze or prepared-childbirth people address themselves only to what goes on in labor and delivery rooms, while La Leche League concerns itself only with the breast-feeding relationship. Leboyer focuses on the care the newborn receives in the delivery room. It is in the home-birth movement that the pieces are being brought together. "You can't," a home-birth midwife told me, "take a woman and tear her apart—that's what the physicians do."

Nor can we treat all of her experiences as "medical." Illich, in *Medical Nemesis,* has addressed the dangers of the medicalization of the life span: an increasing dependence on professional/medical services to solve, even to define, our problems for us. Women are especially vulnerable to this kind of medicalization—we are a minority group, set aside by our biology. It is altogether too easy for patriarchal society to define women by our biology, and to define women's biological functions as requiring medical management.

The midwives and mothers involved in the home-birth movement are part of the larger struggle of feminism to redefine women in women's terms. In part these women are reconstructing the pre–obstetrics-and-gynecology models of women's health. They are coming to grips with a feminism that embraces rather than denies women's biological realities.

2

History of
Maternity Care

The recorded history of midwifery goes back as far as any recorded history. The wife of Pericles and the mother of Socrates were midwives, and in Exodus Moses' midwives, Shifra and Puah, are rewarded by God. Every culture in the history of the world has had its midwives; wherever there have been women, there have been midwives.

The history of maternity care is the history of midwifery. The rise of obstetrics was the fall of midwifery. It remains to be seen what the rebirth of midwifery will mean for obstetrics and for maternity care.

The first half of this chapter traces the rise of obstetrics and the fall of midwifery, women's loss of control over childbirth to men's hands and to men's tools. The second half of the chapter discusses the nurse-midwife, the modern, medically sanctioned answer to the granny or lay or empirical midwife.

Two important things happened in the history of midwifery: midwives lost autonomy, control of their work, to doctors; and doctors and midwives allocated patients according to notions of appropriate "territory." The two problems are interrelated. Doctors carved out as their territory pathological or abnormal births. They then went on to define all births as inherently pathological and abnormal, so that there was no room for the midwife. Doctors continue to control midwives by controlling their support services, especially the services believed to be necessary in case of abnormal or "complicated" births. Because doctors do control these backup services, midwives must work within the restrictions imposed by doctors, even in acknowledged "normal" or "low risk" births.

When we look backwards, midwifery seems to us like a branch of medicine, and the midwife an untrained forerunner of the obstetrician. A historian of the middle ages, for example, noted that midwives were outside of the control of the university physician and stated: "... the university physician generally ignored this whole area of medicine. Midwives might or might not be qualified, but this was not a matter of public concern."[1] Looking backwards lets us see history with all of the prejudices of our own time superimposed on the prejudices of the historical period. Medicalization combines with sexism as we view the history of midwifery. More accurately, free of those prejudices, one might state not that physicians ignored this "area of medicine," but that midwifery and its concerns were outside of medicine, just as matters that were undoubtedly of concern to women were outside of the "public concern." Until pregnancy and childbirth were defined as medical events, midwifery was in no sense a branch, area, or interest of medicine as a profession.

The earliest sign of encroachment on midwifery came from the development of the barber-surgeons guilds. In England, for example, under the guild system that developed in the thirteenth century, the right to use surgical instruments belonged officially only to the surgeon. Thus, when giving birth was absolutely impossible, the midwife called in the barber-surgeon to perform an embryotomy (crushing the fetal skull, dismembering it in utero, and removing it piecemeal) or to remove the baby by cesarean section after the death of the mother. It was not within the technology of the barber-surgeon to deliver a live baby from a live mother. Not until the development of forceps in the seventeenth century were men involved in live births, and so became a genuine challenge to midwives. Interest in abnormal cases increased throughout the seventeenth and especially the eighteenth centuries; this may have been due to rapid urbanization and the resultant increase in pelvic deformities caused by rickets.[2]

In the early seventeenth century, the barber-surgeon Peter Chamberlen developed the obstetrical forceps, an instrument that enabled its user to deliver a child mechanically without necessarily destroying it first. The Chamberlen family kept the forceps secret for three generations, for their own financial gain, and only let it be known that they possessed some way of preventing piecemeal extraction of an impacted fetus. The right to use instruments still resided exclusively with men, and when the Chamberlens finally sold their design (or the design leaked out) it was for the use of the barber-surgeons, and not generally available to midwives.

It has frequently been assumed that the forceps were an enormous breakthrough in improving maternity care, but this has hardly been demonstrated and in retrospect seems unlikely. The physicians and surgeons did not have the opportunity to observe and learn the rudiments of normal birth and were therefore at a decided disadvantage in handling difficult births. And unlike in the pre-forceps days, when a barber-surgeon was called in only if all hope of a live birth was gone, midwives were increasingly encouraged and instructed to call in the barber-surgeon prophylactically, whenever birth became difficult.

Sarah Stone, an eighteenth-century midwife and author of the *Complete Practice of Midwifery*, alleged that more mothers and children had died at the hands of raw recruits just out of their apprenticeship to the barber-surgeon than through the worst ignorance and stupidity of the midwife.[3] The noted midwife Elizabeth Nihell, author of *A Treatise on the Art of the Midwife*, in 1760 questioned the value of instrumentation, as a result of her training in France at the Hotel-Dieu, where midwives practiced without male supervision or intervention.[4] Instruments were, in her opinion, rarely if ever necessary. It is important to bear in mind that the forceps were of a primitive design, not originally curved to fit the birth canal; were used as "high" or "mid" forceps rather than the "outlet" forceps most commonly used currently and so went high up into the birth canal; and were not sterilized. A journalist of the time, Philip Thicknesse, agreed with Elizabeth Nihell that the growing popularity of the man-midwife, the barber-surgeon, and his instruments was not because of his superior skills but because of the power of men to convince women of the dangers of childbirth and the incompetence of midwives. The men were aided by the growing prestige of male birth attendants as a symbol of higher social status, possibly because of their higher fees. Not only did the men use their instruments unnecessarily, resulting in maternal and infant mortality and morbidity, puerperal fever and extraordinary birth injuries, but, Mrs. Nihell complained, were so adept at concealing errors with "a cloud of hard words and scientific jargon" that the injured patient herself was convinced that she could not thank him enough for the mischief he had done.[5] "Meddlesome midwifery," as it was called at the time, was the forerunner of what is today, in a time of increasing cesarean-section rates, called "interventionist obstetrics."

Spurred on by the development of basic anatomical knowledge and increased understanding of the processes of reproduction, surgeons of the 1700s began to develop formal training programs in midwifery. Women midwives were systematically excluded from such programs. Women were not trained, because women were believed to be inherently incompetent. The situation was far from simple, however, and some surgeons did try to provide training for the midwives, sharing with them the advances made in medical knowledge. Such attempts failed in the face of opposition from within medicine, supported by the prevailing beliefs about women's abilities to perform in a professional capacity. The result was a widening disparity between midwives and surgeons. As new and sophisticated techniques were developed by the men, they were kept from the women.[6]

We cannot assume that midwives were incompetent to use instruments when these were available to them. Rather, their basic experience with normal birth probably made them eminently more capable than the inexperienced men. For example, some historians believe that the first cesarean section recorded in the British Isles in which both mother and child survived was performed by an illiterate Irish midwife, Mary Dunally.[7] The training, experience, and competence of the midwives of the seventeenth and eighteenth centuries varied enormously, and went largely unregulated. And the same is true of the training, experience, and competence of the physicians and barber-surgeons.

Midwifery survived the rise of the male midwife and the encroachment of the medical-surgical professions in Europe and in England, albeit with a considerable loss of autonomy. In England, for example, when the Central Midwifery Board was founded in 1902 it had no mandatory midwifery repre-

entation. It was later established that midwives be excluded
from becoming a majority of its membership, and it was not
until 1973 that a midwife became chairperson of the board.
The board outlined in detail the rules covering midwifery
duties, and even now the "moral" or "character" requirements for midwives are still under its purview.

As physicians gained near-complete ascendancy, the midwife was redefined from being a competitor of the physician-
surgeon to being, in her new role, his assistant. Midwives lost
autonomy over their work throughout most of Europe and in
England, to a greater or lesser extent losing control over
their own licensing, training requirements, and the restrictions under which they must function. Once surgeons came
to be *socially defined* as having expertise in the management
of difficult or abnormal birth, midwifery effectively lost control over even normal birth. I emphasize "socially defined"
because it is not at all clear that the surgeons were providing
better services, in spite of the surgical and instrumental techniques. Not all physicians who practiced the new obstetrics
were trained in its use. The iatrogenic results of the new
obstetrics may have outweighed its benefits, particularly for
normal and healthy births. As was demonstrated in Chapter
1, the rise of obstetrics was not associated with clear and
immediate benefits to mothers and babies.

But once the physician or surgeon is held to be necessary
"in case something goes wrong," then the midwife becomes
dependent on the physician and his goodwill for her
"backup" services. When physicians want to compete with
midwives for clients, all they have to do is to withhold backup
services, that is, refuse to come to the aid of a midwife who
calls for medical assistance. In 1913 in England three doctors,
all members of a medico-ethical society, refused to attend a
midwife's emergency call because of a prior agreement that
no member of the society would attend such cases without

immediate payment of a higher fee than usual. (The midwife had previously sent each doctor a letter informing him that the mother was insured and pay would be forthcoming.) The mother died.[8] The issue that troubled public-health officials in setting up midwifery services, an issue clearly stated in the *American Journal of Obstetrics and Gynecology* in 1912, was that the American medical profession could never be forced by law to respond to the call of a midwife in trouble.[9]

Even when physicians are not in competition with midwives but really need midwives to handle the cases that they, the physicians, wish to avoid—such as the rural poor or the tediously normal births—physicians still control the midwives by setting the standards for training and regulating which instruments and procedures they may use, and for which they must call on their backup doctors. While these decisions are ostensibly made to bring about best possible health care for mother and child, by preventing "unqualified" persons from providing particular services, that is certainly not the way it always works out. For example, in a work written in 1736 as a question-and-answer session between a surgeon and a midwife, *The Midwife Rightly Instructed,* the surgeon refuses to tell the midwife how to deal with a hemorrhage. The surgeon warns the midwife not to aspire beyond the capacities of a woman, and says, "I never designed, Lucina, to make you a Doctress, but to tell you how to practise as a Midwife."[10] There is almost no way for a doctor to have been called in quickly enough to save a hemorrhaging woman, even assuming he knew how to do it. Clearly the health of women and children was sacrificed to the furtherance of medical control over midwifery.

The balance of power that has been achieved between medicine and midwifery varies across the Western world. It is only in the United States, however, that midwifery actually failed to survive. When in 1966 a joint study of the International Confederation of Midwives and the International Federation of Gynecology and Obstetrics compiled a report on maternity care, it was necessary to treat the United States as a "special case" in the tables, "because of its tendency not to recognize midwifery as an independent profession."[11]

In the nineteenth and early twentieth centuries, American midwives and physicians were in direct competition for patients, and not only for their fees. Newer, more clinically oriented medical training demanded "teaching material," so that even immigrant and poor women were desired as patients.[12] The displacement of the midwife can be better understood in terms of this competition than as an ideological struggle or as "scientific advancement." Physicians, unlike the unorganized, disenfranchised midwives, had access to the power of the state through their professional associations. They were thus able to control licensing legislation, in state after state restricting the midwives' sphere of activity and imposing legal sanctions against them.[13]

During the course of the late 1800s through the early twentieth century, medicine gained virtually complete control of childbirth in America, beginning with the middle class and moving on to the poor and immigrant population. Midwifery almost ceased to exist in the United States, and for the first time in history, an entire society of women was attended in childbirth by men.

What did this medically attended birth look like, feel like, to the women who experienced it?

The standards for obstetrical intervention that gained acceptance in the 1920s and thirties, and are still used today, can be traced back to a 1920 article in the *American Journal of Obstetrics and Gynecology*, "The Prophylactic Forceps Operation," by Joseph B. DeLee of Chicago.[14] DeLee's procedure for a routine, normal birth required sedating the woman through labor, and giving ether for the descent of the fetus. The baby was to be removed from the unconscious mother by forceps. An incision through the skin and muscle of the perineum, called an episiotomy, was to be done before the forceps were applied. Removal of the placenta was also to be obstetrically managed rather than spontaneous. Ergot or a derivative was to be injected to cause the uterus to clamp down and prevent postpartum hemorrhage.

Why were DeLee's procedures, rather than allowing the mother to push the baby out spontaneously, so widely accepted by the 1930s? On one level, we can answer this in terms of the needs of the still-developing profession of obstetrics: the need for teaching material; the need to justify both the costs and the prestige of obstetrics by providing a special service that midwives and general practitioners had not provided; the need to routinize patients in a centralized facility. I would like to consider, however, the medical rationale, which was phrased in terms of the dangers of labor itself, in order to understand the medical model of maternity care.

The use of the forceps was to spare the baby's head, DeLee having compared labor to a baby's head being crushed in a door. The episiotomy was done to prevent tearing of the perineum, something that is almost inevitable with the use of forceps. Even without forceps use, however, American physicians were finding tearing to be a problem, most likely owing to the use of the American-style delivery table, which required the supine position, with legs in stirrups.[15] The clean cut of the episiotomy was held to be easier to repair than the jagged tear. DeLee further claimed that the stretching and tearing of the perineum resulted in such gynecological conditions as prolapsed uteri, tears in the vaginal wall, and sagging perineums. The first empirical study to determine the long-term effectiveness of episiotomies was not done until 1976, and the results indicate that episiotomies cause rather than prevent these conditions.[16] The episiotomy, DeLee claimed, would restore "virginal conditions," making the mother "better than new." It is not uncommon to hear of obstetricians assuring husbands at current husband-attended births that they are sewing the woman up "good and tight."

For the baby, according to DeLee and his many followers, the labor was a dangerous, crushing threat, responsible for epilepsy, idiocy, imbecility, and cerebral palsy, as well as being a direct cause of death. For the mother, birth was compared to falling on a pitchfork, driving the handle through her perineum. Using these analogies, DeLee was able to conclude that labor itself was abnormal:

> In both cases, the cause of the damage, the fall on the pitchfork and the crushing of the door, is pathogenic, that is, disease-producing, and anything pathogenic is pathologic or abnormal.[17]

The implication of the DeLee approach to birth for the mother is that she experiences the birth as an entirely medical event, not unlike any other surgical procedure. At the beginning of labor she is brought to the hospital and turned over to the hospital staff. The sedation of the thirties, forties, and fifties was "twilight sleep," a combination of morphine for pain relief in early labor, and then scopolamine, believed to be an amnesiac.

A woman under twilight sleep can feel and respond to pain; the claim is only that she will not remember what happened. Women in twilight sleep therefore must be restrained, or their uncontrolled thrashing can cause severe injuries, as the scope leaves them thoroughly disoriented and in pain. Current obstetrical nursing texts include pictures of women with battered faces who were improperly restrained and threw themselves out of bed.

The birth itself was not part of the mother's conscious experience, because she was made totally unconscious for the delivery. Such women required careful watching as they recovered from anesthesia. They were in no way competent to hold or even see their babies; it might be quite some time before they were told the birth was over.[18] The babies were themselves born drugged, and required careful medical attention. It was several hours, or even days, before the mother and baby were "introduced."

That essentially the same management existed through to the 1970s in American obstetrical services has been documented by Nancy Stoller Shaw in her observations of maternity care in Boston hospitals.[19] Shaw reports that obstetric residents went by the book, and the book (the "Procedures and Policies" book of the hospital) says:

The use of premedication for labor and anesthesia for delivery are an integral part of the philosophy of this hospital . . . It is the conviction in this institution that the use of adequate medication for labor and anesthesia for delivery serve the welfare of the mother and baby best, not only when difficulties develop suddenly, or unexpectedly, but also in uncomplicated situations.[20]

And with regard to the interventionist management of labor and delivery, Shaw says:

The Maternity Division staff strongly believes in an activistic controlling approach to labor designed to make it as short as possible. Synthetic labor stimulants [oxytoxics] are injected into the woman, especially the primipara, to stimulate labor . . . In addition, during [the] expulsive stage of labor [delivery] the obstetrician is expected to *routinely* use "episiotomy and low forceps delivery to minimize damage to maternal soft parts, to diminish the need for subsequent gynecologic surgery, and to *shorten the duration of pressure on the fetal head.*"[21]

In sum:

These patients become totally alienated from their birth experience. They are treated like lumps of flesh from which a baby is pulled.[22]

It is against this backdrop that the development of the new midwifery model must be understood. I will in the next chapter discuss the natural-childbirth and prepared-childbirth movements, and La Leche League, as responses to the extreme depersonalization and mechanization of birth. The reemergence of midwifery, however, is a response to the mechanic role of the practitioner, for the self-conceptualization of the practitioner is also tied in to the ideology of the underlying model. Because they view the body as a machine, obstetricians can see their work in treating that machine as essentially mechanical. They will certainly argue that it is highly complicated work which they are doing, but in the medical model any competent physician should be able to do the job. The affective neutrality[23] of the professional depends on that: it is the skill and techniques of the physician, and not an interdependent emotional relationship with the woman, that are believed to determine the outcome of a birth. Midwifery, on the other hand, treats childbirth in the larger context of women's lives. Midwives did not and do not deliver babies. They teach women how to give birth. The role of the traditional midwife was "total"—she helped in the socialization of the mother to her new status, both as teacher and as role model. "The midwife's relation to the woman was both diffuse and affective, while the physician role demanded specificity and affective neutrality."[24] Midwives taught how to birth babies, how to nurse them, and how to care for the babies and the mother's own body. Physicians deliver babies and move on. The physician "isolated the laboring woman and her delivery of the infant from the rest of the childbearing experience, and defined it as a medical and surgical event which required specialized knowledge."[25] As one modern nurse-midwife has said of obstetrics residents: "They want us to stay with the woman in labor and just call them when she's ready to deliver. To them, that's the whole thing."

This is where the story of midwifery in the United States might have ended. Birth had been thoroughly medicalized, and doctors had a complete monopoly. The midwife virtually disappeared.

But midwifery was recreated in the United States, in two different forms and under very different circumstances. One form of midwife, the "lay" or "empirical" midwife, has grown up within the home-birth movement. Women have reinvented the traditional midwife, someone who has had births of her own, seen a lot of other births, and begun to help out at births. These midwives vary enormously as to their experience and training. Some have participated in hundreds of births and developed a unique body of knowledge about birth. Others have simply helped out an occasional friend or neighbor using their own birth experiences. Often, of course, it is from such a beginning that a woman can go on to train herself as an empirical midwife, learning, as the obstetricians do, by doing.

The other version of the midwife was invented by doctors and is a form of nurse-practitioner, or what is called, reminiscent of soybeans in hamburger meat, a "physician extender." This midwife, the nurse-midwife, is in the most difficult of positions. She seeks to develop and maintain an alternative approach to maternity care, but she works within hospitals, under the direction of obstetricians. We turn now to the history of nurse-midwifery.

Nurse-Midwifery:
The New American Midwife Controversy

In 1911 Bellevue opened the first American hospital-affiliated school of midwifery. It was at just that point that medicine was wrapping up what was left of midwifery in America, and in 1936 the Bellevue school was closed.

In 1925 an American public-health nurse, Mary Breckinridge, returned from midwifery school in England and established the Frontier Nursing Service program in Kentucky. Breckinridge imported English-trained midwives and encouraged American nurses to go to England for training. The Frontier Nursing Service provided, and continues to provide, midwifery and family-care services to the rural poor of Kentucky, establishing an impressively safe record for home births with a high-risk population.

In 1932 a Frontier Nursing Service midwife set up the Lobenstine clinic in New York, to train American nurses to be midwives. That later became the Maternity Center Association school, and M.C.A. nurse-midwives provided home births in New York until 1958. One of the nurse-midwives I interviewed in the current home-birth and birthing-center movement is a graduate of that program. In 1958 the program moved to Downstate Medical Center–Kings County Hospital. Nurse-midwifery education programs were also developed at Columbia, Johns Hopkins, and Yale. In 1955 the American College of Nurse-Midwifery (later, Nurse-Midwives) was established as the certified nurse-midwives professional organization. By 1976 there were 1,800 certified nurse-midwives in the United States, and the number is increasing rapidly. There are currently well over a dozen nurse-midwifery education programs approved by the American College of Nurse-Midwives. Some of these will admit any registered nurse with the appropriate experience, and offer certification to a nurse with no further academic degree. Others are open only to degree nurses, and offer the master's degree in conjunction with certification.

Nurse-midwifery licensing is determined by the states. There are still several states, including Massachusetts, in which nurse-midwifery certification is not recognized, and certified nurse-midwives may practice only as nurses.

Exactly what a nurse-midwife is and what she does seem to vary with the eye of the beholder. The ACNM public-information brochure "The Nurse Midwife—A Member of the Modern Obstetrical Team" shows on its cover a surgically capped, gowned, and masked woman holding up a just-born baby. In contrast to the standard obstetrical photos, we see the face of the mother, who is looking at the baby, and the midwife, looking at the mother. The brochure states:

> The nurse-midwife provides complete care for the normal childbearing woman. She is qualified to manage prenatal care and labor, to deliver the baby and to provide methods of family planning.

The next paragraph is accompanied by a photograph of a serious-looking man in a white coat holding a chart and looking at the midwife:

> In the U.S. a nurse-midwife always functions within a physician-directed health service; she is not an independent practitioner.

In other of their brochures, that last phrase, "she is not an independent practitioner," is in italics.

If she is so decidedly not an independent practitioner, does that mean that she is an assistant to physicians, or at any rate dominated by physicians? Ruth Lubic, CNM, director of the Maternity Center Association and one of the most effective proponents of midwifery as a profession rather than an ancillary service, wrote an article for the *American Journal of Nursing,* entitled "Myths about Nurse-Midwives."[26] One of the "myths" which she denounced is that "nurse-midwifery and nurse-midwives are unduly physician dominated." That, she states, "is simply not true," and points to nurse-midwifery control over its own education and certification procedures. "There has been no need to surrender autonomy. We are not exploited." To another "myth," that "nurse-midwives are physician assistants," Lubic responds that nurse-midwifery is not promulgated to "assist any group of professionals with a work load."

The other side of that story comes from physicians, and reads quite differently. A good example of the way midwifery is presented in the obstetrics-and-gynecology literature is a 1964 article by Hellman and O'Brien on the midwifery training program at Downstate.[27] Hellman, who has been called the "father of nurse-midwifery,"[28] was instrumental in getting the certified nurse-midwives recognized as members of the "obstetrical team," as they were endorsed by the American College of Obstetrics and Gynecology in January of 1971. Back in 1964, the approach Hellman and O'Brien took for readers of *Obstetrics and Gynecology* was to first map out the shortage of diplomates of the American Board of Obstetrics and Gynecology for the expected increase in births. They reach the conclusion that "the burden on ward services may become intolerable unless adequate planning is initiated." Not only was there a physicians shortage projected for ward services, but "Even if such manpower [sic] were available by importation, it would be unwise to increase the obstetrical house staff out of proportion to the amount of major gynecological surgery available for advanced training." That is an

interesting predicament one gets into when normal childbirth and major gynecological surgery are to be considered
part of the same specialty. The solution to the problem was
the nurse-midwife.

These nurse-midwives would, because of the nature of
their training programs, have had considerably more birth
experience than junior residents and certainly much more
than interns. In spite of that, Hellman and O'Brien make the
assumption that the certified nurse-midwife will be more
closely supervised in practice. There are other differences as
well:

> The nurse-midwife differs from the intern and resident not
> only in the degree to which she is supervised, but also
> because she cares for one patient at a time throughout both
> labor and delivery. This creates a one-to-one ratio which
> constitutes both the strength and to some extent the weak-
> ness of the program.

This latter point remains unexplained and unelaborated. The
final point Hellman and O'Brien make is that while nurse-
midwives are not the only answer to the "manpower" problem, they are one answer,

> and one that the American College of Obstetrics and
> Gynecology should examine and *should control* . . . It is
> highly desirable that the standards for training and activi-
> ties of these programs be *under the supervision of the
> College,* just as the residency training programs should be.
> [emphasis added][29]

The school of nurse-midwifery at Downstate is still, fifteen
years later, under the control of the medical school and separate from the nursing school.

It is not just obstetricians who see nurse-midwives this way. *Newsweek* ran an article on nurse-midwifery in 1969, which was being distributed through the 1970s by the director of Nurse-Midwives Services Program, MIC project of New York. After making a glowing report on nurse-midwifery, the article concludes:

> Beyond obstetrics, the nurse-midwife represents the first wave of a growing army of "paramedics" who will increasingly take over the burdens of the beleaguered U.S. medical doctor.[30]

So far I have focused on the professional independence and autonomy of nurse-midwifery. A second but related issue is the relationship between nurse-midwifery and midwifery history. The first line of the *Newsweek* article is "The new midwife hardly resembles the ignorant crone of folklore." Rather than questioning whether the old midwives resembled the folklore figure—or the source of the "folklore"—it attempts to show that the nurse-midwife is different from the old midwife.

In her book *The Complete Book of Midwifery,* Barbara Brennan, CNM, spells out the full requirements and training for nurse-midwives, and says:

> I have gone into all this detail to show that certified nurse midwives are very different from Great-aunt Kate and all the lay midwives who have recently appeared on the scene. We are top level professionals with medically sound education and experience.[31]

Brennan seeks to maintain balance between "modern medical management" and "traditional midwifery." In her preface she says:

The midwife who used to be "granny," an untrained birthing assistant, is now a certified nurse-midwife who is a specialist with obstetrical nursing experience and graduate training in midwifery. But she has the attitudes and approaches of the age-old profession, and that is what women today are seeking.[32]

It is this kind of selling of nurse-midwifery as the modern medical answer to the granny that led Suzanne Arms in her critique of American birthing practices, *Immaculate Deception*, to say that nurse-midwifery is "yet another deception in the process of the hospital birth."[33] Arms's book received favorable reviews and was very well received within the natural-childbirth movement. Her biting criticism of the American nurse-midwife seems to have struck certified nurse-midwives very deeply. Arms says of the nurse-midwife:

She is no longer the guardian of normal birth and watchful servant of mothers. She is a registered nurse with a postgraduate degree in a specialty called midwifery. And she looks and acts much like the physician authority whom she is licensed to assist.[34]

Arms's book appeared in 1975. The first issue of the *Journal of Nurse-Midwifery* for 1976 carried an editorial, "We Have a Major Decision to Make," in response to Arms. The editorial begins, "Traditionally nurse-midwives have considered themselves advocates of the childbearing couple. Recently a shocking accusation has challenged this position." The editors say that whether or not there is a basis in fact to the accusations that nurse-midwives have sold out to the medical establishment, the credence given the accusation by the consumer is something which nurse-midwives, "as professionals, must give serious thought." The major decisions nurse-mid-wives have to make center around the appropriate response of certified nurse-midwives to the growing home-birth movement on the one hand, and the proliferation of medical technology in birth on the other. The editorial concludes by calling for "strong support within the College for all view-points and all types of practice that meet the standards of *safe* care." [emphasis added] That begs the question.

The ACNM has not been supportive of home births; in-deed, some certified nurse-midwives doing home births have felt that the college was "out to get them." With acceptance and respect so hard to obtain from the medical profession, some of the nurse-midwifery leadership feels that home births rock the boat. Certified nurse-midwives are very aware of their expendability. An obstetrical resident gets paid approximately the same amount as a certified nurse-midwife, works double the hours, and "manages" several labors at a time. In a time of decreasing birth rates (and increasing gynecological surgery), the "manpower" shortage and the imbalance between births and surgery that Hellman and O'Brien predicted are no longer an issue. Certified nurse-midwives are a luxury.

How different is the position of the American nurse-mid-wife from that of the contemporary midwife in Great Brit-ain? While in the United States hospital-based nurse-midwi-fery was a "manufactured" occupation, in Great Britain the position of the contemporary midwife was created by a suc-cession of legislative controls over traditional midwives, usurping their professional authority. The popular, widely used British midwifery text, Margaret Myles's *Textbook for Midwives,* states:

Doctors who have not been accustomed to the collabora-tion of professional midwives should reconsider the modern situation in which midwives are supplementary to and not substitutes for the doctor. They are an extension of his eyes, ears and hands, and a helpful assistant in abnormal and operative obstetrics.[35]

Myles phrases it as positively as possible, saying that "the modern role of the midwife is that of a team member functioning within an obstetric unit," but it is clear that the midwife is not the professional authority in that team. Her diagram of the entire "team" shows the obstetrician on top, in larger and darker letters than any other team member including the midwife. The introduction of the National Health Service (the British comprehensive medical-care system) in 1948 effectively locked in the power relations between midwives and doctors. The midwife retained her legal right to practice midwifery, but her employing authority requires her to function in collaboration with the doctor, who then delegates part of the maternity care to her. Under the Central Midwives Board Rules, the midwife must send for medical assistance when any deviation from the normal occurs, or any procedure outside her province is necessary.[36] Since the medical profession defines both "normal" and the "province" of the midwife, the costs to her autonomy are obvious. Myles, again phrasing it as positively as possible, says that the introduction of the National Health Service was for the midwife "the inauguration of the team concept of shared responsibility." Critics of the American obstetrical system worry that a national health service introduced at this time would similarly "lock in" the positions of doctors and midwives and effectively ruin all chances of reform.

With all of these limitations on her professional autonomy, what does the "modern" or "professional" midwife have to offer to birthing women? What has distinguished the midwife from the obstetrician has been her attitude and her hands. First, midwives, including nurse-midwives, have been trained with at least the stated definition of birth as a normal, healthy phenomenon. Second, and I think more important, midwives have been denied the use of instruments (notably forceps) and so, in order not to lose patients to physicians, have had to use their hands. Midwives sometimes speak of "hands" as another way of saying "skills," for example: "She has fantastic hands," or, "They may have a lot of theory, but you can't trust their hands."

The new medical technology and instruments that are being developed are being made available to nurse-midwives, and sometimes midwives are required to use them. Fetal monitoring is a good example of this. A hospital-based midwife told me that her hospital's policy demands the use of internal monitors in certain circumstances with the clinic patients, regardless of the nurse-midwives' judgment. She has been forced to rupture membranes, something she thinks is very bad midwifery. Internal monitoring requires the rupture of membranes (the sac containing the fetus and amniotic fluid, which cushions the fetal head during labor), and the use of a screw-in electrode in the top of the baby's head. The metal electrode, inserted through the partially opened cervix, screws into the fetal scalp and allows the monitoring of fetal blood. Somewhat less dramatically, many hospitals require or encourage external monitoring, which means putting a belt, attached to a machine, around the mother's abdomen. That essentially prevents the mother from getting up and walking around during labor, something which is usually considered part of good midwifery practice. Use of IVs is another example of medical technology allowed and sometimes required of midwives. Similarly, midwives can prescribe pain medication and do episiotomies.

This is a recurrent dilemma. If midwives are denied the use of medical technology, then they obviously won't have it when they need it. They will have to turn over every patient who needs any assistance, or even diagnosis, to a physician. That is essentially the policy offered by the medical profession in the 1700s, as outlined in the example given earlier of the surgeon refusing instruction on dealing with hemorrhage. But if she is allowed the medical technology, then what prevents the midwife from becoming a "mini-obstetrician," as critics have claimed? Presumably, it is her training in birth as normal and natural and healthy that distinguishes the midwife. And there's the rub.

Contemporary nurse-midwifery training takes place almost exclusively in hospitals. The only official domiciliary birth program in which nurse-midwives are trained is the Frontier Nursing Service, and the waiting list for that program now extends over several years. Any other home-birth training a midwife now gets is more or less underground. Sometimes a graduate nurse-midwife doing home births takes students out with her on a birth. This is definitely not a part of formal curriculum. The rest of the training takes place with poor clinic populations, and in a situation fairly tightly bound by physician-made hospital regulations. Can one get a sense of birth as normal and healthy by doing hospital-style deliveries with women one has never seen before, who are strapped to a monitor and IV in the labor room and to a table in the delivery room?

Among the major employers of nurse-midwives are inner-city hospital maternity clinics. Certified nurse-midwives have told me that they want to spend a year in that setting because of the volume and variety of patients ("You really get to see a lot"), and because the experience is seen as good for the development of certain kinds of skills: thinking quickly, recognizing pathology, and developing certain hand skills and techniques. On the other hand, the nurse-midwives I interviewed were all quite sensitive to the socialization process that they had been through in school and at work: "It turns your head around," or, more emphatically, "You get totally fucked over." They know that they learned to see birth through medically trained eyes: "If I could deliver a baby in the hospital and get it physically born, healthy and whole, I thought that was enough, that was my contribution." Almost all of the nurse-midwives I interviewed expressed interest in learning from lay midwives, often expressed as an antidote to the hospital experience.

It may be that "nurse-midwife" is a contradiction in terms, with an inherent dilemma. Nurses, in our medical system, are defined by their relationship to doctors, and midwives are, in the meaning of the term derived from Old English, "with the woman." Nurse-midwives operating in the medical establishment, paid by that medical establishment, have a hard time as "advocates of the childbearing couple." The essential elements of cooption—job, prestige, professional recognition—are all right there. As has been demonstrated with lawyers, clients come and go, but the institution and the people working for the institution, be it court or hospital, D.A. or M.D., remain. For a midwife to stand firm as an advocate of the right of any given client to birth in her own way would jeopardize her relationship with physicians, nurses, and hospital administrators. Ultimately, it would cost her her job.

In this context, home birth and midwife-run birthing centers can be seen not only as meeting client needs, but as meeting midwifery needs as well. It may be that the only way for them to get true professional autonomy is for them to opt out of the medical system. Opting out, however, is not easy. It is no easier for the midwife than it is for the physician to practice outside of a professional referral network. Midwives remain—as has been true since the medicalization of childbirth—dependent on physicians for "backup" services. If a laboring woman or a newborn baby, in the midwife's judgment, needs medical assistance, the midwife must have a physician to refer to. Ideally this should be a cordial, collegial relationship. Historically and today, this is frequently not so, and one of the ways physicians have always been able to fight midwives is to refuse backup services.

The nurse-midwives doing home births whom I interviewed were very concerned about backup problems. One, practicing in a birthing center where backup arrangements are formalized with a nearby hospital that accepts their transfers, said she would not herself give birth at home because she does not trust the local backup arrangements for home birth. Almost none of the home-birth midwives ever have the opportunity to follow a client into the hospital but must turn her over to hospital staff and then leave.

—"You definitely don't learn anything. It's sleazy."
—"It's hard in this city because to go to the hospital is such a big deal. I had one couple that went in with a [retained] placenta and they said, 'Where's your baby, did you throw it in the garbage, are you going to sell it?' "
—"It becomes such an emotional trauma to send someone to a hospital, it's a very painful decision to make. It's very hard on the client."

Also, doing the births is of borderline legality in some cases, depending on the backup arrangements. With firm physician backup, nurse-midwives in some states can legally do home births. But firm physician backup has been interpreted to mean that a midwife is employed by the physician, and not paid independently by the client. There is currently no midwife in New York, for example, hired by a physician to do home births. For self-protection, as well as protection of their clients, nurse-midwives would prefer not to bring clients into the hospital and call particular attention to themselves. They too are subject to a great deal of pressure, to "hassles."

—[about agreeing to do a home birth for someone] "It's this whole identity thing—because you are so responsible for these people and you feel you have to be sure they're going to represent you well [laughter], going to have a normal birth and not freak out on you at the end. You're so much more involved in the whole relationship than midwives in hospitals."

—"I just had this letter from the board [licensing] last week saying that it's come to their attention that I'm doing home births—after two years they just decided to notice—it's ironic because my license comes up for renewal this year."

—"You're kind of keyed up; your neck's on the line somehow."

For midwives, professional autonomy does not come cheap.

To Sum Up

The medicalization of childbirth has been extraordinarily successful, so successful that the competing profession, midwifery, has ceased to be a profession and become an ancillary service to medicine.

This cannot be explained on the basis of a superior technology, as standard histories of medicine claim. For one thing, at each point where medicine extended its control, we lack evidence that its technology was superior, and on the contrary have evidence to show the superiority of midwifery for maternal and infant survival and health. Even more important, one cannot explain power by the development of tech-

nology—power is a prerequisite for the opportunity to develop technology and especially to maintain control over
that technology. If the barber-surgeons had not had the
power to monopolize instruments in the first place, it would
not have been a barber-surgeon who developed the forceps.
Whether or not the technology is superior, it takes power to
maintain a monopoly over it.

The barber-surgeon, and later the physician, organized in
order to gain and to maintain power. As high-status males,
they were (and are) in a position to make alliances with the
state. When midwives did organize, earlier in European history, they were burned as witches.[37] Later on, the women
and the few lower-class men-midwives still lacked the social
power with which they could have negotiated with the state.

The technique that the barber-surgeons of earlier times
and the obstetricians of today have used to maintain power
over midwives is to define the skills that they (the surgeons)
monopolize as being essential for abnormal birth. The midwife is therefore dependent on the surgeon for backup services, which he holds the power to provide or deny. In this
relationship, the midwife loses all autonomy in her work. The
surgeon can define what is normal and abnormal, as well as
control the training of midwives and the services they can
provide. For example, American physicians have defined the
"need" for an episiotomy (surgical incision to widen the birth
outlet) as normal, and have allowed midwives to provide this
"service," while all other surgery and use of instruments are
defined as "abnormal" and not permitted to midwives.

American nurse-midwives have bought in to medical control, in much the same way other ancillary occupations have.
They have sought power by "upgrading" the profession, notably by extending educational requirements. But no matter
how much the midwife models herself on the surgeon, no
matter how long she trains in his hospitals, no matter how

many of his techniques she masters, she has not changed the fundamental balance of power. The only route to professional autonomy for midwives is the demedicalization of childbirth, and as the social-power factors remain essentially what they were in the 1700s, demedicalization might not be possible.

As Krause has pointed out in referring to how physicians got rid of nurse-anesthetists when "the job became more interesting in profit terms to the physician":

> The issue here is a general one. The physician can claim expertise over any and all activities in the health-care field, and if the setting is one over which he has actual control, that is that. Attempts to develop "specialist expertise" upon a physician's turf lead to the eventual limitation of the occupation by the group at the top of the technological hierarchy.[38]

As long as childbirth remains in the hospital, that may very well be that.

3

Consumer
Movements in
Maternity Care

When one considers the extraordinary diversity of the population using maternal and infant-care services in America, the homogeneity of the settings in which such services are provided is all the more striking. Hospital births in Peoria, in Manhattan, in the South Bronx, in Santa Cruz, in cities, in suburbs, in small towns and large look remarkably alike. The maternal and infant-care services have been effectively monopolized by the medical profession, making pregnancy, childbirth, and infant care and feeding all medical events, handled according to standardized medical protocols.

The medicalization of maternity care has not gone unchallenged. Once medical control over birth was firmly established, by the 1930s or earlier in the United States, the first major challenge came from the natural-childbirth movement. That movement began with the responses of obstetricians in other countries—notably Grantly Dick-Read of England and Ferdinand Lamaze of France—to the excesses of medical management. American women responded warmly to these new ideas, and the natural-childbirth movement in the United States was born.

"Natural childbirth" is a slippery concept: it may mean anything from there being no surgical incision at the time of the birth (episiotomy), whether or not the woman was conscious, to consciousness alone, even with an epidural or spinal anesthetic.[1] "Prepared childbirth" is a more useful concept for viewing American hospital births; it has come to mean the use of breathing and/or relaxation techniques. A nationally broadcast television program in 1974, praising the wonders of prepared childbirth, showed a woman using such techniques throughout early labor, and following them with the administration of an epidural that numbed her totally to the sensations of contractions and delivery. Her ability to be "awake and aware" was the source of admiration and satisfaction as, strapped to a delivery table, she watched the obstetrician pull out her baby with forceps. How did this come to be the 1970s resolution of the natural-childbirth movement?

It is widely held that the childbirth practices developed in the 1920s, including heavy medication, make up "traditional" childbirth, and childbirth preparation is a revolution against that tradition. That is not what happened. The childbirth-preparation movement, far from being a revolution, is at most a reformation movement, working within the medical model. This was not true of the earliest childbirth preparation, Grantly Dick-Read's natural childbirth, which developed in England. But Read's approach failed in the United States because it did not prepare women for the social situation they had to face in labor. Actually to use the Read method would have necessitated a revolution in childbirth management in the United States, not unlike what is happening in the birthing-center and home-birth movement. It was a revolution that did not happen.

Very little about the medical management of childbirth has changed in American hospitals in the past fifty years, apart from an increase in medical technology and intervention. What has changed has been the patient who comes in. The modern patient is frequently *prepared:* she knows what to expect and how to behave appropriately. Consciousness and lack of medication, the main achievements of childbirth reform in America, make an enormous difference in the experience of the individual woman—but they do not necessarily mean change in the medical management of birth. Natural childbirth implies a nontechnological approach to birth, and that is not consonant with the medical model. Prepared childbirth is socialization into the medical model. Consciousness does not equal control, and control over pain is not control over birth.

Making Pain the Issue

In the medical management of childbirth, the experience of the mother is viewed by physicians and other health workers primarily in terms of pain: pain experienced and pain avoided. There are a number of reasons why pain becomes a central issue in hospitalized births. For one thing, birth in hospitals is almost certainly experienced as more painful than birth outside of hospitals. The lack of emotional support and the simple lack of distraction play a large part in the experience of pain. Before the pressures of the prepared-childbirth movement brought husbands into the labor room, laboring women were routinely left alone. Their only companionship might have been another laboring woman on the other side of a curtain. For many women, this is still the situation. A nurse will stop in now and again, but for hour upon hour the woman lies alone, with no one to comfort her, hold her hand, rub her back, or just talk to her, and nothing to do to take her mind off her pain. Consider what a tooth-ache feels like in the middle of the night, when you're all alone and just lying there, feeling it ache and watching the clock tick away hours.

Second, the physical management of birth in hospitals may make it more painful. Confinement to bed prolongs labor, and the comparatively inefficient contractions in the hori-zontal position may make it more painful. When a woman is upright, each contraction presses the baby down against her cervix, opening up the birth passage. When she is lying down, the weight of the baby presses on the mother's spine, accomplishing nothing except to increase her discomfort.

Third, the mother's experience needs to be conceptual-ized as pain in order to justify medical control. Conceptualiz-ing the mother's experience as *work* would move control to the mother. This is clearest in the medical management of the second stage of labor, delivery, in which the mother is so positioned as to make the experience as painful as possible and at the same time to minimize the value of her bearing-down efforts. When the mother is in the lithotomy position (flat on her back with her legs in stirrups), the baby must be moved (pushed or pulled) upwards because of the curve of the birth canal. Doctors felt that this position gave them the most control, with total access to the mother's exposed geni-tals. But doctors' control came at the expense of mothers' control. The lithotomy position renders her totally unable to help herself, and she feels like "a turtle on its back" or a "beached whale."

This is not to say that labor, even under optimal conditions, is not painful. It is. As one of the nurse-midwives doing out-of-hospital births said: "Labor is pain—I have no question in my mind that it's really painful, and I think this idea of painless childbirth is off the wall, because most people do experience real pain." But there is a difference between experiencing pain and defining the entire situation in terms of pain. Pain may be one of the sensations people experience in sexual relations, for example, but most do not take it as the key element in sex. Any particular stimulation or pressure produces many complex sensations, and pain may be a part of what one feels. Certainly a pressure, irritation, or pinch during sexual intercourse that would be experienced as painful *by itself* may not even be noticed. Pain means different things at different points. What would be taken by itself as a painful sensation, when felt at orgasm, may be incorporated into the orgasm and never felt as pain at all. And birth does have much in common with orgasm: the hormone oxytocin is released; there are uterine contractions, nipple erection, and, under the best circumstances for birth, an orgasmic feeling. But the lithotomy position, like the missionary position, puts women flat on their backs and makes attaining orgasm a lot less likely.

Pain itself—felt pain, real pain—can be handled in different ways. It can be met with chemical, pharmacological technique (at its extreme, rendering people unconscious so that they do not feel pain—or anything else); with physical contact and comfort (as we rock a baby with a bellyache); with reassurance of the pain's normalcy and its passing ("There, there, you're okay, it's almost over now!"); or any combination of these. The techniques medicine uses to handle pain in labor are often not the most appropriate.

The felt pain of birthing women does not correspond to the medical expectations for their pain. For one thing, women who have experienced unmedicated births almost always find the first stage of labor, cervical dilation, to be painful, and the second stage, the actual birth, to be much less painful. Pushing the baby out is very hard work but for most women is not experienced entirely as pain. By contrast, in the medical model, it is the second stage of labor that is conceptualized and therefore treated as the most painful. Relatively mild pain-relieving medications are offered for first-stage labor, but for second stage, the "big guns," the anesthetics, spinals, and epidurals, are brought out. Pain in birth is sanctioned only in the delivery room because it is only there that the hospital provides the means to handle pain in an affectively neutral fashion—namely, by anesthesia. For doctors particularly, pain has been accepted and dealt with as pain only in the delivery room.[2] Dealing with pain by the most affectively neutral (and efficient) means available is not unique to childbirth. For surgical patients, the most frequently mentioned method of handling *any* complaint is the use of sedative or narcotic drugs.[3] In the situation of childbirth, the mother's demands for attention in labor are responded to with pain medication, thus in turn reaffirming the conceptualization of her needs as stemming from pain, and reaffirming the view of her as a surgical patient like any other surgical patient, and the delivery room like any other operating room. A laboring woman might really want some reassurance, some human contact. If she rings for the nurse, she will most likely be offered pain medication. Her fear, her need, will be met as if they were pain, teaching her that they are pain, thus reaffirming the medical view of her needs as stemming from pain.

The techniques that medicine developed for pain relief in labor were entirely impersonal. Through the 1950s women were given narcotics and scopolamine (an amnesiac), a combination called "twilight sleep," for labor, and anesthesia for delivery. Twilight sleep, or being "scoped," along with relieving pain made the woman forget the pain, and so willing to repeat the experience. This may be at least in part a response to the growing availability of and acceptance of contraception—if the woman forgets the pain, perhaps she will be ready to get pregnant again, now that contraception has given her a choice in getting pregnant. Sylvia Plath's heroine in *The Bell Jar* says that the amnesiacs sound just like "the sort of drug a man would invent." Twilight sleep also had advantages for institutional management: it could be attended to by lower-level staff, on "standing orders" from the doctor. And, in the next-best thing to having the patient's social self go home while the physical self is left for repair, the patient had no recall of her treatment. Doctors needed to have no contact with the patient until delivery. Delivery is of course the task for which the affectively neutral, technically competent surgeon-obstetrician is prepared.

Read: Childbirth without Fear

There were instances of women rejecting one or another aspect of modern obstetrics before any "movement" began. Margaret Mead, for example, writes in her autobiography, *Blackberry Winter*, of her attempt to re-create for herself in an American hospital the kind of natural, unmedicated birth she had seen so often in the South Seas. The first major thrust of the childbirth movement, however, was the publication of *Natural Childbirth*, by Grantly Dick-Read, in 1933. Read was an English obstetrician, and so his work must be understood in the light of a very different cultural experience surrounding birth. English midwifery survived the growth of obstetrics, as outlined in the previous chapter; and English obstetrics, quite possibly balanced by the existence of midwifery and relatively uninterfered-with births, never became as interventionist as American obstetrics.

Read developed his concept of "natural childbirth" as a result of a home-birth experience, just the kind of radicalizing experience I shall later discuss in connection with the nurse-midwives. He attended a woman in labor in Whitechapel, in a leaky one-room hovel lit by a candle in a beer bottle. As the baby's head was crowning (beginning to emerge) he offered the mother a chloroform mask, which she rejected. She went on to have a calm, peaceful, and quiet birth. When Read asked her later why she had refused medication, she gave an answer that has become a classic statement of the natural-childbirth philosophy: "It didn't hurt. It wasn't meant to, was it, doctor?"[4]

In the years that passed, Read observed that most women seemed to suffer a great deal in childbirth, but occasionally he met the "calm woman who neither wished for anesthetic nor appeared to have unbearable discomfort . . . it gradually dawned on me . . . that it was the peacefulness of a relatively painless labor that marked it most clearly as being different. There was calm, it seemed almost faith, in the normal and natural outcome of childbirth."[5]

Read decided that no, it was not "meant to hurt," and developed a theory of natural childbirth. He outlined that theory:

Civilization and culture have brought influences to bear upon the minds of women which have introduced justifiable fears and anxieties concerning labor. The more cultured the races of the earth have become, so much the more dogmatic have they been in pronouncing childbirth to be a painful and dangerous ordeal. This fear and anticipation have given rise to natural protective tensions in the body, and such tensions are not of the mind only, for the mechanisms of protective actions by the body include muscle tension. Unfortunately the natural tension produced by fear influences those muscles which close the womb and prevent the child from being driven out during childbirth. Therefore, fear inhibits: that is to say, gives rise to resistance at the outlet of the womb, when in the normal state those muscles should be relaxed and free from tension. Such resistance and tension give rise to real pain because the uterus is supplied with organs which record pain set up by excessive tension. Therefore fear, pain and tension are the three evils which are not normal to the natural design, but which have been introduced in the course of civilization by the ignorance of those who have been concerned with attendance at childbirth. If pain, fear and tension go hand in hand, then it must be necessary to relieve tension and to overcome fear in order to eliminate pain.[6]

In a nutshell: "If fear can be eliminated, pain will cease."[7]

Read's is a fairly sophisticated statement of psychosomatic relationships, and notably, one that does not "blame the victim." Unlike many other statements by physicians which held the "weakness" or "delicacy" of "civilized" women to blame for pain in childbirth, Read places responsibility with birth attendants for the "evils" of fear, pain, and tension. That is an important theme in his work: although he holds the most Victorian and traditionalist attitude toward women's role and purposes, Read shows respect for the laboring woman. While viewing motherhood as a woman's "ultimate purpose in life,"[8] her crowning achievement, and so on, may not do much for women's place in the larger society, it is not necessarily a bad perspective with which to approach a laboring woman. Seeing the laboring woman as fulfilling her most important function in life, drawing closer to God as she works to bring forth her baby (and Read definitely viewed labor as work, "hard work"), may be of more value to the laboring woman than the prevailing American philosophy, which saw the laboring woman as essentially no different from someone in the hospital for gallbladder surgery.

Read's philosophy had considerable appeal in the United States as well in Great Britain, and it is its Americanization that concerns me here. *Childbirth without Fear: the Principles and Practices of Natural Childbirth* was published in the United States in 1944. In 1947 the Maternity Center Association invited Read to the United States for a lecture tour. While Read's book and method appealed to many American women, the Americanization of Read was in practice something of a disaster.

Read called attention to the socio-emotional context in which birth takes place: he did not speak only of its psychological meaning for the individual woman. Having a "good attitude" is not enough. Read taught women relaxation techniques, how to find and then release muscle tension throughout the body—by unwrinkling the brow, letting loose the hunched shoulders, and unclenching the fists. He taught these techniques before labor, but then reaffirmed that teaching throughout labor. He stated: "No greater curse can fall upon a young woman whose first labor has commenced than the crime of enforced loneliness." He relates his own fear during a wartime battle in which he "learned the meaning of loneliness."[9] He said that women needed *continual* comfort and emotional support throughout labor. While that may have been possible for Read's patients in-hospital, and was certainly possible for his home-birth patients, it was not provided for the American women who "failed" at natural childbirth. The majority of American women who attempted to follow Read's advice did so under hostile conditions. They shared labor rooms with women who were "scoped," and their screams, combined with the repeated offering of pain-relief medication by the hospital staff, reinforced the very fear of birth that Read set out to remove. The results were generally perceived as failures of the method or failures of the individual woman, rather than the result of systematic interference by the institution.

Because the Read method developed in a social situation entirely different from the American hospital, it was impossible to transplant it intact. Loneliness of the laboring woman was the most severe handicap to the use of the method in this country, but not the only one. American physicians, rejecting the English style of side-lying birth and Read's advice, continued to use delivery tables, routine episiotomies, and local anesthetics even for "Read" births.[10] Rather than helping to produce the peace and calm that Read called for, the move to the delivery table, the strapping into the lithotomy position, the episiotomy, and so on, all created tension. Results with the Read method at Yale Hospital Clinic in 1946 showed that Read-style preparation did reduce the amount of anesthesia in comparison to that used for unprepared women, but where Read had averaged nine out of ten births without medication, the Yale group used drugs in half the cases. As time went on, the differences between the two groups, prepared and unprepared, lessened. Richard and Dorothy Wertz, in their comprehensive study of the history of birth in America, *Lying-In*, argue that the earlier success may have come from the "newness" of the technique, "since patients desiring prepared birth received extra attention and were welcomed with open arms as subjects for research. Once the newness and special attention lessened, so did the favorable results."[11] That is a very interesting argument to make in this instance. It is certainly true that many new drugs have most favorable results when special attention is paid to the subjects in the first studies. With the Read method, however, attention is *part* of the method. As some few American hospitals routinized the method, or, conversely, other hospitals which were not supportive at all had women using it anyway, the method itself was so severely compromised as to be worthless. When the special attention —or emotional support—was taken away, all that was left of the Read method were some relaxation techniques and the "knowledge," in contradiction to all that the woman saw and heard in her hospital labor, that birth is a normal and healthy phenomenon.

What was needed was a childbirth method designed to meet the needs of hospitalized women. Women needed preparation not just for the physical event of the birth itself, as Read provided, but for the birth as it occurs in hospitals. The Lamaze, or psychoprophylactic method, met these demands.

Lamaze: Childbirth without Pain

The psychoprophylactic method grew out of Pavlovian conditioning techniques. Uterine contractions were held to be stimuli to which alternative responses could be learned. Most women had learned pain and fear responses; it was believed that with training, these responses could be unlearned, or deconditioned, and replaced with such responses as breathing techniques and abdominal effleurage, or stroking. Furthermore, it was held that concentration on these techniques —techniques based on the methods used by lay midwives— would inhibit cerebral-cortex response to other potentially painful stimuli. The method was developed in hospitals in the Soviet Union and in 1951 was established there as the official method of childbirth.

In that same year, 1951, two French obstetricians, Ferdinand Lamaze and Pierre Vellay, traveled to Russia and observed obstetrical practices. After making some relatively minor changes, Lamaze introduced the method in Paris. In 1956 he published a book on the method, *Painless Childbirth*, and Pope Pius sanctioned its use. Worldwide acceptance followed swiftly.[12] The method was brought to the United States not by an obstetrician but by a mother, Marjorie Karmel, an American who gave birth with Lamaze in Paris in 1955. In 1959 she published *Thank You, Dr. Lamaze: a Mother's Experience in Painless Childbirth.* In 1960 Marjorie Karmel, along with a physiotherapist, Elisabeth Bing, and a physician, Benjamin Segal, founded ASPO, the American Society for Psychoprophylaxis in Obstetrics.

From its inception, ASPO has been geared to the American hospital and the American way of birth. The only challenge ASPO offered to the American birth concerned the use of anesthesia. ASPO substituted psychological for pharmacological control of pain. While the difference between consciousness and unconsciousness may be all the difference in the world for the mother, from the point of view of the institution that single factor is relatively minor. In the original ASPO training course, written by Bing and Karmel and published in 1961, it is stated:

> In all cases the woman should be encouraged to respect her own doctor's word as final. . . . It is most important to stress that her job and his are completely separate. He is responsible for her physical well-being and that of her baby. She is responsible for controlling herself and her behavior.[13]

This certainly poses no threat to the control of birth by obstetricians. As Vellay himself, one of the French developers of the method, was to say in 1966, "We have always maintained that *Painless Childbirth belongs above all to the obstetrician.* They can estimate and understand better than anyone else the very special behavior of the pregnant woman."[14]

Even on the question of pain medication, the doctor's rather than the woman's perceptions were to be valued and trusted:

> If your doctor himself suggests medication, you should accept it willingly—even if you don't feel the need for it—as he undoubtedly has very good reasons for his decision.[15]

It is important to note that this was written long before obstetricians were familiar with the technique, and so could not possibly be accurate in their judgment of the need for pain relief—if in fact one person can *ever* judge another's pain.

The physical trappings and procedures surrounding the American birth were written into the original course, including the perineal shaves, enemas, delivery tables (although women were taught to request politely that only leg and not hand restraints be used), episiotomies, and whatnot. To consider just the example of the episiotomy, Lamaze instructors even today are often taught to think of it as a merciful aid to the mother. At a birth-movie showing, several Lamaze instructors expressed to me their disgust at the sight of a slowly stretching and bulging vaginal opening, as depicted in a French film in which the baby is delivered over an intact perineum (without cutting). The untrained members of the audience, in marked contrast, were visibly disturbed by the sight and sound of skin being cut for the episiotomy in another, American-made, Lamaze film. Even more basically, ASPO accepted the medical model's separation of childbirth from the rest of the maternity experience, stating in this first manual that rooming-in (mother and baby not being separated) and breast feeding are "entirely separate questions" from the Lamaze method.

ASPO thus managed to meet on the one hand the demands of women for a "natural" childbirth and, on the other, the demands of obstetricians for "good medical management." The issue became resolved over *consciousness*. The title of the first book to be published by an American obstetrician supporting the Lamaze method makes the point: *Awake and Aware: Participation in Childbirth through Psychoprophylaxis.*[16] Control over one's behavior (notably pain response) was interpreted to mean control over the situation. At first glance, the Lamaze method may appear to center on autonomy, but that confuses consciousness and pain control with power. Women, especially the middle-class educated women of the 1960s and seventies who used the method and made it so popular, may have felt that it met some of their desire for control over their bodies. But this was a deceptive thing, a false consciousness. The method succeeded where Read had failed because it was the only practical method designed to deal with the hospital situation. In the chapter on childbirth, I will show just how the Lamaze techniques fit into and support the hospital birth.

ASPO and the Lamaze technique still dominate prepared childbirth. ASPO teachers, or Lamaze instructors, as they are frequently called, work both in hospitals and privately, offering the ASPO childbirth-preparation course, which has changed very little since the first manual in 1961. The childbirth-education classes begin in late pregnancy—the seventh month is believed to be ideal—so that the conditioning will be fresh and the level of motivation high. Classes, usually consisting of approximately six to ten couples and an instructor, meet weekly for six weeks, to learn the mechanisms of labor, breathing and relaxation techniques, and about hospital procedures. The entire course deals with labor and delivery, though some brief mention is usually made of how a newborn baby looks and acts. As with the medical model, birth is separated both from pregnancy and from parenthood.

The course is given for pregnant women and their husbands. Husband participation is considered advantageous but not strictly necessary for the use of the method. "Enforced loneliness" is not considered an insurmountable handicap. Over the past twenty years the majority of American hospitals have allowed husbands into the labor rooms and, now, the delivery rooms. The husband acts as his wife's "labor coach," a position held by the *monitrice* in the French version of the Lamaze technique. The coach provides the continual emotional support that Read talked about, but is seen by ASPO as really being there to provide very specific coaching in the method. Since there is no *monitrice,* no member of the American hospital staff assigned to help the laboring woman, the husband takes on both roles in the American version, and so must be trained along with the wife. In essence, the method keeps the woman quiet by giving her a task to do, making being a "good"—noncomplaining, obedient, cooperative—patient[17] the woman's primary goal. And as is not uncommon with relatives of institutionalized people, the husbands are coopted into doing the staff's work, moving the patient through the medical routines as smoothly as possible. Mother, coached by father, behaves herself, while doctor delivers the baby.

Within the institution of the hospital, medical dominance, and thus the medical model, is so powerful and entrenched that it cannot be modified. Attempts at reform either fail outright or become so coopted that they end by supporting the system. The contrasts between Read's "childbirth without fear" and Lamaze's "childbirth without pain" can be understood only in the social contexts within which each method developed.

Read saw birth as a woman-controlled event, something that a woman works to bring about. The women Read saw were only minimally medicated, and physically unrestrained. Because at least on occasion he dealt with women at home, in their usual social settings, Read was able to see the influence of a supportive environment. Furthermore, he saw birth in the social context of motherhood. Immediately after birth the women were *mothering*—holding, talking to, comforting, playing with their newborns. The baby, in Read's view, was the woman's prize for her work.

Those who dealt exclusively with hospitalized births, and particularly American managed births, saw birth as a physician-controlled event, something that physicians work to bring about. The women the American childbirth movement saw were both heavily medicated and physically restrained, as well as cut off from all social support. Birth was thus seen as a mechanical-surgical event. After birth, the babies were taken away and the mothers sent to recovery rooms. Birth was to be witnessed, rather than "done," by mothers. The orgasmic and spiritual nature of birth of which Read spoke was replaced by a businesslike matter-of-factness. Emotional support was traded in for technique coaching; spirituality, for athletics. The crisis nature of birth was retained from the medical model, and childbirth, as practiced by the Lamaze, prepared-childbirth instructors, continued to be defined in terms of medicine rather than motherhood. It is the home-birth movement that presented genuine challenges to the medical model.

Feminism and the Womanly Arts

The home-birth movement across the United States represents an extraordinary and sometimes uneasy alliance of feminist and traditionalist women and men. For the feminists, childbirth tends to be one of many fronts on which the struggle for women's control of their lives is taking place. For the traditionalists, the childbirth issue is rooted in the context of the traditional wife-mother role. For the traditionalists, the issue is frequently not so much that of a woman's control over her body as it is one of family involvement and control over birth.

The struggle around childbirth is essentially a question of autonomy and control, a basic power issue. One of the sides of that power struggle is the profession of medicine, which has established itself in the United States as the legitimate authority on all matters relating to maternal and infant health—contraception, fertility/infertility, pregnancy, childbirth practices, postpartum management, infant feeding, and much of early child rearing. The other side of the struggle for control over childbirth is not nearly so organized, and makes up the home-birth and "alternative birth center" or out-of-hospital birth movement. This side includes within it this schism between feminists and traditionalists. While both challenge the medical model and the profession of medicine, the feminists go beyond that and challenge the patriarchal family structure as well. The insistence on women's control over women's bodies, so essentially a part of the feminist movement, presents threats to the traditional family structure (women deciding whether and when to have babies) as well as to the profession of medicine (women deciding how and where to have babies).

Norma Swenson, active in the prepared-childbirth movement and in recent years active in the women's-health movement, and one of the authors of *Our Bodies, Ourselves,* [18] has pointed out the incompatibility of the prepared-childbirth movement with the feminist movement. The long-standing rule of the childbirth movement was that the *doctor* has the final responsibility for birth. The feminists see women as having the right to control their bodies, and the responsibility that goes along with that right.[19]

Swenson goes on to say that feminists and nonfeminists alike are increasingly resolving this contradiction in favor of the woman. Maybe. From my observations of the home-birth movement, I would say that is not necessarily true. Both feminists and traditionalists are engaged in wresting power from medicine, resolving the contradiction *against* the doctor. But where the feminists see the birthing woman as an individual with the right to control her own body, the traditionalists see the birthing woman as part of a family unit, with *family* rights and obligations.

The issue is highlighted in the question of abortion. Feminists in the home-birth movement see freedom of choice in childbirth and the right to abortion as two sides of the same coin: women's right to control their bodies. Many feminists became involved with women's-health issues through organizing around abortion, where the right of women to control their own bodies was being denied by the state. Feminists are increasingly coming to see childbirth in the same way. For the traditionalists, on the other hand, abortion is a very different issue, and for some, a contradiction to the home-birth movement. For some traditionalists, home birth is above all a way of strengthening the family. The interest in the home-birth movement has moved from simply bringing the father in, as was the case with the prepared-childbirth movement, to greater interest in birth as a family event, with other children present. There is talk about "family bonding," cementing ties between parents and siblings and the newborn at the time of birth. These same traditionalists, on the other hand, often see abortion as threatening the family structure. Many of the traditionalists also have a religious or spiritual commitment to home birth, in which birth is seen more as a spiritual than a medical event, and abortion is forbidden. *Spiritual Midwifery,* by Ina May and the Farm Midwives, of the Tennessee commune "The Farm," prints the Hippocratic injunction against abortion facing the opening page of "Instructions for Midwives."[20]

Feminists are often uncomfortable with the traditionalist women in the childbirth movement, with their commitment to fulltime motherhood, their dependence on men as husbands, fathers, and doctors, and even their political opposition on such basic issues as the Equal Rights Amendment. The traditionalists, for their part, are not trusting of the feminists. The Hathaway family, joint authors of the book *Children at Birth*, for example, warn against the feminist movement:

> A word about the feminist movement. Lately there is an assumption the FEMALE attendants are naturally better than male—that all women are sisters and only a woman can empathize with another woman. Maybe this is right but I doubt it. Cast your mind back over the history of childbirth—Dick-Read, Lamaze, Bradley, Brewer, DeLee, Semmelweise, Leboyer—all were males. These MEN have contributed greatly, not only to the technological safety of birth but also to the feelings, joy, pride of the MOTHER, the FATHER. Today we have many concerned females— and more power to them—but also we have unconcerned, sadistic and political women.[21]

Because this split between traditionalists and feminists (or political women) is recognized, and because both the feminists and the traditionalists recognize their mutual need if they are going to effect change, and probably also because the political heritage of both (especially the ASPO and La Leche League experience of the traditionalists) has taught them the value of the single-issue group, specifically feminist issues—particularly abortion—are never raised outside of small, homogeneous groups.

Abortion is somewhat tangential to childbirth practices; it may be a perfect simile, as the feminists see it, a situation in which women's control of their bodies is at stake; or it may be the exact opposite, as the traditionalists see it, a threat to the integrity of the family they so strongly support. But in time and space, abortion is removed from childbirth practices. Other areas of conflict need to be faced more openly.

Fathers at Birth: Coaches, Partners, or Helpers?

The effect of feminist versus traditionalist orientation on the way birth is done is more directly discernible. Take, for example, the question of the role of the father/mate in childbirth. This role may be conceptualized in a variety of ways: fathers may be 1) kept away from births; 2) expected to physically and emotionally support the mother in labor; or 3) given authority and control over the birthing woman. The last is the most traditionalist, patriarchal role. I found the clearest statement of that role in Marion Sousa's *Childbirth at Home.* [22] Sousa presents the traditionalists' argument for childbirth at home, writing for "parents who feel that the birth of their child ought to be a family event rather than a surgical operation . . ."[23] Sousa writes, paraphrasing Elisabeth Bing, the physiotherapist founder of ASPO:

> . . . in a healthy marriage, the husband ought to be the dominant partner. As such, he needs definite scope to exercise his directive role when the child is born. In ideal circumstances, the husband must be able to both supervise and support his wife during labor.[24]

Another mode of childbirth preparation, the Bradley method (like the Lamaze, named after the male obstetrician who developed the technique), is called "husband-coached childbirth."[25] The Bradley method, unlike the Lamaze, has been closely linked to the home-birth movement and particularly to the National Association of Parents and Professionals for Safe Alternatives in Childbirth (NAPSAC), the national umbrella organization for the alternative-birth movement. I have seen, at a NAPSAC conference plenary session, birth films in which the father wore a Bradley "coach" T-shirt, while the mother gave birth with only the father and her other children in attendance. At an entire session of birth films, not a single film was shown with a woman (lay midwife, physician, or nurse-midwife) as birth attendant. All birth attendants were male doctors or fathers.

The father as a "coach," or "directive" and "supervising," while the woman is in labor, is clearly playing a traditionalist, patriarchal role. The implications of the other two potential roles of the father, absent or supportive, are less clear. The absent father may exemplify the feminist ideal of strong female solidarity, in which birthing is woman's business, with women supporting each other. Then too, the father's absenting himself from the birth may be an example of the strong, "macho" male role, in which men would wish not to be sullied with women's work around children.

The same alternative interpretations are applicable to the father in the supportive role. The father who participates actively in preparing for birth, helping the mother do the exercises, learn breathing techniques, and so on, who actually supports her in labor, may be significant of a truly supportive and mutual relationship preparatory to nonsexist, cooperative child rearing. On the other hand, this suggests couvade rituals, in which the husband imitates the wife's pregnancy and to some extent her birth rituals. Among the Arapesh and Balinese studied by Margaret Mead, for example, fathers share pregnancy taboos with mothers and lie beside the woman after birth, resting from labor. Such practices as cutting the umbilical cord, preparing a birth feast, and helping with the wife's daily chores are similar in form if not in intensity to the couvade.[26] These are all typical of the father's role as an active participant in birth. I have seen numerous birth films in which the father appears to be laboring as hard as the mother, doing the breathing exercises, holding her up during contractions, even placing the nipple in the baby's mouth. (For a good example of this kind of supportive-imitative behavior, see the childbirth film *Lynn and Smitty.*) These birth rituals, like the couvade, may represent specific mechanisms by which the children produced by women are claimed by men.[27] From a different perspective, the benefits of "participatory birthing" are male role enrichment;[28] and the participatory birthing of a child can be a "peak experience" for the father, as it has been called for mothers.[29] The line between sharing and controlling, support and "who's having this baby anyway?," is not at all clear.

The modern example of the couvade ritual is best represented by the "Leboyer birth." Frederick Leboyer is a French obstetrician who has defined birth as a trauma for the child. He seems to try to make amends for the supposed nightmare of being born by repeating the birth more "gently."[30] Shortly after birth the baby is placed in body-temperature water and then massaged. The bath and massage are done by Leboyer himself, as he describes it, but in this country the Leboyer bath is typically done by the father. The symbolic reemergence from the amniotic fluid and the rebirthing by the father's hands is the male improvement over the female's birthing.

Learning by Doing:
Mothers' Experiences with Birth

For feminists, the commitment to home birth or midwife-run birthing centers grows out of their ideological commitment to women. Midwifery is a feminist issue, even for those not actively engaged in childbearing. The traditional women, on the other hand, seem more likely to come to home birth out of their own childbearing experience. Strongly traditionalist women may have large families and in the course of three or four hospital deliveries have learned quite a bit about the hospital management of birth as well as about birth itself. With repeated exposure to the situation, a certain amount of demystification is inevitable, and the mother may come to feel that she knows more about her body in labor than does the hospital staff. But medical management of birth is based on "objective" criteria, rather than on the "subjective" experience of the mother; that is, cervical dilatation and fetal monitor graphs count for much more than the mother's statement of how far along she is. I have heard countless stories of hospital births in which the staff discounted the mother's reports, went with the "objective" criteria, and then found that the mother had been right. Most common is the story, often told in the first person, of the staff's ignoring the mother's pronouncement that she is ready to birth *now.* While the staff consults her chart and assures her that she has time to go, the mother pushes the baby out on the labor bed. Another story I have heard, albeit less commonly, is of the staff's suddenly expressing great concern for the fetus, based on the monitor, while the mother insists that nothing has changed. The problem, as the story is told, is eventually diagnosed as being in the monitor itself, whether it is a loose connection or even, in one instance, a pulled plug. Such stories of course argue in favor of the midwifery model: trusting the mother to know her own body. That is why they are so popular among home-birth advocates. But these episodes also occur repeatedly and are radicalizing experiences for the mother.

Whether it is the relatively dramatic instance, such as

those told in these stories, or the more mundane, repeated experience of the inappropriateness or irrelevance of medical management for her history and needs, a number of experienced mothers turn away from the hospital.

—The way they scrub at you and get you ready—as though you have no feelings whatsoever . . . We couldn't see any real advantage to hospital deliveries. (Mother, after three hospital births)[31]

—I just got to thinking about the kind of noncare I got in the hospital that I paid so much for . . . (Mother, after five hospital births)[32]

And reflecting total disillusionment with the power of the physician, Marion Thompson, a founding mother of La Leche League, described one of the three hospital births that preceded her home births. She was a rarity, twenty-five years ago in that hospital, having her second "natural" childbirth, and a number of spectators were invited by her doctor (after she was told that there would be no room for her husband):

So I was wheeled right into the delivery room, asked to please keep my legs together and not to bear down, and then left alone. When my doctor arrived it reminded me of those triumphal processions where the king enters the captured city. All it really lacked were the bugles. First came a nurse walking backwards, the better to put his gloves on, and directly in back of him another nurse, tying up his gown. Behind them, the spectators, who quickly filled the room. "Doctor, they won't let me push," I said. "Marion, you can push now," he said. So in three pushes, no tearing and no screaming, my beautiful dark-haired Deborah was born. And as I joyfully reached out to touch her, one of the residents rushed up to my physician and said, "Doctor, how did you do it?"[33]

It is not only the mother's experience with giving birth that may disillusion her with medical management. There is also the factor of her experience with mothering. In Chapter 7, I discuss how the relationship between birth practices and later infant care, such as timed and scheduled feedings, fear of "spoiling" infants with too much holding, and so on, coincided with the hospitalization and medicalization of birth. But for now let us consider the opposite relation: the effects of infant care and child-rearing practices on later birth choices, and consider the implications of a strong traditional mother role for later birth choice.

La Leche League and Home Birth

On a July day in 1956 two mothers at a Christian family-movement picnic in Franklin Park, Illinois, sat under a tree and nursed their babies. Throughout the afternoon mothers at the picnic walked over to them and said, "I had so wanted to nurse my baby, but . . ."

> That's when it really hit us that the problems we had in trying to nurse our babies were common to a lot of mothers," Marion [Thompson] recalled. "It wasn't just Mary's particular rare problem or my particular rare problem."[34]

That kind of mental leap, made between one's personal problems and a common situation, has variously been called the sociological imagination[35] and consciousness raising. These two women, along with five others, took that idea and joined together in what eventually became La Leche League International, with more than 3,300 groups in the United States and forty-two other countries.

The League began with the idea that what was necessary

for successful breast feeding was support and encouragement, which women were not getting elsewhere. The League set out to provide support groups, a telephone "hot line" for individual counseling, and role models. Any interested woman, whether she was pregnant, nursing, or neither, could come to La Leche League meetings and watch other women nurse and hear their discussions. She could see for herself healthy five-month-old infants who had never gotten any nourishment other than breast milk.

In the 1950s we were at least a full generation removed from midwifery and home birth. Grandmothers of the 1950s had more often than not given birth in a hospital, attended by a physician. They had likely had their own babies on scheduled feedings and weaned early to a bottle. Add to this the frequently great geographical distance between the new mothers of the 1950s and their female kin, and the role of the League becomes clear. They provided in a formal structure what the medical and family systems were unable or unwilling to provide informally.

Medicine had taken over the grandmother's or midwives' role in infant care beyond the period of hospitalization, in the sense of becoming the "authority," having the ultimate word. Consider the following from an early (1946) edition of Dr. Spock's *Common Sense Book of Baby and Child Care:*

—Your doctor will prescribe the baby's schedule on the basis of his needs, and you should consult him about any changes.[36]
—The baby's doctor is the one to make the decision and prescribe the formula.[37] [Note that formula is "prescribed."]
—If you are particularly interested [in demand schedule] you can discuss with your doctor whether he thinks it is practical or advisable for your baby.[38]

—If he is on the bottle, draining every one, and regularly waking early, consult the doctor about increasing the formula.[39]
—If he's regularly not getting enough, he'll probably cry for more. Take his word for it, and get in touch with the doctor.[40]

Note that this is from the "common sense" approach to baby care. What made Spock "commonsensical" is that he told mothers to trust the baby's judgment as well as the physician's. The only person whose judgment is clearly not to be trusted is the mother's.

Spock is hardly unique in this reliance upon the doctor for the normal care of babies. A 1953 "Happy Mealtime for Your Baby," published by the Beech-Nut Packing Company (makers of baby foods), says:

Before we go any further, let's emphasize one important point: your doctor knows your baby—and he knows you. How your particular baby should be cared for, *whether he's sick or well,* is a matter that should be decided by your doctor—not by the neighbors, relatives or books.[41]

This is the prevailing tone of the times for middle-class mothers, and this is what the League responded to. Even when medicine began to create the idea of easing up on schedules, it was not the mother's judgment they relied on, but the baby's. Think about what it means when we say "demand" feeding—that the newborn makes demands, demands which the mother then meets. This is like the model of the fetus in pregnancy, as a consuming parasite. How different it is if we instead think of "need feeding,"[42] babies being fed when they need it. La Leche League provided continual reassurance that only the mother knows her own baby and is best able to interpret its needs.

The League came up with specific, concrete suggestions for infant care and parenting that were directly counter to prevailing medical advice, including taking the baby into the parent's bed for night feeding, "baby led" weaning, and the late introduction of solid foods. Doctors thought that babies needed solid food early, and that breast milk could not really sustain a baby beyond the first six weeks or so. League mothers trusted the baby to indicate when it needed more than milk, and trusted the mother to recognize these needs. Rather than coaxing and patiently pushing spoonfuls of "baby food," League mothers said it was fine to wait till babies reached out for food.

Even today this remains controversial. A mother who rejected her pediatrician's "prescription" of cereal for her six-week-old, when she remarked that he was gaining weight and growing well on breast milk, showing no interest in anything else, was greeted with "Oh, no, you're not one of those La Leche fanatics, are you?" The case of the Bruners of Boise, Idaho, is a more dramatic and more frightening example. The Bruners angered their pediatrician by having a home birth. When he saw that their older child, a two-year-old, was still nursing, he accused them of child abuse and nutritional deprivation. Unfortunately, the political power of the profession of medicine is such that the child was forcibly taken to a hospital for observation. There was of course no evidence of neglect or deprivation, and the child was released to the parents.[43]

The League mothers began to deal with these questions of baby care in political terms, asking not only what is best for babies, but asking *who knows best.*

We were bucking the whole medical establishment when we recommended late solids. These were the problems we dealt with at board meetings.[44]

And in regard to late weaning:

"I remember I was so excited about those articles when Edwina was writing them," Marion said. "I felt they were such important breakthroughs. As I was typing them up for the NEWS I felt they were so important because I had never seen it down in print before. This was the first real exploration of the issue from the mother's and the baby's viewpoint. I felt it was very exciting and important. You couldn't find that information any place else in the United States at that time."[45]

What the League has contributed to the home-birth movement is an awareness that medical knowledge is incomplete and systematically inaccurate. A good proportion of home-birth parents and people actively involved in the home-birth movement are League members, who learned a lot with baby number one (or two or three) and turned to home birth with the League philosophy of faith in mothering. Most of the founding mothers of La Leche League had their last babies at home, though this has not been widely publicized. La Leche League has remained a single-issue organization, taking on only breast-feeding, just as ASPO takes on only birth.

Unlike prepared-childbirth groups, however, La Leche League has not been coopted by the medical establishment. They have not accepted the medical model, nor have they found places for themselves in the medical establishment. League leaders are all volunteers, unlike ASPO teachers, who are paid for their time. (LLL is organized around "groups," which have "leaders." ASPO is organized around "classes" and "instructors.")

Baby care is potentially more resistant to medicalization than is childbirth, for a number of reasons. Infant feeding is not a "crisis" situation, and it is difficult to invoke the "life or death" drama one can call up for childbirth. Weight is gained or not gained over time; disagreeing with the doctor does not threaten a mother with the imminent loss of her baby's life. In childbirth, a medical procedure can be phrased as being for the life/health of the baby, and whether or not that has basis in fact, the mother is in no position to determine. Then too, infant care cannot be isolated the way childbirth has been. Most women have never seen a birth when they are wheeled into a delivery room for the first time. ASPO provides films for role models, but the league provides the supportive presence, including round-the-clock telephone help, of other mothers.

The League presented an alternative model of infant care and parenting, one that emphasized "mother-wisdom" at the same time that it pointed out flaws in medical knowledge. These ideas became an important part of the ideology of the home-birth movement.

La Leche League presents a woman-centered model of mothering, where the mother is the expert on mothering. The League is certainly not "feminist" in any modern sense of that word. Women are, in their view, bound totally to home and child, and mothering is the only role they seem to see for a woman. On the other hand, within that domain, she is in control and her judgment is valued. The League wholeheartedly rejects male doctors' telling mothers how to mother. That is very close to the attitude of eighteenth-century midwives, who felt it was ludicrous for men to try and take control over birth:

I should not despair of seeing a great he-fellow florishing a pap-spoon as well as a forceps, or of the public being enlightened by learned tracts and disputations, stuffed full of Greek and Latin technical terms, to prove that water-

gruel scotch-porridge was a much more healthy aliment
for new-born infants than the milk of the female breast,
and that it was safer for a man to dandle a baby than for
an insignificant woman.[46]

That is of course precisely the extreme to which it has been
taken, with Similac and Enfamil replacing water gruel and
Scotch porridge.

La Leche League has combined a strongly traditional
model of mothering, emphasizing "mother-wisdom" and the
"womanly arts," with a rejection of medical authority. It has
succeeded, to the extent that it has grown enormously and
provides services to many thousands of women and children,
without being coopted by medicine. Its success is based on
its ability and its willingness to work outside of medicine.

The Feminist Contribution

Even though much of the active leadership in the home-
birth movement is strongly traditionalist, the reemergence
of feminism plays a supportive role. The contemporary
women's movement has created both a climate and a rheto-
ric that are used by home-birth advocates; one hears phrases
like "taking our bodies back," "consciousness raising," and
"patriarchal dominance" from women whose entire life-style
expresses strongly traditionalist gender-role values. The
women's movement legitimizes these women's desires for
women birth attendants, and, even more important, for
women *controlling* birth.

The women's movement can also be credited with much
of the growing awareness and skepticism of health-care con-
sumers about medical practice in general. It was women
organizing around the issue of abortion who began to raise

questions about medical expansion into ethical concerns, bringing essentially moral issues under medical control.[47] And women, pointing out the sexist structure and practice of medicine, brought to public awareness some of the limitations of medicine. The movement to "demystify" medicine grew out of feminist consciousness.

Feminism also provides a social support for women birth practitioners, both the empirical and the nurse-midwives. Many, if not most, of the empirical midwives are women who became midwives as a result of their own birthing experiences. They, like some of the nurse-midwives, are working mothers, whose irregular hours do not allow them to play a traditional wife-mother role.

The home-birth movement and midwifery strike a responsive chord in both feminist and strongly traditionalist women, because the underlying ideology is strongly woman centered. The more traditional women are more comfortable when the woman is linked into a family structure, and the more feminist women, when the woman is considered as an individual; but they share a view of the mother as having both the right and the ability to mother in her own way.

At a time when one hears so much about the splintering of the women's movement, I find it heartening to see counterculture women from communes, suburban "housewives," and feminist activists all organizing around a single issue.

PART II
Maternity Care
in America

4

Infertility: Getting Pregnant

A woman seeking medical assistance for infertility has the following encounter with her doctor:

Dr. C.: Have you thought of adopting a child?
Mrs. A.: We're at opposite ends of the pole on that. George would like to very much, and I guess I'm kind of selfish about it, but at this point I'm balking.
Dr. C.: In other words, you want George's baby.

This conversation was presented in a 1972 medical-journal article as an ideal model for physicians to follow in such situations.[1] But is it? A woman who is seeking assistance for infertility may or may not care about having George's baby, but she almost certainly is interested in having her *own* baby. She comes seeking assistance in getting pregnant. But just what does pregnancy mean? Dr. C., working within the patriarchal model of medicine, thinks of pregnancy as a woman's carrying the child of a man. This idea of pregnancy has a long history within our culture in general, and within medicine in particular.

One of the first uses of the microscope was to examine sperm and to view the child carried within each spermatozoa. This "little man," homunculus, was one of the earliest medical discoveries made by using the new technology of the microscope. In time, of course, medicine acknowledged the embryo to be the product of two genetic contributions, with women as creators as well as hosts or nesting places for embryos. That conceptualization of sperm as actually being the baby in miniature has strong social support in the patriarchal view of women as bearers of men's children and has not entirely disappeared.

In the medical model, the sperm continues to be seen as the active "life force," and the female as a passive receptacle containing an ovum waiting to be fertilized. Fertilization is defined in *Gould Medical Dictionary* as the union of male and female gametes, but also as the act of making fruitful and as impregnation.[2] The male fertilizes the female; the female is fertilized. The sperm is said to move up the female reproductive tract as if under its own power, "swimming" up to reach the ovum. Yet biological evidence exists that indicates that a bit of inert matter will be pulled up the female reproductive tract just as quickly as sperm. In the same way that sexual intercourse can be described as the penis entering the vagina, *or* as the vagina encircling and grasping the penis, so conception can be described as the sperm swimming up the female reproductive tract to find and fertilize the waiting ovum, *or* as the female reproductive tract pulling up the sperm, which the waiting ovum then incorporates. No, the egg is not necessarily sitting around waiting for the phone to ring. Medicine, as an institution of patriarchal culture, prefers thinking of the waiting ovum and the active sperm, along with the thrusting penis and receptive vagina.

Shades of the early theory of the homunculus are still with us. This patriarchal perspective is part of mainstream American culture; consider recent popular songs with lines such as "You're having my baby," and "Would you marry me anyway, would you have my baby?" Our language embodies the idea: to father something is to generate it; to mother it is to nurture it. And where is the corollary for a "seminal" theory?

Infertility and the Boundaries of Parenthood

In any serious consideration of infertility, the problem of defining biological as well as social motherhood and fatherhood emerges. Biological fatherhood is genetic parenthood; a biological father contributes half of the genetic basis for the child to be. Normally genetic parenthood is combined with the sexual contribution to conception; the biological father is the sexual mate of the mother. But that no longer has to be the case. Biological fathers can make their genetic contribution to conception without mating with the mother, substituting an artificial form of insemination for sexual intercourse.

The first recorded case of artificial insemination comes from an Arabian manuscript of 1322. A horse breeder left a wad of wool in a mare's vagina overnight, and then held it to the nostrils of a prized stallion. The breeder caught the stallion's ejaculate on the wool and put the wool back into the mare, which conceived.[3] The procedure, with slight variations, is now a basic part of animal husbandry. But it appears to have taken five hundred years before the process was tried with humans. In the 1890s an American doctor, Robert Dickenson, with great secrecy artificially inseminated women whose husbands were unable to produce sperm. The continued secrecy surrounding artificial insemination makes it hard to determine how many children have been "produced" this way, but estimates are at between 5,000 and 10,000 children born each year in the United States.

Biological motherhood encompasses both aspects of biological fatherhood—the genetic and the sexual—and a great deal more. Biological motherhood also involves pregnancy, the birth process, and suckling the baby. As the technology has become and continues to become available to make substitutes for one or another of these aspects of motherhood, the problem of defining female infertility gets more complicated. Before the invention of the rubber nipple, the pasteurizing process for cow's milk, and the development of formulas to substitute for breast milk, if a woman could not produce milk, she could not be a mother; her babies would die. Her only alternative was to find a substitute mother, a wet nurse. But a wet nurse is possible only in an adequately fed population. When people or animals are able to scrounge up only enough food to keep themselves alive, any female who cannot nurse her baby cannot be a mother. This has been the case among all people living on the borders of starvation, whether they are tribal nomads or people living in nonindustrialized parts of the world, or in modern nations in times of war-created starvation. In modern American society we no longer think of the breasts as necessary for fertility, now that we have found substitutes, although their symbolic value of course remains powerful.

A woman with a very small pelvis, perhaps deformed from an accident or from rickets in childhood, cannot "give birth" —her baby must be removed surgically. Before the advent of the techniques necessary to do cesarean sections, women with small pelvises were perforce infertile; they could not produce a live baby and survive. According to Jewish law, a child delivered by cesarean section may not fulfill the obligations of a "firstborn,"[4] which places the mother in the rather strange position of being socially "infertile" in spite of the presence of her child. It is no longer necessary for a woman to go through a birth, to move through the stages of labor, in order to be a mother. Pregnancy can be ended before labor, the mother made unconscious, and a live baby delivered surgically.

It is not yet possible for a human female to avoid pregnancy and still "reproduce," but it is possible in animals and doubtless will soon be possible for people. Embryo transplants have been done with several species, including mice and cows.[5] The embryos have been removed from the mother in which they were conceived and transplanted to another mother in which they were carried and from which they were born and by which they were presumably suckled. Very expensive British lamb embryos, for instance, are flushed out of ewes after conception and are placed in rabbits and flown to the United States and South Africa. One rabbit can serve as a packing crate for several embryos and is much cheaper to transport than several pregnant sheep. Upon arrival, the rabbits are disposed of and the embryo sheep transplanted into ordinary ewes, where they develop normally until birth.[6] It is just a matter of time, and probably not much time at that, before human embryos can be flushed out of one woman and placed in another. A very similar procedure has already been successfully done with extrauterine conception, but using the same woman as genetic parent and for pregnancy. The great fanfare which greeted the British baby Louise Brown, who was "produced" this way, was in recognition of technological barriers being pushed further along, challenging our traditional ideas of parenthood.

When embryos, or just ova, can be transplanted from one person to another, it is debatable whether the "donor" or the "host" will be considered the biological mother. The donor, the one who mates and conceives, can in one sense be thought of as a biological father; she contributes half of the genetic material, and there her biological contribution ends. Women who are "infertile" because they cannot conceive would enter biological motherhood at the point after conception, carrying and birthing transplanted embryos. The mother-host would not be a genetic parent, but there would be a biological tie between mother and child, and social motherhood would begin normally, with pregnancy.

Finally, there are women who enter biological, not only social, motherhood only after birth, women who cannot conceive or bear children, but who nurse their adopted children. They are using their breasts and their milk to establish a physical and biological tie to their social children.[7]

The modern, anonymous adoption, so different from taking in a relative's children, and the use of artificial insemination have raised new distinctions in defining parenthood: there are now "real" parents, "biological" parents, and "adoptive" parents. Embryo transplants push those distinctions further. The use of an artificial placenta, a true "test-tube" baby, or the use of animals as hosts for human embryos, which comes close to the myth of the feral child raised by the wolves, push all our nice, comfortable ideas about mommies and daddies and babies—that cats can't have puppies and dogs can't have kittens—over the brink. Enormous moral and ethical dilemmas are raised under the heading of infertility, questions every bit as awesome and complicated as those raised by abortion or genetic counseling. Social relationships are redefined to meet the changes in our technology; we define these relationships in different ways as our technology changes what it means to be a mother or a father.

Providing formula, doing a C-section, and incubating a premature baby are all "routine" procedures, so much so that the "true motherhood" of women who rely on any or all of them is never questioned. As step by step the technology gets more powerful, we as a society have to find a way of incorporating it, redefining "motherhood" and "fatherhood." Alternatively, we have to find a way of controlling the technology, taking from it what we want and not taking what we do not want. We do not have to take everything technology and science have to give.[8]

The issue is raised again with the possibility of cloning—yet another potential technology to influence our thinking about parenthood. Cloning replaces genetic motherhood and fatherhood, as we know them, with direct genetic transfer. A clone is not a new combination of genetic possibilities but an exact duplicate of its "parent." How will the advent of cloning for humans affect our thinking about parenthood? Cloning replaces genetic parenthood, but a cloned cell, like a zygote, the single-celled product of conception, needs a biological mother in which to be implanted and develop. While genetically very different, cloning is socially not very different from genetic fatherhood. As Judith Lorber has said:

> Whether the method is implantation of an embryo, artificial insemination, or sexual conception, until we have artificial wombs, a man has to have the cooperation of a woman for the pregnancy and delivery. In order to have a biological child of his own, he must find a woman at her fertile time, get her pregnant, get her to inform him if she is pregnant, persuade her to take care of herself physically and carry the child to term, give birth and not kill the child, but deliver *his* child to *him*. Even if he does not want this woman to bring up his child, it is clear that a man has to use strong means of persuasion on a woman—physical, psychological, social, or economic—in order to reproduce himself in his own image.[9]

Some things change, but some things remain constant; until the development of either an artificial placenta or a willingness to transplant human embryos into the uteri of other species, every human baby, cloned or not, will have a human mother. Lorber contrasts the difficulty of a male's trying to have his own child with the situation of women, who need only to get live sperm—and in the event of cloning not even that—in order to have a child of their own. Rather than seeing the demands of biological motherhood as restrictive, putting women at a physical disadvantage, Lorber focuses on the potential power women have in the ability to control reproduction. However:

> Now the question must be asked, how is it that women, who have superior biological control over reproduction, do not have social power in most societies? That is, how did they lose social control over their children; how were they deprived of the control of what is probably the most valuable social resource a group can have?[10]

It is a question that cannot be answered in a fully satisfying way. Lorber points to the socially created need of women for men institutionalized in marriage and the family. The creation of the family, and thus kinship rules, gives men claim on the children of women; she carries George's baby.

This leads back to basic questions of what a family is and what parenthood means. Perhaps for people who will have very little to do with raising the child, it is particularly important to have a genetic tie; hence the distinction between fathering as largely genetic and mothering as largely social. The coming technology, which will allow women to "father" children, may present new possibilities for women who feel this way. Some people have expressed concern over the possibility of women's using other women as mercenary host-mothers for their children, as indeed some women have done. There has never been much of a pattern, however, of women bearing children and then turning them over to men and disappearing. Male-fathers have seen the usefulness of keeping the mother around as a readily available source of dependable child care. Women who want to "father" children will probably also discover the usefulness of a wife-mother. The women who have come to use other women as mercenary mothers have been infertile women using mercenary donor-mothers, not women with normally functioning reproductive organs using mercenary host-mothers. Very few infertile women lack a uterus that could host an embryo, and probably the opportunity to have normally beginning social motherhood, starting with pregnancy, would be welcomed by many of them. The surrogate mothers who have been in the news lately have not been used for "convenience," to avoid pregnancy. Rather they have been used by women who are, at least at this point in our technological development, infertile.

The preceding analysis of how parenthood is and may be defined is useful in understanding the medical model of fertility-infertility. Let me now turn the discussion from the world of embryo transplants, artificial placentas, and cloning to the here and now of the medical management of the infertile couple.

The Treatment of Infertility

Infertility investigations usually begin when the woman of the infertile couple goes to a gynecologist. Starting with the woman rather than the man is for social rather than physiological reasons. Physiologically it makes as much if not more sense to begin an infertility evaluation with the male partner; but socially, infertility as well as fertility is seen primarily as the woman's problem. For women, the single most common cause of infertility is her mating with an infertile man. (Conversely, the single most common cause of infertility in men is mating with an infertile woman.) Some researchers suggest that only 40 percent of infertility is attributable in whole or in part to the male, and others claim that half of all fertility problems may be due to male factors alone, including some cases of repeated miscarriages caused by defective sperm. There are numerous reasons why a male may be infertile, some of them treatable and some not, but from the woman's point of view they can all be lumped together. When male infertility is the problem, as it will be for approximately half of all women with a presenting complaint of infertility, the solution lies with the male: either treatment or a change of mate. When the man cannot be treated, the woman can use another man as the father and be an entirely "natural" biological mother.

This leads to the medical route to changing the mate: artificial insemination. Most of the literature on artificial insemination (both in and out of medicine) discusses it as an aid for the woman married to a sterile man. The reader is asked to sympathize with her plight and view artificial insemination as the solution to *her* problem. In one of the clearest statements of this view, Gerald Leach, author of *The Biocrats*, writes that artificial insemination with donor sperm (A.I.D.) will be a psychological success, "above all if the wife realizes that a husband's agreement to A.I.D. is a profoundly important gift to her."[11] This is the theme of the medical-literature discussions of A.I.D. counseling.

Historically, when infertility was assumed always to be the "fault" of the wife, husbands were given the recourse of divorce. Part of the marriage contract was the agreement to produce children, and if the wife could not live up to her obligation, the contract was voided. In Jewish law, part of the American heritage, ten years of marriage without the production of a child entitled a husband to divorce his wife. Remarriage was possible for him, but not for her as a "barren" woman. Now, given the technological sophistication sometimes to prove beyond all doubt that the male is responsible for the "barren" state of the couple, in this situation maternity is a privilege rather than an obligation of the wife. The husband, having been diagnosed as infertile, can "allow" the wife to be treated. A.I.D. does, after all, turn conception into a series of medical treatments for the woman. But it is important to bear in mind that it is the husband whose infertility is being overcome by means of these treatments. When the wife is on the examining table, it is hard to remember just whom A.I.D. is aiding.

While girls are raised to be mothers, from the first doll to teenage baby-sitting jobs, the channels by which women can achieve the goal of motherhood are strictly limited; this leaves the woman who is married to an infertile man in a difficult situation. If she adheres to traditional goals (motherhood), then the traditional means, getting pregnant within her marriage, won't work for her. The more traditional she is in her goals, that is, the more she defines herself in terms of motherhood, the greater the pressure she is under to use innovative means to achieve these goals. It may really be the most traditional women who are the most willing to use innovative, even radical, means to achieve this goal. In the case of the infertile woman, innovation may mean the use of medical services to accomplish what is usually accomplished naturally, that is, ovulation, implantation, and, recently, "test tube" conception of her own ova. Adoption is another alternative. For the fertile woman married to the infertile man, there is much more room for innovation. Adoption is a possibility in this situation as well, but other, possibly more satisfactory solutions are also available.

For the fertile woman married to the infertile man who

accepts the cultural goal of motherhood and wishes to make her "innovations" as unobtrusive as possible, becoming pregnant is the logical choice. Following the argument up to this point, the medical literature then branches into a discussion of artificial insemination as a "gift" husbands can give to their wife. The kindness, goodness, and open-heartedness of the husband is usually stressed in discussions of artificial insemination. In a strikingly radical note, one (female) doctor at a discussion of the law and ethics of A.I.D. raised the following question:

> Why should insemination be artificial? Why is it not acceptable that she might have a baby from another person by natural insemination? This channeling of the woman's needs and the ways in which she may accomplish these needs through a male morality deserves more attention.[12]

An alternative way of looking at the situation is that artificial insemination is a treatment for male infertility which wives can give as a profoundly important gift to their husbands. Rather than finding another, fertile, husband, or simply taking a lover, the wife agrees to be inseminated like a prize cow, with doctor's appointments and syringes and cervical caps replacing the warmth and intimacy of sexual relations. Whether she does this just to meet her husband's needs, or has her own reasons for not wanting to take a lover, she does give her husband the normal family life and full experience of fatherhood he would be denied if she replaced him with another husband, and spares him the discomfort, feelings of inadequacy, and jealousy he might experience if she took a lover as a more natural "donor." She turns over the choice of donor to the doctor (having no choice in who the father of one's child will be is paralleled only in rape) and accepts the anonymity and unnaturalness of A.I.D. Some women request for their second child that the same donor be used again. This has been interpreted by doctors as simple satisfaction with the "product," but might more truly represent the woman's attempt to regain control. Rather than having an unknown donor of the doctor's choice, the second pregnancy has a known, specific donor (baby one's genetic father) whom she has chosen.

From the perspective of a patriarchal society, in cases of artificial insemination the husband is "allowing" his wife the pregnancy, rather than adopting or remaining childless, as if those were *her* only possible recourses, and even more important, as if adoption or A.I.D. or even childlessness would all be the same for the husband. In the emphasis on genetic ties as defining fatherhood, the sharing of a pregnancy and birth by the woman's husband have been dismissed as meaningless. In some states in the U.S. as well as in some other countries, the husband of a woman who has had artificial insemination (even at his written request) must formally adopt the child in order for it to be considered his. In the medical literature, he is referred to as the "stepfather."

Patriarchal society has reduced the potential of fathering to the single-cell genetic contribution. Many centers for infertility make it a policy not to offer A.I.D. unless it is first requested by the "patient." The medical profession, in what it does and does not research, what it does and does not offer willingly, dismisses the importance for men of having children to raise, or being someone's father. Any responsibility that a man undertakes willingly to control reproduction, whether it is male contraception or male treatment of infertility, is seen as a sacrifice and a kindness on his part for his wife.

This same point can be demonstrated in medical treatment at the beginning stages of an infertility evaluation. The first logical step is to determine whether the woman is producing ova, and the man, sperm. Since ovulation is by far the more difficult to determine, a semen analysis for the presence of adequate, healthy sperm is the usual first step. One way of doing a semen analysis is to collect the ejaculate in a glass jar after masturbation and have it analyzed within two hours. A second way is to recapture the semen from the vagina of the man's sexual partner, in a "postcoital examination." In order for it to be most informative, the postcoital test must be done within two hours of intercourse, which means that the couple has to have intercourse by appointment, at a time convenient to the physician. The woman then has to get dressed immediately, travel to the doctor, get undressed, and get on an examining table. At later points in a fertility analysis such a procedure may be necessary, but for a semen analysis it turns the woman into a substitute for a glass jar. In a symposium on diagnostic procedures in infertility,[13] four male doctors discussed the pressures on the male in a postcoital test, the requirement that he "perform" on demand. The pressures on the female, to have that "performance" followed immediately by an examination (almost always by a male doctor), were ignored. One doctor concluded:

> We've been talking about possible pressures involved in preparing for a postcoital test. A great deal of pressure can also be generated in preparing for a semen analysis. I frankly think it is easier to obtain a postcoital test, at least in the initial phase of the evaluation.

The male "prepares" for the postcoital test, but it is the woman who is actually examined. Using a postcoital test as a substitute for a semen analysis alleviates pressure on the male; he is being examined through the female, so that he does not undergo the pressure of having to masturbate on demand, and probably even more important, so that he is provided a "discreet" way of being examined without being made to feel that his fertility (read power, maleness) is being questioned. The male in the infertile couple is treated as fertile until proven otherwise, while for the female, infertility is assumed and implied even though the chances are about the same for both. Examining both of them initially would imply that either or both of them could be infertile. One of the major textbooks dealing with this area states:

> Because the female has been a more willing patient, more research has been accomplished in female infertility. As a result, current therapeutic possibilities are greater for the correction of female than male infertility.[14]

Then too, this pattern may not be a result only of the willingness of the female to be a patient, but of the relative willingness of doctors to treat the reproductive system in females. With regard to contraception, in which there are many more techniques available for women than men, physicians believe that the male system is easier to interfere with because it is more complicated.[15] The corollary, that infertility in the male system is easier to repair because it is simpler, has not been examined. The same doctors who debate the relative emotional trauma for the male of a postcoital versus postmasturbatory semen analysis (for neither of which does the male have to be seen or touched by doctors) are unlikely to suggest elaborate testing or treatment procedures for their male patients. As with contraception for men, we cannot really know how unwilling men would be to take over responsibility for either fertility or infertility, as long as the medical profession "protects" them in this way.

The Treatment of Genetic Problems

Very closely related to the management of infertility is the medical management of certain genetic diseases and conditions that affect pregnancy and fetal development. Two of the best-known of these genetic diseases are Tay Sachs, predominantly affecting European Jews, and sickle cell anemia, predominantly affecting blacks. Both of these are recessive traits; for a couple to have an affected baby, both genetic parents must be carriers. The genetic-counseling programs that have been established in order to deal with these and similar disorders attempt to identify carriers in the target population before they become parents, and when a double-carrier couple is identified, to counsel childlessness, adoption, or amniocentesis and selective abortion. The social couple is treated as a genetic unit. Donor semination, artificial or otherwise, is not suggested in the medical literature, although that would allow normal social parenthood for both parents.

A similar situation is found in the management of Rh incompatibilities. In Rh incompatibility a perfectly normal baby who is Rh positive is reacted to as if it were a foreign invader in its perfectly normal Rh negative mother. The destruction of fetal blood cells creates severe anemia and the condition called erythroblastosis fetalis. The fetus is bloated, may have heart failure, may be born dead or convulsing, or may become severely jaundiced. It may escape death but be left severely brain damaged. It is not a genetic disease, because there would be nothing wrong with the fetus if only it were in an Rh positive mother, and nothing wrong with the mother's ability to carry a fetus if only it were Rh negative. It is simply an incompatibility.

The most logical step, then, in dealing with Rh problems is to prevent the incompatibility by preventing Rh negative women from mating with Rh positive men. The Rh factor is a dominant gene; for a baby to be Rh positive it has only to inherit the Rh factor from one of its parents. Therefore, it is only if an Rh negative woman mates with an Rh negative man, who like herself has no genes for the Rh positive trait, that she can be assured of having "compatible" babies.

For most Rh negative women, the problem was solved in 1968 with the discovery of RhoGAM, a gamma globulin which destroys Rh cells before the mother's body begins antibody production. However, the *American College of Obstetrics and Gynecology Technical Bulletin* on the Rh factor reported that in 1974 between 10 and 20 percent of women at risk were not given the protection of RhoGAM and that particularly after abortion it was frequently not given. Because there are women who were sensitized before RhoGAM was developed, because not every woman who should be given RhoGAM is given it, and because some women become sensitized in spite of the use of RhoGAM, Rh sensitization does still occur. Depending on fetal age and how badly the fetus is affected, medical management of erythroblastosis fetalis consists of induction of labor, cesarean section, or transfusion in utero, each of which carries risks to both mother and fetus. Fetal transfusions, for example, involve injecting dye into the amniotic fluid and doing an amniogram (X-ray procedure) to determine whether the fetus is hydropic (bloated). Once the fetus is hydropic, there is very little chance of saving it. Fifty to 60 percent of nonhydropic fetuses are saved with transfusions, though just how many of these would have lived without the transfusions is not known. Using fluoroscopy (more radiation), the physician inserts a needle through the mother's abdomen, into the uterus, and directly into the peritoneal cavity of the fetus, and blood is transfused. This procedure is repeated every ten days to three weeks until the fetus is mature enough to be born. While more than half of the fetuses die anyway, the survivors appear to be quite normal. However, the long-range hazards of both the radiation and the transfusions are not readily ascertained.

While I found repeated discussion of this and related treatment procedures in the medical literature, I found no suggestions for recommending donor semination by an Rh negative man to the sensitized Rh negative woman. Being Rh negative was discussed as a risk condition for *women*. Bear in mind that a woman who has lost any number of fetuses and babies to Rh incompatibility is perfectly capable of carrying an Rh negative baby to term without any medical complications at all. Again, the problem, here an interactive genetic problem and not a pathology on either side, is defined as the woman's problem in fertility, and is treated as such.

This way of seeing the problem comes back to the way pregnancy itself is conceptualized within the medical model. As long as pregnancy is conceptualized as the presence of a man's baby in a woman, fatherhood will be seen as genetic parenthood, and motherhood as the ability to provide an adequate nest for George's baby.

5

Pregnancy

Not everybody who gets pregnant can be a tall, well-nourished, Rh positive twenty-four-year-old who has never miscarried or had a stillborn, never been sick except for rubella and toxoplasmosis* many years before, and has given birth three years earlier to a healthy baby weighing between seven and nine and a half pounds. Yet virtually any deviation from this ideal makes a woman "high risk." While she and her doctor may accept in principle the current popular idea that pregnancy is a normal and healthy condition, the many tests, the careful watching, the constant screening will help her think of her own particular pregnancy as being precarious, even dangerous. If she is thirty-five or older, she is obstetrically "elderly," and will be encouraged to have amniocentesis to test for genetic disorders, and will be

*Rubella is German measles; toxoplasmosis, like rubella, is a usually mild disease that can cause complications in pregnancy.

watched for obstetric complications. If she is too young, had no children or had too many, even if she is simply poor, she may find herself classified as "high risk," an exception to the supposed norm of pregnancy as healthy.

In fact, even if a woman does have all the healthy characteristics medicine can ask for, she still won't be called healthy, or even normal. She will be classified "low risk." In that sense, all of us are at some risk for developing virtually any disease and even dying of it in the next year. But what if you went for an annual checkup, and instead of being told you were healthy, were told instead that you were at low risk of dying of leukemia, lung cancer, or heart disease this year? Virtually any house can be struck by lightning; do you care to think of where you live as being "low risk" for lightning? This is just what contemporary medicine has done to pregnancy. It has distinguished between "low risk" and "high risk" pregnancy, with the emphasis always on risk, and then gone on to define an ever increasing proportion of pregnancies as "high risk." That is, normal pregnancy may exist and be only "low risk," but there are many factors that will make any given pregnancy "high risk." Some of these factors are engendered by the changes of pregnancy itself, such as the phenomenon of "preclinical diabetes," or "mild pre-eclampsia," which I will discuss later in this chapter. Other "risk factors" are natural characteristics of women, such as parity (number of previous pregnancies) and age. The tendency is clearly to broaden the "high risk" category. For example, a grand multipara is considered a high risk-patient. A grand multipara was, until recently, defined as a woman who had had five or more previous births. Now that women are having fewer pregnancies, "grand multipara" is being redefined to mean "having had three previous births." Presumably the objective and inherent risk of a fourth or fifth pregnancy has not increased just because it has become a less frequent occurrence, yet it is a newly created "high risk" situation. Similarly, the age for amniocentesis for genetic disorders has been moved from forty to thirty-five within just the past ten years. As the categories expand, more and more pregnancies are subsumed under the heading of "high risk."

Medicine used to simply define pregnancy itself as pathological, a condition of illness, quite frankly a disease. That was of course how medicine gained control over the management of pregnancy. It justified requiring medical care during pregnancy by calling it a disease state. Doctors are, after all, society's experts on disease. Having called childbirth a pathological condition and moved that under medical control, their next step was to call the entire pregnancy pathological and to develop medically oriented prenatal care.

Remnants of this definition of pregnancy as a disease remain in modern obstetrics. For example, a physician introducing a discussion on a particular phenomenon of normal pregnancy began by stating:

> For those who regard normal pregnancy as a disease, the terms "physiological" and "normal pregnancy" will probably appear as contradictory or even mutually exclusive.[1]

In the new (1980) edition of *Williams Obstetrics* the authors explain:

> A priori, pregnancy should be considered a normal physiologic state. Unfortunately, the complexity of the functional and anatomic changes that accompany gestation tends to stigmatize normal pregnancy as a disease process.[2]

Even when the specific pronouncement is made that pregnancy is not a disease, as in *Williams,* the seductive vocabulary of illness remains. Every text and article I consulted in my review of the medical literature on pregnancy referred to the determination of pregnancy as the "diagnosis" of pregnancy, and to the changes of pregnancy as its "symptoms." And in discussions of one or another phenomenon of pregnancy the word "normal" is frequently used to refer to the nonpregnant state (e.g., the hormonal level in pregnancy is "higher than normal," or the uterus in pregnancy is contrasted to its "normal state").

The Medical Model of Pregnancy

Until the 1960s, medicine in this country viewed the pregnant woman as a body with an insulated, parasitic capsule growing inside it. The capsule within was seen as virtually omniscient and omnipotent, knowing exactly what it needed from its mother-host, reaching out and taking it from her—taking vitamins, minerals, protein, and energy, at her expense if necessary—while protected from all that was bad or harmful.

The pregnancy in this model is almost entirely a mechanical event in the mother, who differs from the nonpregnant only by the presence of this thing growing inside her. Differences other than mechanical changes, such as the enlarging of the uterus, are accordingly seen by physicians as symptoms to be treated so that the woman can be kept as "normal" as possible through the "stress" of pregnancy. Pregnancy is not necessarily unhealthy in this model, but it is frequently associated with changes other than the mechanical growth of the uterus and its contents, and these changes *are* seen as unhealthy. For example, the hemoglobin count, which is lower in pregnant women than in nonpregnant women, makes pregnant women appear (by nonpregnant standards) anemic. The result is that they are treated for this anemia with iron supplementation. Water retention, or edema, is greater in pregnant than in nonpregnant women. This "condition" is treated by the placing of limits on salt intake and by the prescription of diuretics. Pregnant women tend to gain weight in addition to that accounted for by the fetus, placenta, and amniotic fluid. They are then treated for this weight gain by being put on strict diets, and sometimes are given "diet pills." Knowing that these changes are very likely to occur in pregnant women, American doctors set out to treat all pregnant women with iron supplements, limits on salt and calorie intake, and diuretics, all in the name of "preventative medicine."

What are the sources of this model? How did pregnancy come to be considered as a stress situation—as not normal? How did the fetus come to be thought of as a parasite and the mother as a host? One answer is that medicine as a profession gained control over pregnancy by calling it a disease. The other answer I have discussed in the previous chapter, where I considered the essentially patriarchal ideology of medicine in its definitions of pregnancy and parenthood. Medically, pregnancy is viewed as being a man's baby growing inside a woman. When the fetus is thus seen as a product of the male's body, it follows that its presence in the female body must be an intrusion. *Obstetric-Gynecologic Terminology*[3] entitles its chapter on the fetus "The Fetus (Passenger)." Despite all the technological advancements, the dominant organizing belief for medicine about pregnancy is that daddy plants a seed in mommy. Thus, for doctors, pregnancy is an adversary relationship, in which the needs and interests of the mother-host are pitted against those of the fetus-parasite.

The Modern Management of Pregnancy: Staying Pregnant

In 1961–62 an unprecedented outbreak of phocomelia, a congenital malformation characterized by severe defects of the long bones, resulting in what were commonly known as "flippers," missing limbs, was observed in Western Germany primarily, and throughout Europe and the United States to a lesser extent. At least 5,000 infants were involved. It was later documented that the defects were related to the use of a tranquilizing drug, thalidomide, during the thirtieth to fiftieth day of pregnancy. In many cases the thalidomide was taken on prescription from obstetricians for the control of nausea during pregnancy.

That thousands of infants were dramatically damaged by a substance ingested by their mothers directly contradicted the medical model, which believed the fetus to be insulated and protected within the womb. The placenta, as a result of this experience, was no longer seen as a shield or barrier for the infant; instead it came to be seen as a "bloody sieve."[4] The 1971 edition of *Williams Obstetrics* stated:

> The most important practical lesson to be drawn from the experience with thalidomide is that no drug should be administered to the pregnant woman *unless it is urgently indicated.* This injunction applies particularly to drugs administered during the first half of pregnancy for nausea and vomiting.[5]

The sixteenth edition, in 1980, substitutes "in the absence of a real therapeutic indication" for "unless urgently indicated," somewhat softening the statement. But in both the older and newer editions, 600 pages earlier, in a discussion of the nausea of pregnancy, several drug recommendations are made, including one that *Williams* reports may be teratogenic (causing malformation), although "evidence is not convincing."[6] *Williams* paints the thalidomide disaster as graphically as possible; there is a photograph of an entirely limbless baby, a formless column of flesh with a baby's head. Yet the evidence that another drug is teratogenic must be "convincing" enough before they will stop recommending it.

Rapidly on the heels of the thalidomide discovery came a new awareness of the danger to the fetus of radiation. While some acknowledgment of the hazards of radiation resulted from the experience of the Hiroshima bombing and its effects on fetal development, in the early 1960s chest X rays were still considered an important part of good early-prenatal care, and X rays were used routinely to determine fetal position (and number, when multiple pregnancy was suspected), to measure the pelvis, and even to determine pregnancy itself. It is now recognized that exposure to radiation in utero greatly increases the incidence of malignant disease in the exposed children.

A further blow to the model of the protected fetus came from the DES research, in which diethylstilbestrol, a synthetic hormone given to some women in the 1940s and fifties to prevent miscarriage, has now been found to cause cancer in their daughters ten, twenty, thirty, and, potentially, fifty years later. This most recent revelation, that a baby which appears fine may nonetheless have been profoundly damaged by a prenatal exposure, may have permanently shaken the idea of the baby as being insulated. But medicine does not even now fear tampering with the prenatal environment, which would lead it to absolutely avoid all but life-saving medications, radiations, and other procedures. There is rather an increased selectivity. For example, while radiation is being used less and less frequently, the use of sonograms (sound-wave pictures) is becoming widespread, along with the claim that they are, unlike X rays, not harmful. The technique is too new to have had long-term follow-up, nor are sonogram-exposed fetuses being studied in large-scale, systematic ways.

Even the use of drugs for pregnancy-related complaints

has far from disappeared, and *Williams* is not alone in its drug recommendations. I have before me two major obstetric texts, both published in 1975. One includes, on its list of drugs so widely used as to be considered safe, meclizine.[7] The other lists several that have been shown to cause birth defects in animals and should thus be avoided; included in this list is meclizine.[8]

It is only in the 1980s that Bendectin, long considered a perfectly safe treatment for the nausea of pregnancy, has come under scrutiny. In this instance it was a parents' lawsuit that raised the safety issue. They claimed that the thalidomide-like damage done to their child was caused by Bendectin. Bendectin has not been declared totally unacceptable, but the medical establishment now calls for greater caution in its use. Drugs, it seems, are innocent until proven guilty.

Similarly, the antacid drugs still widely recommended for heartburn in pregnancy (*Williams* calls them "innocuous"[9]) have been linked, by at least one reputable researcher, to stress on fetal kidneys, leading to metabolic alkolosis and edema, congestive heart failure, or an increase in kidney disease in the newborn, magnesium poisoning, and damage to fetal neurological and neuromuscular systems.[10] It is because of contradictions such as these in the literature that I say the medical model of the fetus as protected by a placental barrier has not entirely disappeared. It is interesting that there seems to have been a more widespread *public* acceptance of the idea of the permeability of the placenta and the care that women are therefore obliged to take with what they eat and drink. Many people seem to be aware of the hazards of smoking, drinking alcohol, or using caffeine during pregnancy, and many hesitate to use any over-the-counter medications without (or even with) the recommendation of their physician. In fact, some women find that they are more cautious than their physicians are about using medications.

In sum, medicine sees the common physical discomforts of pregnancy, such as nausea or heartburn, as the symptoms of an underlying diseaselike state, brought on by the stress of bearing a parasitelike fetus. The prescribed treatments, ranging from some old "treatments" using parts of the husband's body—his blood or testosterone—to treat the problems caused by *his* fetus in *her* body, to the variety of drugs and procedures now in use, are limited only by the growing body of evidence that treating the mother has direct and sometimes disastrous effects on the infant.

The Midwifery Model

In the midwifery model, on the other hand, the emphasis is on pregnancy as a healthy and entirely normal condition for mammals. This position is, of course, politically necessary if lay midwives are to claim that nonmedical personnel are competent to attend to the needs of pregnant women. How then do they respond to these common physical complaints of pregnancy? Being nauseated certainly does not *feel* healthy. How can midwives maintain that this is a normal and healthy part of pregnancy?

The primary resolution involves on the one hand minimizing these complaints, and, on the other, responding to them as nutritional problems. There is very little discussion of problems of pregnancy in the home-birth and lay-midwifery literature, and very little talk about it among midwives whom I have interviewed and at home-birth meetings I have attended. Discomfort is not denied, but it is minimized, because it is not seen as "symptomatic" of disease. Even though nurse-midwives, when working under a physician, such as

those at the birth center, can prescribe medications, I have
rarely heard drug use recommended for nausea. Vitamin B₆
is widely suggested, however, along with dietary recommendations. For example:

> Nausea or queasiness usually comes when there has been
> a period of fast or little eating, such as in the morning or
> late afternoon. In this way, it ties in with low blood sugar,
> a condition which can be corrected with frequent high-
> protein meals and plenty of B vitamins.[11]

Statements basically like this one by Hazell are found in the
writings of Adelle Davis[12] and in *Spiritual Midwifery,* [13] all
of which are widely read by lay midwives and home-birth
advocates.

In interviewing nurse-midwives doing home births, the
question of how they dealt with the physical discomforts of
pregnancy was never raised until I asked. Frequently my
questions went unanswered until I pressed. The responses
varied. Those who were more medically oriented recommended some of the standard medications, "if really
needed." Those who were further away from the medical
model responded as follows:

—"It passes."
—"I would help you to understand your basic physiological
mechanisms involved so you could take a very active role
in dealing with some of these minor discomforts, especially
through nutritional and dietary management."
—"Surprisingly few complaints about the body. People
tend to be very well read, so that they kind of know and
have an idea what these things are. They'll come in and
say, 'I have cramps in my legs, do you think I'm getting
enough calcium?' so the issue is resolved right there."

One midwife answered in a way that showed how aware she was of the difference between the medical model under which she was trained and the midwifery model she was coming to accept:

> "Women do get heartburn, but it's a very small issue. I just don't find it a big deal. I remember, though, in [the] training I had that's all we did—we spent days studying heartburn. Maybe five minutes of a visit is spent on that kind of thing."

Laboratory Definitions of "Normal"

The physical discomforts are not the only "symptoms" of pregnancy that receive medical attention. Pregnancy is a total body condition in its physical effects; virtually no part of the body is unaffected by pregnancy. Of all these changes a number are seen by medicine as pathological deviations from the norms for the nonpregnant, including some deviations that show up only on laboratory tests.

Along with the development of techniques for measuring body functions, like urinalysis and blood tests, came a set of standards for the measurement not only of what is, but of what should be. I found one indication of medical self-consciousness about the way these standards are used in clinical medicine in a volume called *Diagnostic Indices in Pregnancy*.[14] These authors stated, as was clear to me from my research into the medical literature, that many clinicians rely on laboratory tests so heavily that deviation from an accepted range of measurements is in itself sufficient to justify treatment. That is, if a person looks and feels well, but has laboratory values outside the normal range, she must be treated anyway. It is a debatable approach under any circumstances.

Should someone with no symptoms and no problems be treated if her blood sugar, for example, is above or below normal? Some clinicians would say yes, that it is just a matter of time before symptoms are seen. Others would want to observe for a longer time before treating, partly because they do not know what is "normal" for that particular person. In pregnancy the situation is even more confusing. The physiological situation is totally changed and continuously changing. What is normal for nonpregnant women may not be normal at all for those who are pregnant. Normal measurements, some medical scientists say, can be defined only as they occur in normal pregnancy.[15] What is more, medical attempts to deal with what are normal physiological changes and adjustments in the pregnant woman may in fact harm her and her baby.

Changes in the blood are typical of those that show up in laboratory testing of pregnant women and are often treated as deviation from the norm. Blood is like an enormously varied soup, of which plasma is the stock. Most blood tests are measures of concentrations of a particular ingredient in a given amount of blood. Just as we can speak of one soup as having more vegetables and fewer noodles per cup than another, so too can we speak of blood as having varying concentrations of red blood cells, white blood cells, platelets, and so on. If you add half again as much stock to the mixture, obviously the concentration of the other ingredients is going to lessen. This is the basis for what is called "physiological anemia of pregnancy." Hemoglobin is measured in grams per 100 ml. of blood, like ounces of carrots per cup of soup. (The hematocrit is another measure of the same thing.) In nonpregnant women a hemoglobin of 12–16 is normal, with 13.5–14 a good, healthy average. A nonpregnant woman with a hemoglobin of 11 or 12 could be just borderline anemic. But what happens in pregnancy?

Starting at approximately six to eight weeks after conception, the amount of plasma in circulation begins to rise, until by the twenty-eighth to thirty-fourth week there is approximately half again as much plasma as in the nonpregnant woman. The increased blood volume is needed not only because of the blood flow to the uterus and breasts, but also to enable the skin and kidneys to eliminate the extra wastes of pregnancy in urine and increased perspiration. The increased blood flow to the skin eliminates the heat generated by the pregnancy. The increased flow to the kidneys helps them function more effectively to remove the wastes of the fetus as well as of the mother. Both require plasma rather than whole blood for these functions. The increase in plasma volume is related to the size of the fetus; the larger the fetus the greater the rise in plasma volume. Women with a history of repeated abortions or stillbirths often have particularly small increases, or even no increase, while women with multiple pregnancies have a much greater than average rise.

In pregnancy the actual amount of hemoglobin increases by about 33 percent. But plasma is increasing by about 50 percent. The measures of hemoglobin thus show a relative decrease. The National Academy of Sciences report *Maternal Nutrition and the Course of Pregnancy* reports average pregnancy hemoglobins of 11 to 12 grams.[16] Other sources say that hemoglobin as low as 10 may be seen in a *normal* pregnancy. Here we have the basic dilemma—if a woman goes to a doctor and has a blood test showing a hemoglobin of 11.5 and is not pregnant, she would be treated with iron supplements. But what if she is pregnant? Is she or is she not anemic?

The use of iron supplements during pregnancy to combat the alleged anemia is standard clinical practice, as reported in medical texts and journals. Yet there is a gap often found in medicine between standard clinical practice, that is, what the average doctor does in his office, and the scientific, research arm of medicine. The National Academy of Sciences points out that there is no evidence that added iron makes any improvement in the health of mother or fetus and generally makes no changes in the hematocrit.[17] Similarly, British and Australian studies show that folic-acid supplementation, prescribed for the same reason in pregnancy, has no discernible effect on the health of the mother or fetus, birth weight, or duration of pregnancy.[18] These supplements are prescribed not on the basis of any scientific evidence of their effectiveness, but as the appropriate medical response to a deviation from the norm on a laboratory test—a norm established on the nonpregnant.

This simple example documents the way in which medicine, with its patriarchal ideology, sees pregnancy. Femaleness can be understood only in male terms, and so pregnancy must be a "stress" on the system. The role of medicine thus becomes one of keeping the woman as "normal" (i.e., nonpregnant) as possible throughout the stress of having the parasitic "passenger."

Treating "Normal"

The diagnosis of anemia based on a blood sample, and its treatment with iron or folic-acid supplements, appears to be relatively harmless, if not necessarily helpful. Other diagnostic procedures and treatments may not be so benign; testing for diabetes is a good example here. Diabetes is an endocrine disorder that makes the maintenance of a healthy pregnancy difficult. On the other hand, pregnancy makes the management of diabetes more difficult. Pregnancy may also trigger diabetic reactions in some previously nondiabetic women. This is where the question of standards for normal becomes complicated. Does a blood-sugar level that would be diabetic in a nonpregnant woman indicate diabetes in a pregnant woman? Are the same standards of measurement for diagnosis appropriate in pregnant women and in nonpregnant women? Medicine's answer has been "yes" to both questions. Many women are diagnosed as having "preclinical" or "chemical" diabetes, a diabetes that shows up only on laboratory testing, during pregnancy, who show no signs or symptoms of diabetes prior to, during, or after pregnancy. The diagnosis is based entirely on laboratory standards and testing. The diagnostic procedure that is carried out when urinalysis indicates the possibility of diabetes includes fasting and then flooding the body with glucose: a glucose tolerance test. I found no discussion in the medical literature of the effects of the procedure itself on the fetus. If the woman is diagnosed as a preclinical diabetic, then that is considered a diagnosis of diabetes. The women, called "class A diabetics," are then classified as "high risk" patients and are monitored as such. They are placed on low-calorie diets, not by any means a benign procedure itself. Their labors are not allowed to go past term—that is, labor will be induced or their babies removed surgically if they do not go into labor before their due dates. Each of the procedures involved in the induction of labor and/or cesarean section carries very real risks to both mother and fetus. These procedures are carried out on "preclinical" or "class A" diabetics on the basis of clinical experience with women who had full-fledged diabetes before they became pregnant. It is not at all clear whether the experience of diabetic women is relevant to these cases of "gestational diabetes."

The issue of diabetes is a difficult one for midwives. Lay midwives claim expertise only in helping normal women through normal pregnancies. Almost all believe that if a woman is not healthy, a physician should be managing or consulting on the case. A diabetic, by definition, is not a normal, healthy woman. But how to define normal when medicine has the monopoly on defining and treating illness remains problematic for those who question the medical approach. The dilemma seems to be better understood by the nurse-midwives I interviewed than it is in the literature of the lay midwives. The nurse-midwives have occasionally expressed their skepticism over the frequency with which preclinical diabetes is diagnosed in the pregnant woman, and what precisely that diagnosis should mean for the management of pregnancy.

The question of anemia is also interesting and somewhat ambiguous for the lay midwives and the home-birth movement. Good nutrition is one of the strong points of prenatal care within the midwifery model, and eating properly is always discussed as the most important thing women can do for themselves in pregnancy. Many contemporary lay midwives have adopted the hematocrit as a measure of nutritional status and pride themselves on setting and achieving higher levels than physicians do. They may thus be following the same policy as medicine in not establishing health and normality standards on pregnant women for pregnant women, or their growing body of knowledge may be establishing precisely those standards. The midwifery literature is split on the issue of supplementation; some sources say pregnant women should be taking iron (and other) supplements, and others stress the importance of getting all nutrients from a "natural" diet.

Several of the nurse-midwives I interviewed set a relatively high standard for hematocrit levels, and then expected pregnant women to achieve that level through diet:

—"... and I got into threatening them with this hematocrit thing—if they didn't have a certain level at a particular

time—useful just as a threat to make them eat well."
—"Women are really proud when they bring up their hematocrits. It's a big thing. 'Oh, I made it to 40! Great, I'm doing it by myself.'"
—"I think there's a ritual that develops in the prenatal visits over hematocrits and anemia. Large amounts of time spent over nutrition."
—"It becomes symbolic for everything that food means in our culture: are you treating yourself right?"

It appears within the midwifery model that the laboratory value itself is less an issue than is its use as a symbol for nutritional status, and nutrition itself has meanings in the midwifery model different from those in the medical model.

Toxemia of Pregnancy

American medicine, as many of its critics have pointed out, is not concerned with nutrition. This is very evident in the case of pregnancy, although obstetricians have supervised the diets of pregnant women. Up until recently, the main dietary concern of obstetricians was with limiting weight gain, which grew out of concern over toxemia, a disease of pregnancy also known as pre-eclampsia and eclampsia. Eclampsia refers to convulsions, the most severe form this disease takes. Toxemia is a disease unique to pregnancy and, interestingly, almost unique to human pregnancy.

One of the early symptoms of toxemia is generalized edema (swelling), which shows up as a sudden weight gain. Obstetricians, screening for the sudden weight gain of toxemia, began to be critical of any weight gain whatsoever in their patients.

Not all of the increased fluid in pregnancy is in the blood.

The increased fluid in the body cells, edema, is frequently noticed in swelling of the ankles and legs, which when limited to these areas is called dependent edema. Blood pooling in the legs, because of the pressure of the uterus, and water retention combine to make the legs swell during the day. At night, as the woman lies on her side (allowing better circulation), the water is returned to the kidneys, frequently necessitating several trips to the bathroom. By morning the dependent edema is gone, or almost gone, and the buildup starts again. Each leg may accumulate one liter or more of water during the day. Some obstetricians have regarded any sign of edema as abnormal, as indeed it would be in the nonpregnant, and treated it with salt restrictions and with diuretics. Yet is hard to reconcile the idea of edema as "pathological" with the fact that it occurs in 40 percent of normal, healthy pregnancies resulting in the birth of normal, healthy babies.

Edema, however, can also be a symptom of toxemia. A generalized edema—noticeable swelling of the face and hands as well as the legs—is frequently the first sign of toxemia. The disease develops after the twentieth to twenty-fourth week of pregnancy, and most frequently after the thirty-second week. The second major part of the syndrome is a rise in blood pressure; the third is the presence of protein in the urine. Most obstetrical prenatal care is organized around screening for these three signs: edema, elevated blood pressure, and protein in the urine. At a standard medical prenatal visit a woman is weighed (sudden weight gain is indicative of water retention), her blood pressure is taken, and her urine is tested.

There is no clear-cut agreement on just what is and what is not the beginning of toxemia, or mild pre-eclampsia. Just how much edema, how much of a rise in blood pressure, or how much protein in the urine must be shown are all subject to debate. Each author, researcher, and physician states clearly what the standards are, yet no two state exactly the same thing. Some authors believe that any one of the three conditions is sufficient for diagnosing a woman as pre-eclamptic, while others state that the woman must have high blood pressure and either edema or proteinuria or both in order to be diagnosed as pre-eclamptic. Given this kind of difficulty in defining the terms, research studies are of course confusing. Some studies, for example, are looking at women with edema and no other symptoms. For these reasons, as well as the variations in populations being studied, the incidences of pre-eclampsia being reported are as low as 2 percent and as high as 29.9 percent.

Women who develop toxemia recover if the uterus is emptied in time and show no long-term effects after recovery. But it is an important cause of maternal and infant deaths. The earlier in pregnancy and the more severe the toxemia, the greater the likelihood of fetal death. The decrease in blood flow to the uterus associated with toxemia results in fetal malnutrition, yet the fetus is too premature to be delivered with a good chance of survival. Because of the various ways in which pre-eclampsia is defined, the outcomes of the diseases have been found to be very different. The same researcher who claims that generalized edema alone is a sign of mild pre-eclampsia states that mild pre-eclampsia is not associated with increased fetal or maternal loss.

Those who think that edema is pre-eclampsia try to prevent edema and use the same techniques that would be used with nonpregnant people: limiting salt intake and using diuretics. Salt restriction and the use of diuretics have been widely used in obstetrics as preventative measures. Yet there are absolutely no data to show that this regimen has prevented anyone from developing toxemia. The subject is a complex one, and open to much argument between physicians. It does appear that toxemic women do not have the plasma increase that is normal for pregnancy, and limiting salt does not help expand blood volume.[19] It has, however, become common practice in American obstetrics to curtail the use of salt by pregnant women showing signs of edema, and frequently to use diuretics as well. There are no data to show that this regimen cures edema and toxemia any more than it prevents it. Again we see the gap between the scientific, research arm of medicine and clinical practice.

The use of diuretics in pregnancy raises the same questions as any other drug use does, in addition to the harmfulness of "curing" a physiological phenomenon. That is, both its unintended and its intended effects can be dangerous. The diuretics may have many side effects, including the creation of dangerous potassium deficiencies, and the causing of diabetes. One rare but serious complication that has caused several maternal deaths affects the pancreas. Years after the evidence is available, though, studies are still being conducted, with results that support the conclusion that the diuretics present a potential hazard to the fetus.[20]

Weight Gain

Especially because of toxemia, but also in order to maintain "normal" standards throughout pregnancy, obstetricians have stressed weight control. An average full-term infant weighs about seven and a half pounds (though midwives would claim that a well-nourished mother will produce a larger baby), a placenta weighs about a pound or a pound and a half, the amniotic fluid and fully developed uterus each weigh about two pounds, and the breasts together gain about one and a half pounds during pregnancy. Add a few more pounds for the increased blood volume, and a weight gain of fifteen pounds can be "accounted for" in the entire pregnancy. Accept that a few extra pounds of fat are stored for energy for lactation, and the figure goes up to twenty pounds. Physicians who worked with the model of pregnancy in which women "contain" pregnancy as a host contains a parasite expected to see a weight gain among their patients of only fifteen to twenty pounds. Larger weight gains were seen as symptoms of pathology, especially because of their similarity to the weight gain of toxemia. Here we have the basis for the classic scenario of the eight-months-pregnant woman nibbling lettuce and cottage cheese because she must step on the scales at the doctor's office the next day.

Birth weight, however, is the single most important factor in the health and survival of newborns. Birth weight is even more strongly related to infant mortality than length of gestation.[21] Well-grown babies survive premature birth better than poorly grown babies survive full-term birth. And birth weight is directly related to maternal nutrition. Better-nourished mothers have better-nourished infants. Specifically, the more weight the mother gains during pregnancy, the larger the baby.[22] Maternal weight gains of thirty to thirty-four pounds or more are optimum for infant survival. A major study shows that there is even a diminution in infant abnormality rates, given increased maternal weight gain.[23]

Most of the fetal weight gain takes place in the third trimester. This points up one of the major problems in setting up any weight-gain limits at all, even the new, more "liberal" standards. When weight gain is limited, there will be women who reach that limit before the end of pregnancy and will try, or be encouraged by their doctors to try, to gain no more weight. The result is malnourishment for the fetus at its time of maximum growth.

Good nutrition is not just a matter of getting enough vitamins or minerals or even protein. Calories are also important.

Our diet-conscious, overweight society treats calories as if they were the bad stuff that exists in food. Yet there is no such thing as a well-balanced pregnancy diet that is low in calories. If there are too few calories available from carbohydrates, the body will use protein for energy, creating a protein shortage even when the daily protein intake seems high enough. Poor women who have been eating starchy, sweet, and fatty diets all their lives and are then put on restricted-calorie diets during pregnancy are the least equipped to provide for their babies from their own stores.

If a woman is burning her own fat for energy—the goal of a reducing diet—or remaining at the same weight while the fetus grows, she is in danger of developing ketosis, an acid-base imbalance of the blood. Maternal ketosis has been related to neuro-psychological defects in the offspring, and the effects are more pronounced in the last trimester.[24]

Although there are signs that these attitudes are changing, within recent years (certainly all through the 1960s and into the 1970s), medicine believed that pregnant women should aim for a weight gain at term of their ideal weight plus fifteen to twenty pounds. That is, a woman ten pounds overweight would be allowed a weight gain of five to ten pounds in the course of her pregnancy, and a woman thirty pounds overweight would be asked to *lose* ten to fifteen pounds. The omnipotent, omniscient fetus was expected to draw its needs from the maternal store. Maternal nutrition, it was believed, had no bearing on the birth weight or the condition of the baby.

The 1962 edition of Alan Guttmacher's widely read *Pregnancy and Birth* is fairly typical of the advice obstetricians were giving to pregnant women. Guttmacher followed the rule that at term the pregnant woman should weigh twenty pounds more than her ideal weight, whether that meant a weight gain or loss during pregnancy. He offered three reasons why weight gain should not be "excessive" during pregnancy.

First, it may impair health. A definite correlation exists between excessive weight gain during pregnancy, especially when rapid, and the development of high blood pressure complications.

"High-blood pressure complications" refers to toxemia. The correlation does exist, but it works the other way; it is the toxemia that causes the sudden weight gain of fluid retention.

In the second place, excessive weight gain makes the pregnant woman more clumsy and prone to stumble or fall.

The issue here is a weight gain limited to twenty pounds, as opposed to the unrestricted weight gain, which is usually not higher than thirty to thirty-five pounds. Having pudgy thighs does not make one accident prone.

Finally, the pregnant woman ought to control weight within normal bounds for vanity's sake alone.[25]

In the late 1960s and early 1970s studies began to appear which indicated that birth weight and maternal weight gain were positively correlated, and that in newborns, bigger really is better. For example, a study published in *Obstetrics and Gynecology* confirmed that greater weight gain was related to higher birth weight, and went on to show that there was a relation to better growth and performance during the first year of life.[26] The authors' proposal, repeated in a 1974 obstetrics text, was to do away with the "traditional obstetric practice of keeping weight gain during pregnancy to a minimum." Researchers also noted that there are twice as many low-birth-weight babies in the United States as in Sweden, and this can, at least in part, account for the much better infant-mortality statistics in Sweden.[27] The working group of the National Academy of Sciences stated in 1970:

> Current obstetrical practice in the U.S. tends to restrict weight gain during pregnancy. In view of the evidence available, one may raise the question of whether this practice is in effect contributing to the large number of low birth weight infants and to the high perinatal mortality rates.[28]

This was another major attack on the medical model of the fetus as located within yet somehow separate from the mother. If the fetus is a parasite, it is, at any rate, not an especially effective parasite, not the all-knowing and all-powerful being medicine had thought it was. The fetus cannot, medicine began to acknowledge, reach out and take what it needs from the mother, regardless of her own health and nutrition. Yet, as with the discovery that the fetus is not perfectly protected, this realization too has not yet brought about fundamental changes in medicine's concept of pregnancy. Just as the drug-use modifications were made without any basic change in the principles of interventionist pregnancy management, so too are weight-gain modifications made. The same charts of how many pounds can be "accounted for" are offered in the current medical texts, with just some modification to allow for a few more pounds, and a caution against weight reduction during pregnancy.

The current home-birth movement and lay-midwifery revival were developing as this research was becoming available, and that may explain part of the midwifery model, in which nutrition is the single most important aspect of pregnancy care. But that is a superficial explanation at best. There is much that is part of current medical knowledge which midwifery rejects. And midwives are not talking about pounds at all, apart from requiring some reassurance that a woman is gaining steadily throughout her pregnancy. Weight-gain expectations are not discussed in the midwifery literature, but good nutrition is a recurrent theme. The midwifery approach to nutrition—that is, that good maternal nutrition is essential to the health of the baby as well as that of the mother—is in accord with the underlying ideology of the midwifery model as woman centered, with the baby as part of its mother. Caring for the mother is therefore the best way of reaching the fetus. The midwifery model consistently sees the needs of the mother and of the fetus as being in total accord and harmony, again because the fetus is part of the mother and the two are one organic unit. In order to have a healthy baby, the mother must have a healthful environment.

There is not in the midwifery model a sense that the needs or desires of the mother must be sacrificed for the good of the fetus, or that the mother would indeed have needs that are other than good for the fetus. For example, it is repeatedly stated that if the mother gives up "junk food" and eats better food for the baby's sake (less refined, more "natural" foods), the mother will feel better and healthier. There is much talk in midwifery and alternative-birth circles about a woman's "getting in touch with her body." That makes sense only if pregnancy is viewed as a normal condition of the female body. The introspection, the psychological turning inwards and self-absorption which may accompany pregnancy, is seen as an opportunity for the woman to learn more about her body and its needs and rhythms. A woman's pregnant body is still very much her own in this model, and is not a host to a parasite. Where the medical model sees pregnancy as a stress and a drain on the mother, the midwifery model sees it as a period of physical and emotional growth and development for both mother and fetus.

Prenatal Care: Two Approaches

I have briefly documented some of the major differences in the models of pregnancy developed by obstetrics and by midwifery and the home-birth movement. The differences between the two are based on both their underlying ideologies and their political necessities. Medicine must emphasize the diseaselike nature of pregnancy, its "riskiness," in order to justify medical management. Midwifery, on the other hand, must emphasize the normal nature of pregnancy, in order to justify nonmedical control in a society in which medicine has a monopoly on illness management. As a patriarchal institution, medicine focuses on the presence of the fetus during pregnancy and sees that fetus as the child of the man. Thus pregnancy is a stress and diseaselike state caused by the presence of the fetal parasite. In the midwifery model the emphasis is on the woman, and pregnancy is a normal condition for women. Women are not compared to a hypothetically stable, noncycling male system but are expected always to be in one or another phase of reproductive life. There is no single "normal" from which to judge deviations; ovulation, menstruation, pregnancy, lactation, menopause—these are not deviations from some abstract norm, but are themselves normal states.

Medicine attempts to maintain the normalcy of the mother throughout the stress of the pregnancy, viewing deviations from normal (nonpregnant) status as symptoms of disease states. This, in turn, of course justifies medical control. Midwifery, on the other hand, views the changes of pregnancy as demonstrating the health of the mother. Rather than seeking to change the mother back in the direction of nonpregnant normality, its goal is to provide the best possible environment in which the changes of pregnancy can occur.

In the medical model, prenatal care is the *management* of pregnancy. The term "management" is used routinely. As an example of its extreme version, a physician in 1971 stated that pregnancy should be viewed as a disease which has an "excellent prognosis for complete, spontaneous recovery if managed under careful medical supervision."[29] The pregnant woman places herself under the care of a physician for the duration of the pregnancy. Alan Guttmacher states: "Once the patient has carefully selected her doctor, she should let him shoulder the full responsibility of her pregnancy and labor."[30]

Obstetricians believe, and so, it would appear, does most of American society, that prenatal care is important in promoting health and preventing disease, that prenatal care saves mothers and babies. And we do have any number of studies showing us that more prenatal care is associated with lower infant mortality rates. These studies can, however, be misleading. For one thing, measures of good prenatal care count prenatal visits—the more visits, the lower the infant mortality. But if births are premature—a leading cause of infant mortality—there is less opportunity for prenatal care. This does not show that having fewer visits causes prematurity. An analysis of this relationship shows no effect of prenatal care on prematurity rates.[31]

Probably even more important in the relation between prenatal care and infant health and survival is the selective process involved: who does and who does *not* seek out prenatal care. Women who have had early and frequent prenatal visits have shown their interest in the pregnancy, their commitment to it, and their willingness and ability to use health services. The same factors that enter into a woman's decision to use health-care services during pregnancy—financial, educational, cultural, and psychological—enter into her decision to seek health services for her baby. Presumably, if a woman has had prenatal care she is more likely to seek medical help, if for example her newborn becomes jaundiced or develops diarrhea, than is a woman who has refused, not been able to afford, or not known about prenatal care. It is this relationship which may explain why prenatal care is related to better infant survival.

What does happen in obstetrically managed prenatal care? Much of it, as stated earlier, revolves around screening for toxemia. The pregnant woman sees the obstetrician each month during the first two trimesters, twice a month for the seventh and eighth months, and weekly for the last month. These visits typically take ten to fifteen minutes or less. The woman is weighed, her blood pressure is taken, and her urine is tested for protein and possibly for sugar. She lies on an examining table and the fetal heart rate is noted, as is the position of the baby. If the woman has symptoms to present, these are noted, and remedies may be prescribed. As is often the case in physician visits, a prescription is handed over as a way of resolving questions and terminating the interview. Time, one feels, is of the essence as the doctor moves from one examining room to the next.

Screening for pathology is part of prenatal care in the midwifery model but is clearly not where the emphasis is placed. Nancy Mills is one of the best-known lay midwives in the United States. She outlined prenatal care at the lay-midwife-run California birth clinic in which she worked:

We do nutritional history when the woman comes in and nutritional counseling on the very first visit. On the second visit we do a complete physical examination, and because the clinic has been operating four years now, women are coming in during the first and second months of pregnancy ... We do pretty much a complete lab work—we do everything that a regular OB practice does, but we do a few more things. I think one of the most critical parts of the care we have to offer is our home-visiting aspects. ... We do several home visits before the birth to get to know the families. And we do this whether they are planning their births in the hospital or in the home, so that when labor comes we are ready to go to the hospital and "labor coach" or to the home. We want to feel like we know the families, we want to know who is there.[32]

And from the Birth Collective at the Fremont Women's Clinic in Seattle:

Our prenatal program includes the usual medical care, i.e., complete history and physical exam, pelvic exam, pelvimetry and laboratory work; lots of discussion about nutrition. ... We encourage people to participate actively in their own care, checking their own urine, weight and blood pressure, learning as much as possible about pregnancy and the birth process. Educational and discussion groups led by various prenatal and pediatric staff happen weekly and provide a forum for people to become acquainted and share questions and experiences. ... We operate from a non-interventionist point of view—the less we do the better.[33]

And from a Madison, Wisconsin, lay-midwifery home-birth center:

The major point of emphasis for our prenatal counseling is nutrition. ... We respect the influence of unconscious emotional and psychic factors on the physical body and encourage mothers and fathers to share dreams, fears and fantasies.[34]

This same midwife spoke of the purpose of her birth center:

> We strive to create a milieu that is safe and supportive in which individuals can discover for themselves what it means to give birth. To open themselves on physical, emotional, and spiritual levels to another person—to give birth.

Thus the first major difference between the two models is that while the medical management is organized around a search for pathology, the midwifery model approaches pregnancy as essentially normal and healthy, a period of *psychological* as well as physical growth and development.

The second major difference is in the conceptualization of responsibility. In the medical model, responsibility is something shouldered by the doctor. This is of course not unique to obstetrics, but has long been a part of the traditional clinical mind. In the medical model the practitioner is expected to see himself as responsible for the outcome of treatment, and since pregnancy is a diseaselike state, its care comes under the treatment model. The physician "manages" the pregnancy, attempting constant, usually minor, adjustments in order to bring the physiological picture of the woman back to "normal." In the midwifery model the mother herself holds the responsibility for her pregnancy and makes her own decisions. The midwife is a teacher and a guide for the pregnant woman and her family during the experience.

Thus, where a physician might spend ten to fifteen minutes at each prenatal visit (or even less, if ancillary staff does part of the work), a routine midwifery prenatal visit takes thirty minutes, an hour, or even more. Essentially the same physical screening procedures are performed (frequently by the mother herself), but the socio-emotional context of the pregnancy is also evaluated and discussed. One might make the argument that the physicians' prenatal visits are limited to just a few minutes based on purely economic motives. While I do not doubt that efficiency and financial gain are important considerations, from the point of view of the medical practitioner the essential business of the visit takes only a few minutes. The machinery of the body is what matters. If the woman's signs are good, then she needs no further treatment until the next visit. If her signs are not good, then the appropriate treatment is prescribed. The job of the physician is to diagnose and to treat, and in the relatively straightforward work of pregnancy management, these routines are handled quickly. But creating a "milieu that is safe and supportive in which individuals can discover for themselves what it means to give birth" is a more time-consuming goal. Getting to know women and their families, educating and sharing information, all take time and involve the midwife in the lives of her clients to a greater extent than does checking blood pressure.

I asked the nurse-midwives I interviewed how they dealt with prenatal care for their home and birthing-center clients, and found that in this regard the midwifery model was clearly becoming dominant. I asked what goes on in prenatal visits:

—"I'm usually interested in why they wanted the pregnancy in the first place; why they want to do it at home and what that means to them, this decision for responsibility that they've taken; their relation as a couple; how they relate to the baby—these are the principal issues to deal with, usually at the first meeting."

—"[I ask] what are your goals for pregnancy and delivery?

Did it occur to you that you have alternatives, that you have control, or do you think that pregnancy and birth are just something that is done to women? Looking back on the experience, you have to have had the chance to make choices. . . . The goal is to look back on pregnancy and birth and say 'I'm really happy I did *X.*' "

—"Sometimes we don't even talk about the pregnancy; sometimes somebody is interested in talking about the work they're doing in their lives, and I consider that really important just because you learn so much about people."

—"Well, it's interesting the way how I handle prenatal care is to answer a lot of questions. A lot of people who ask for home birth know what they're doing; they've done a lot of reading, more than I have, and what I mainly do is clarify anything they're not sure of. . . . Some people will say "I have no questions," and then I will have to find something from what they've said before, go in this avenue or that avenue. But it's basically answering their questions, getting them straight in their mind, and building up a personal rapport, that's basically what it is."

Responsibility and personal rapport probably loom so large for the nurse-midwives as well as the lay midwives because of the personal responsibility and risks they take on in agreeing to attend the home birth.

6

Childbirth:
The Social Construction
of Birth

The first thing to remember is that obstetrics is a surgical specialty. The management of childbirth within hospitals is essentially the same as the management of any other surgical event. While obstetrics is a patriarchal institution, that fact becomes almost irrelevant in the management of childbirth. Certainly women in labor are treated in a dehumanizing way, are condescended to and ignored, patted and punished. But that treatment is hardly unique to obstetrical patients. It is part of the way in which hospital patients in general, and surgical patients in particular, are treated.

In surgery the ideology of technology is dominant. Perhaps more clearly than anywhere else in medicine, the body is a machine, the doctor a mechanic. In the typical surgical situation the unconscious patient is waiting, like a car upon a hydraulic lift, when the surgeon arrives, and is still in that condition as the surgeon leaves. The surgeon and the rest of the medical staff may care about the person whose body lies before them, but for the duration of the surgery, the mind-body dualism theorized by Descartes is a reality. It seems genuinely difficult for surgeons to respond to patients as conscious human beings at the same time they are working on their bodies. Marcia Millman reports, from her observations of surgical wards, that when patients have been given local rather than general anesthesia for an operation and are thus awake, their serious remarks about the operation or their attempts to take part in the doctors' conversations as the surgery is underway often bring the staff to laughter.[1] To them, the talking patient is incongruous, almost as if a car had sighed while one of its flat tires was being replaced.

When women are sedated through labor and made unconscious for delivery, as the obstetrician DeLee outlined in his 1920 article in the *American Journal of Obstetrics and Gynecology*,[2] then the only possible description of birth is as an "operation" performed by a surgeon on a patient. DeLee's article, "The Prophylactic Forceps Operation," set the standards for obstetrical management of birth, routinizing such procedures as forceps extraction, episiotomies, manual extraction of the placenta, and the lithotomy position (flat on the back with the legs up in stirrups). Although in recent years the use of heavy sedation and anesthesia has been less frequent because of the dangers they pose for the mother and the baby, the surgical nature of the event remains constant.

Nancy Stoller Shaw described the physician-directed, in-hospital deliveries she observed in the 1970s in Boston as all following the same pattern. The patient is placed on a delivery table that is similar in appearance to an operating table. The majority of patients had spinal anesthesia, or its equivalent, the epidural, which numbs the woman from approximately the waist down but leaves her conscious. She is placed in the lithotomy position and draped; her hands may be strapped to prevent her from contaminating the sterile field. She cannot move her body below the chest, and "Her active participation in the birth is effectively over."

This does not mean that the woman becomes unimportant, only that her body, or more specifically, the birth canal and its contents, and the almost born baby are the only things the doctor is really interested in. This part of her and, in particular, the whole exposed pubic area, visible to those at the foot of the table, is the stage on which the drama is played out. Before it, the doctor sits on a small metal stool to do his work. Unless he stands up, he cannot clearly see the mother's face, nor she his. She is separated as a person, as effectively as she can be, from the part of her that is giving birth.[3]

The Birth Process

The medical literature defines childbirth as a three-stage physiological process. In the first stage the cervix, the opening of the uterus into the vagina, dilates from being nearly closed to its fullest dimension of approximately ten centimeters (almost four inches). This is referred to as "labor," and the contractions of the uterus that pull upon the cervix, as "labor pains." In the second stage the baby is pushed through the opened cervix and through the vagina, or birth canal, and out of the mother's body. This is the "delivery." The third stage is the expulsion of the placenta, the "afterbirth."

In any situation the possibility exists for alternative definitions of the situation, different versions of what is *really* happening. Which version is accepted and acted upon is a reflection of the power of the participants. Those with more power can have their definition of the situation accepted as reality. Often this involves some bargaining or negotiating between the people involved. Take, for example, a child with a sore throat who doesn't want to go to school. The parent may say the throat is not *that* red, and the child counters with "But my head hurts too." Might the child be experiencing some soreness and pain? Certainly. But is it bad enough that the child should stay home from school? That depends. Medical authorities may function just like the parent in this situation. Patients recovering from tuberculosis, for example, may claim that they really are well enough to have a weekend pass,[4] and patients and doctors in mental hospitals negotiate over the patient's mental health.[5] Frequently, pregnant women come to the hospital claiming that they are in labor, but by medically established judgments they are not. The state of being in labor, like illness or any deviance, is an ascribed status: that is, it is a position to which a person is assigned by those in authority.[6] But one can also negotiate, to try and achieve that status or have one's claim to it recognized.

When people have negotiated a definition of the situation, that becomes reality for them, and they have to work within that reality. Let us take as an example a woman at term having painful contractions at ten-minute intervals, who has not yet begun to dilate. Whether she is or is not in labor will depend on whether she then begins to dilate, or the contractions stop and begin again days or weeks later. Whether a woman is in labor or "false labor" at Time One depends on what will have happened by Time Two. If she presents herself to the hospital claiming that she is in labor, and by weeping, pleading, or just because she seems educated and middle-class, she is admitted, the medical acknowledgment that she is in labor will have been established. If she does not begin to dilate for twenty-four hours, and then twelve hours after that—thirty-six hours after her admission—she delivers, that woman will have had a thirty-six-hour labor. The medical authorities will see it as a thirty-six-hour labor, and so will she. That reality which they negotiated, when labor began, becomes the only reality they have. On the other hand, if she is denied or delays admission and presents herself to the hospital twenty-four hours later for a twelve-hour in-hospital labor, she will have had a twelve-hour labor preceded by a day of discomfort. From the point of view of the institution that is "responsible" for her labor, and thus her pain, only from the time of her admission, the latter is preferable, the longer labor being easily perceived as institutional misman-agement. Yet from the point of view of the woman, the *physical* sensations in both cases are precisely the same. It is the *social* definitions—calling it labor or not—that make the difference between a terribly long labor or a pretty average labor with some strange contractions beforehand. Because medicine wants to define labor as a situation requiring hospi-talization, but at the same time wants to avoid prolonged labor, "real" labor is defined not in terms of the sensations the woman experiences, but in terms of "progress"—cervical dilatation.

The pregnant woman therefore wants to be accurate (in medical terms) about defining the onset of labor. Otherwise, if she gains early admission, she will have helped to define the situation as an overly long labor. In addition to the stress inherent in thinking oneself to be in labor for thirty-six hours, the medical treatment she will receive presents its own prob-lems. Laboring women are routinely confined to bed in hos-pitals, a situation that is as disturbing psychologically as it is physically. Not only is the labor perceived as being longer, but the horizontal position she must assume in bed physically prolongs labor, as may the routine administration of seda-tives during a long hospital stay. In addition to the variations in treatment during the first hours of labor, the treatment she will receive is different in the last hours, when the woman is hospitalized in either case. Women who have been in a hospital labor room for thirty hours receive different treatment from women who have been there for only six hours, even if both are equally dilated and have had identical physical progress. Which woman, after all, is more likely to have a cesarean section for overly long labor—the one who got there just six hours ago, or the one who has been there through three shifts of nurses? What the woman experienced before she got to the hospital—how strongly, how frequently, and for how long her contractions have been coming—does not enter into the professional decision making nearly as much as what the medical attendants have seen for themselves.

It is also important for the pregnant woman to be accurate in identifying labor, because if she presents herself to the hospital and is denied admission, she is beginning her relationship with the hospital and her birth attendants from a bad bargaining position. Her version of reality is denied, leaving her with no alternative but to lose faith in her own or the institution's ability to perceive accurately what is happening to her. Either situation will have negative consequences for the eventual labor and delivery. That is why childbirth-education classes frequently spend considerable time on the defining of labor and so-called false labor.

The same issues arise when a decision has to be made about when a woman should be moved from a labor to a delivery room. In American hospitals, unlike those in most of the rest of the world, the first and second stages of labor are seen as sufficiently separate to require different rooms and, frequently, different staff. Women attended by nursing and house staff throughout their labor may not see their own obstetrician until they are in the delivery room. Since a woman will be moved from one room to another to mark the transition from one stage of labor to another, the professional staff has to make a distinction between laboring and delivering, and then apply that distinction to the individual woman. A cut-off point has to be established at which a woman is no longer viewed as laboring but as delivering. If the point is missed, and the woman delivers, say, in the hall on the way to the delivery room, then she is seen as having "precipped," having had a precipitous delivery. If the point is called too soon, if the staff decides that the woman is ready to deliver and the physical reality is that she has another hour to go, then concern is aroused about the length of second stage, because she has spent that extra hour in a delivery rather than a labor room.

Why must the hospital make arbitrary decisions in defining labor and its stages? Because the use of the facilities requires scheduling. The staff has to know when a labor room will be freed and a delivery room needed. It becomes necessary, therefore, periodically to examine the woman internally to judge cervical dilatation and to predict delivery time. This is usually done by the nursing staff. Some examinations may be necessary in order to evaluate the physical condition of the laboring woman and her fetus, but repeated examinations of cervical dilatation are equally necessary for scheduling purposes. Still others are done for teaching purposes. Such examinations are usually quite painful, so that here we see the institutional demands *inflicting* rather than alleviating pain.

There is one more reason for the examinations. The staff has to do *something* to laboring women; otherwise they needn't be there. The hospital has its own work of maintaining its prestige as, in this instance, a baby-making institution, processing or "treating" the laboring women. The labor process is usually self-contained; left to her own devices the woman can produce the baby, in nine cases out of ten, with absolutely no professional assistance. Not only may the examination, at its most useful, locate the minority of women needing assistance; it also constitutes "treatment" of all laboring women, thus justifying the existence of the institution. The woman can therefore be seen, and see herself, as being in the hospital for the purpose of such treatment, or "medical care."

Nancy Stoller Shaw, in her study of maternity care, *Forced Labor*, notes that for a woman giving birth in a hospital, childbirth involves a "continual inability to protect herself and control the access of others to her body."[7] Standard "prepping" procedures, like admissions procedures to the army, jail, a mental hospital, or any total institution, reinforce the idea that the individual loses control over her body and self, including a "systematic removal of all personal effects as well as parts of the body (hair, feces) and its extensions (eyeglasses, false teeth)."[8] The custom of shaving the perineum has been repeatedly demonstrated to serve no medical purpose at all, having developed, with the invention of the disposable razor, from the clipping of any very long pubic hairs to a full shave.[9] While it is a pointless, humiliating, depersonalizing, and irritating experience, it is explained to the woman and staff as being necessary, with the latter being best equipped to provide this "service."

The Impact of Prepared Childbirth

Prepared childbirth has tried to humanize medical management—not to do away with the medical approach, but to make it more pleasant for women, more responsive to their needs. Many compromises have been made even with this modest goal. The American Society for Psychoprophylaxis in Obstetrics, ASPO, as the first (and foremost) source of child-

birth preparation, has supported the way medical procedures are viewed, as is made clear in an unpublished "Guidelines for ASPO Teachers" (c. 1970). The guidelines state, for
example, with regard to examinations:

> It should be pointed out to patients that internal examina-
> tions during labor in the hospital can be performed by the
> patient's own physician, by a resident physician, an intern,
> or a nurse. This depends on the procedures established by
> hospital policy. Examinations will be given either rectally
> or vaginally, again depending on hospital rules or individ-
> ual physicians, but it is not for the parturient to decide who
> should or should not examine her during labor.

This is far from being a consumer-oriented approach and
is in fact in direct opposition to the legal rights of the woman.
The American Civil Liberties Union Handbook *The Rights of
Hospital Patients,* states, "All patients have a right to refuse
to be examined by anyone in the hospital setting."[10] Similarly, while the patient has a right to refuse any treatment or
procedure,[11] ASPO guidelines say, with regard to the "prepping" procedures, "It is not worthwhile to make an issue out
of this."

ASPO has not supported childbirth outside of the hospital,
and home-birth advocates have been denied acceptance into
ASPO teacher-training programs. The hospital is unchallenged as the location for birth, and the training the pregnant woman receives usually does not teach her to understand and manipulate the hospital environment. For the
most part, rather than teaching in detail about hospital facilities and personnel, the childbirth-education classes instruct
the woman in ways to avoid dealing with external events.
The laboring woman is taught to take a "focal point"—a
picture or flower she brings from home, or simply a spot on

the wall—and focus on that alone, blocking out all other happenings during a contraction. Rather than being alerted to which hospital procedures are arbitrary or might be unnecessary in her case, the woman is taught instead how to ignore—"breathe through"—enemas, perineal shaves, repeated examinations, transfer from bed to stretcher, and so on. The focusing technique is thus one for dealing with the hospital, and may not be directly related to the birth experience itself.

The cues available to us in a situation include not only physical objects and sensations, but also perceived behavior and even the way we see ourselves acting. The cues we get from our own behavior are an important part of how we understand what is happening. This has interesting implications for childbirth.

All of the childbirth-preparation programs teach the use of breathing techniques for labor. Margaret Myles, author of one of the most widely used textbooks of midwifery in the world,[12] has said that it has been her experience that no matter what childbirth-preparation breathing techniques a woman used, as long as there was a regular pattern of breathing, it worked. Whether it was Lamaze puffing and panting in rhythm, or plain puh-puh-puh, they all worked. The usual explanation for the effectiveness of these methods is that the concentration on breathing blocks out sensations of pain. Yet women practice their breathing exercises while driving or watching television or reading—all activities that require some level of concentration. Anything that won't take one's mind off the road, or away from a TV program, is unlikely to distract a woman from the sensations of labor. I believe the real reason that breathing exercises work so well in the control of pain in childbirth is that they present the woman with positive cues regarding her situation. If she were not doing the breathing, she might very well be crying or calling out. Her ability to evaluate her own situation, taking cues from her own behavior as well as that of others, becomes very important. The woman who has just gotten through a contraction without crying out has presented herself with evidence that the pain is bearable. If it were not bearable after all, she knows, she would be crying. The woman's perceived pain and perceived composure are conflicting elements. As long as the composure can be maintained, then the conflict can be resolved by the sensations being defined as bearable. In a sense, it is a more structured version of "Whenever I feel afraid, I whistle a happy tune."

When a laboring woman is lying in a hospital bed, an intravenous needle in her arm (as is standard hospital procedure), listening to doctors being paged, with strangers coming in and out of the room, then the cues available to her are objectively no different from the cues she could expect if she were dying. People cannot be placed in hospital gowns on hospital tables under hospital lights wearing little bracelets that will identify them, whether consciously present or not, without there being created for them as well as for those who care for them, the image of patient. All that the birthing woman can work for in that situation is control over pain and her expression of pain.

In emphasizing pain and its control, the childbirth-education groups reinforce the medical model of childbirth as a crisis situation. The substitution of self-hypnosis, breathing techniques, and the like for control by drugs does not challenge the essential model of what is occurring in the birth. Both the educators and the physicians are in accord that childbirth pain requires professional assistance in its control. The two groups are, or more accurately *were*, vying for dominance or political control over pain relief. The resolution that was reached can be seen, certainly in the case of ASPO, as cooption by the medical establishment of the childbirth educator. Withdrawing all fundamental challenges to the medical profession, ASPO worked toward having breathing techniques seen and used as one of a potentially escalating series of analgesics.

To Be Delivered or to Give Birth

The messages that the woman picks up from the cues available to her are not limited to the normality, health, and relative painfulness of her condition. The definition of the situation goes much deeper than that, to the very heart of the process and who controls it. This is best exemplified by the use of the word "deliver." Both mothers and birth attendants are said to deliver babies. When the *mother* is seen as delivering, then the attendant is assisting—aiding, literally attending. But when the *doctor* is delivering the baby, the mother is in the passive position of *being delivered.* The words are of course the least of the cues that the laboring woman receives regarding the importance of her contribution to the event taking place, the delivery of her baby.

Three basic patient-practitioner relationships—ways doctors and patients can deal with each other—have been identified.[13] The first is the *active-passive* relationship, particularly applicable to the unconscious patient in an emergency situation. The doctor makes all decisions, and the patient is "worked on," much the same way as mechanical repairs are done. In childbirth this relationship is typified by the doctor using forceps or surgery to pull the baby out of an unconscious mother. What is particularly important to note is that the doctor not only has complete control once the mother is unconscious, but it is also the physician who has the authority to define normal, variations from normal, and obstetric emergencies, as well as the "state" of the patient. The physician in a hospital birth always holds the power to create an active-passive relationship by having the mother anesthetized.

The original ASPO teacher-training course states:

> If your doctor himself suggests medication, you should accept it willingly—even if you don't feel the need for it—as he undoubtedly has very good reasons for his decision.[14]

The 1970 teacher-training guidelines state that "the final decision on the use of drugs has to be with the individual physician," a statement again contradicting the legal rights of patients, as outlined by the A.C.L.U., to refuse "any medical or surgical procedure [from] being performed on them regardless of the opinions of their doctors as to the advisability of the treatment."

The second possible practitioner-patient relationship is one of *guidance-cooperation.* The practitioner guides and directs the patient, who, if she is a good patient, takes guidance and direction easily. In childbirth, this is best typified by the in-hospital "prepared" birth. The laboring woman is there to be "coached," a word frequently used in childbirth-preparation classes. All the preparation she has had has taught her to work within the framework of institutional rules. ASPO teacher guidelines have this to say about doctor-patient relationships:

> The patient should be encouraged to have a good "rapport" with her physician. If her doctor is not acquainted with the Lamaze technique, she should try and get his confidence, show that she is not a fanatic, and perhaps see if he will read the ASPO "Physicians Communique" or the ASPO training manual. It should be pointed out that, quite

obviously, physicians do not cherish to be told by their patients how to conduct their labor and delivery. However, it can certainly be tactfully discussed, and from our experience a great deal can be gained from this.

Note that physicians *conduct* labor and delivery, and if the "patient" (note too the acceptance of the patient role for the laboring woman) makes it clear that she is not fanatic, her labor may be conducted in accord with some of her wishes. The burden is on the patient to be tactful, and the suggestion is pointedly not made that she select another physician. The legitimate basis of the authority of the physician is not questioned.

The third possible relationship is one of *mutual participation,* in which practitioner and patient work together toward a common goal. In essence, it is a denial of the "patient" role and thus of medical control. But the institutionalization of childbirth works against the development of this relationship. The hospital patient is in no position to be an equal participant in her birthing. She is outnumbered and overpowered. She may be allowed to act as if she were an equal participant, even bringing a patient advocate (husband, coach) with her, but should she stop playing by the rules and become disagreeable, difficult, or disruptive, as defined by the birth attendants, her true powerlessness is made clear. Her "advocate" is there only as long as the hospital attendants choose to allow him to be there, only so long as he continues to coach the woman in accord with institutional rules. The ASPO teacher guidelines state:

ASPO very much encourages "Family Centered Maternity," i.e., a husband and wife team during labor and delivery when possible. It is understood, however, that only husbands who have taken a formal course with their wife in the Lamaze technique can be of real help to the wife.

Rather than demystifying childbirth, this sentiment moves birth further into the sphere of medical activities, too complex for a lay person to understand without special training.

It is perhaps for these reasons that so much emphasis is put on control of both pain and the expression of pain in preparation for childbirth classes. According to the rules of the game, if the laboring woman chooses to deal with her pain by crying or calling out, she has entirely forfeited her right to make decisions. Much is made in childbirth-preparation circles of the woman's being in control during labor, but all that is meant by that is control over her expressions of pain. A woman who maintains a fixed, if somewhat glazed, cheerful expression and continues a regular pattern of breathing is said to be "in control," as she is carted from one room to another and literally strapped flat on her back with her legs in the air.

Certainly a woman who was unconscious, semistupefied, amnesiac, or simply numb from the waist down cannot have experienced giving birth as an accomplishment, something over which she had control. But what of the woman who is encouraged in childbirth-preparation classes to see herself as a member of a "team" delivering her baby? Though she may help and watch in a mirror, she is not the primary actor. Positioning and draping her in such a way that she cannot directly see the birth, not allowing her to touch her genitals or the forthcoming baby, tells the mother that the birth is something that is happening to her or being done to her, not something she herself is doing. The birth is managed, conducted, by the other members of the team, those who are telling her what to do, and physically manipulating her and her baby.

A birth is an exciting, thrilling thing to see. It is an even more exciting and thrilling thing to *do*. Encouraging a woman to watch herself in a mirror giving birth moves her from being a participant to an observer of the birth. The emphasis on "seeing" the birth comes out of the context of prepared, in-hospital, doctor-directed births. The woman is awake, encouraged to see herself as part of the team, and help the doctor by following suggestions and taking direction. But the hospital members of that team have had most of their experience delivering babies without the active participation and help of the mother. They know that they will get that baby delivered with or without the woman's cooperation: that is their purpose in being there. If the mother wants to be awake, "be there" for the birth, then the only role they have to offer her is that of observer. She can watch the birth like anyone else, and is—no differently from the anesthetized, "unprepared" mother—expected to be grateful to the physician specifically and the staff generally for the wonderful job they have done. The closing words of a 1973 film produced by ASPO for parent education are "How lucky I was to have witnessed this miracle"—spoken by the mother![15] In prepared childbirth no less than in the pre-1950s medical model, the status inherent in the ability to make a baby is shifted from the birthing woman to the medical profession. In the case of prepared birth, the "coach" becomes a member of the medical team, and joins it in teaching the woman to cooperate with institutional demands, keeping her in her place.

The Role of the Birth Attendant

Physicians control birth because it is done in their territory, under their expertise. That control over their work space is what makes them "professional." As the senior professionals around, they obviously control all the other workers—the nurses, orderlies, and aides all have to function under the physician's supervision. But they also control the patients. The medical management of birth means the management of birthing women; to control or to manage a situation is to control and manage individuals.

The alternative to physician and institutional control of childbirth is childbirth outside of institutions, and, most important, outside of the medical model. In this alternative, birth is an activity that women *do*. The woman may need some help, but the help is, for the most part, in the form of teaching her how to do for herself. As important as the word "deliver" is in understanding the medical model of childbirth, so too the word "birthing" clarifies the midwifery model. Birthing, like swimming, singing, and dancing, is something people do, not have done for them.

Nancy Mills is a contemporary lay midwife and an important figure in the home-birth movement. She began as a midwife by visiting a friend in labor, and has since attended over 600 births. Her words are the most eloquent statement available of the midwifery approach to birth:

> I see myself going in and being a helper, being an attendant. Sometimes I play with the kids, or I do some cooking. Sometimes I sit with the woman. Sometimes I help the husband assist the woman. Some families need more help than others, but it is easy to go in and see where you are needed and how you can fill that role.[16]

The birth is not made to fit the routine, but the attendant to fit the birth. The birth is something the mother does by herself, but:

> It is important for that woman to be able to look at you, to know you are there, to hold your hand, to be reassured. I know it helps when I say to a woman, "I know how you feel. I know it's harder than you thought it was going to be, but you can do it."[17]

Similarly, the lay midwives of the Fremont Women's Birth Clinic say, "We feel that people should be in control of their experience, and we'll fit in accordingly,"[18] and a lay midwife from Madison, Wisconsin, says, "People come to us not so we will care for them but so we will help them care for themselves."[19]

I asked the nurse-midwives I interviewed what they saw as their role in a birth, and what they did when they got to the home:

—"Nothing, first. Which is very important, because they expect me to do something, like I'm supposed to do something. But they're doing it already and that's what we're going to be doing, so I find it very important to just come in and sit down."

—"If I go in and I find the mother is agitated, I'll say 'Hi,' and go straight to the mother. If I find that she's not agitated, I'll take a slower 'hi,' you know. . . . If she looks comfortable, I don't feel there's any rush, and I let her continue to feel that she's doing okay."

—"I try to get the main support person involved in doing the birth because it's really their birth and not mine. . . . My role is to listen to what's being said."

—"They see me as a consultant, that I do have special skills and knowledge, but that they participate in the decisions too, and except for something really outrageous most decisions are made collectively. They're not giving me their body and they have to understand that."

And most clearly of all:

—"My aim is that when I leave that family feels they birthed it. I was there and I helped, but they did it . . . so that in their whole recollection of the experience I will be very minimal. That's my goal and that's my aim."

Both this social role and this goal are very different from the role of the doctor in a hospital birth, a role that Shaw sums up as being "the director and the star."[20]

Childbirth, in the medical model, is a surgical procedure performed by an obstetrician on the pelvic regions of women, involving the removal of a fetus and a placenta. The fetus is turned over to a pediatric staff, the mother to an obstetrical-nursing staff, and the placenta disposed of or sold for its hormones. The procedure is usually performed vaginally but, as is increasingly the case, may be performed abdominally. Some physicians have expressed their inability to understand why women so much prefer delivery "from below" (vaginally) to delivery "from above" (abdominally). The social setting is essentially the same in either case.

Childbirth, in the midwifery model, is an event in the lives of women and their families. Birthing is something that women can do, but usually require emotional support and teaching to do well—that is, to the mother's own satisfaction.

In this chapter I have focused primarily on the role of the birth attendant vis-à-vis the birthing woman. The attendant can take the active role, and take on the responsibility for the birth, as in the medical model. Or the birthing woman can take the active role, with the attendant in a supportive position; then the birthing woman and her family take the responsibility for the birth as in the midwifery model. The former is based on the ideology of technology, in which the body is viewed as a machine, the performance of which can be improved by a competent mechanic. The latter is based on an integration of mind and body, so that physical events can be seen as socially done. A woman at home is not delivered. She gives birth.

7

The Care and Feeding of Babies

The development of separate medical specialties of obstetrics and pediatrics, or the newer subspecialty neonatology, the care of newborns, may be both a reflection and a cause of the medical view of mother and child as being entirely separate "problems in medical management." Medicine has separated, both physically and conceptually, the mother from her infant, denying the biological as much as the emotional relationship and interaction that home-birth midwives see as continuing in the postbirth period. That the development of separate specialties reflects the conceptual separation is obvious. One reason for this may be the nature of medical education. With their "rotations" through the various specialties, physicians—and nurses—learn about mothers and babies in different places and at different times, and about other family members, notably the father, not at all. The moment the cord is cut may very well be the last time any physician sees mother and baby together in the hospital.

Home-birth midwives, on the other hand, unlike obstetricians, maintain responsibility for both mother and baby as an interdependent unit in the hours and days after birth. None of the home-birth midwives I interviewed suggested that any health-care worker but her be responsible for the infant at the time of and immediately after birth. Most suggested that the baby be "checked out" by a pediatrician sometime within a week following the birth, but all indicated their own responsibility for the baby at the birth and in the follow-up phone calls and visits. The responsibilities that the midwives expected mothers and their support people to take for the birth extended to their responsibility for the baby. After it was ascertained that the baby appeared well and normal, further primary responsibility for the baby passed to the parents. Midwives were careful to point out the problems and signs to look for, notably infant jaundice; but being alert for the signs and seeking assistance, it was made clear, was the parents' responsibility. The assumed competence of the parents to observe their own babies contrasts strongly with the current medically defined "necessity" of keeping infants under medical observation for the first seventy-two hours. That is the reason many doctors and hospitals have been giving for objecting to same-day discharges for maternity patients. The midwives see it differently. One midwife told me:

When the mother is really the first human being to have contact with the baby and that contact is continuing within several hours, she is the expert for her baby, and feels it, and develops a tremendous amount of confidence, even skills: fathers too, and others. They all feel very close to the baby, very responsible for the baby. There is no third party interfering with this. The role of the midwife in that instance is really just to point out little things, to enhance this feeling of responsibility.

The medical model of pregnancy is mirrored in the medical separation of mother and baby. The needs of infant and mother, not necessarily perceived as harmonious during pregnancy, are certainly not perceived as interactive after birth. For example, since pregnancy and birth are thought of as illnesses or crisis situations, the mother is expected to "need her rest," to recuperate or recover from the experience. Consequently, in most American hospitals, mothers are sent to a "recovery room" from the delivery room. Infants, however, are perceived as "demanding" attention and feeding. The infant's "demands" are then counter to the mother's "need for rest." Since rest in a hospital is defined as something that takes place quietly and in solitude, and infant care is seen as an activity, the two are contradictory. That is why mother and child are routinely separated immediately after birth, just when the desire and the need for intimacy are greatest.

Within the midwifery model, however, both maternal and infant needs are defined quite differently. The mother's need for rest is defined as the need to be freed from everything but herself and her baby. The infant's needs are perceived as body contact, colostrum, and then milk. Far from being contradictory, these needs, it is believed, all come together as the mother lies in bed, dozing and nursing her baby.

—"More often than not I advise the mothers that the baby might be most happy right in bed with her, and that'd be the best way to get some quality rest in the early days because the baby's so content being close to her."
—"Then when we leave, the family can all get into bed together and get some rest."

[184]

Breast Feeding

The distinctions between the midwifery and the medical models of postpartum and infant care are made especially clear in the "management" of infant feeding. The differences involve three factors: the underlying physiological model of the relationship between fetus/baby and mother; an ideology of "nature" versus an ideology of interlocking techniques; and an emphasis on prevention versus an emphasis on cure.

Most cultures have acknowledged a physiological interdependence of mother and baby extending past birth, and have therefore expected mothers and babies to be physically close most of the time, allowing for easy and casual breast feeding. This is especially true in the first hours and days after birth. In our own society, it is only since the establishment of separate newborn nurseries in hospitals in the past fifty years that mothers and infants have been considered entirely separate and independent beings. Instead of being dependent upon each other, both are dependent on a wide range of technological developments, most obviously on artificial formulas and foods, but on antibiotics and artificial hormones as well.

Lactation is of special interest because it is the sole reproductive process that has commercial competition. The substitution of artificial for natural infant feedings is a recent phenomenon, available on a widespread basis only since the development of the rubber nipple and the creation of a dairy industry capable of meeting the needs of an urban population. In the history of evolution, that is very recent indeed. To date, women's other reproductive services, such as the incubation of embryo and (early) fetus are not yet available commercially. (See Chapter 4 for an elaboration of this point.) Therefore infant food is a unique commodity, essential for human survival, and available through two distinct production systems: as a human biological product, and as an industrial product.

As a biological product, milk can be viewed—as the midwives, home-birth advocates, and La Leche League view it —as part of mothering. Beginning with the 1958 edition of the La Leche League pamphlet "Why Nurse Your Baby?," a paragraph entitled "Mothering Is Our Objective" is included. It states in part:

> Our aim is to help mothers give and enjoy happiness and security to their babies through breast feeding. The unique relationship between mother and her breast-fed infant affords a natural and sure start in good mothering. Much more than the best food for baby, breast feeding is the best start in living.

As an industrial product, on the other hand, milk is a commodity, a product rather than a relationship, subject therefore to "comparison shopping," advertising, and technological refinement. Of crucial importance is the role of the producers of artificial formulas, and the sales methods they use to compete with breast milk. The profession of medicine has acted in support of commercial interests just as they have with the drug industry, that is, by patient education, formal and informal, and by selective prescribing. Medicine, most important, has adopted the underlying assumptions about maternal and infant health care that are entirely in accord with the formula industry. The medical model has followed commercial and industrial needs. Milk, in this model, is a product, something that can be synthesized and, with technological know-how, quite possibly improved on.

What Is in a Milk?

Artificial formulas are not, as one might think, close dupli-cates of breast milk, but differ in many important ways. For example, the artificial formulas are considerably lower in fat and cholesterol and higher in iron than is human milk. Re-search on fat and dietary-cholesterol levels with adults seemed to indicate to physicians that these are "bad" for people, and iron, according to other research, "good." Low-ering the one and raising the other then *should* result in an improvement over human milk. These divergences from the composition of human milk are indicative of the technologi-cal orientation of the medical model: the assumption is not made, as in the "nature-oriented" ideology of the midwifery model, that whatever milk evolution has produced is best. (I have heard that view expressed in such sentiments as "If babies needed orange juice, one breast would make milk, the other juice," or "If babies needed Gerber food, we'd all have two breasts and a food mill.")

Yet meeting an infant's nutritional needs is more compli-cated than just putting the right ingredients in a bottle and getting the baby to drink it. That is made particularly clear in the case of the problems of iron-deficiency anemia in artifi-cially fed babies. All milk is low in iron, although there is some iron in human milk. Babies on breast milk alone usually get enough iron, combined with the iron stored from fetal life, to last until they are about six months old, without any iron supplements. However, even with the use of iron sup-plements, and iron added to the formula and baby cereals, artificially fed infants are more likely to become anemic than are breast-fed infants.[1] "Improving" the formula by adding iron does not solve the problem. The breast-fed infants get less iron, but are apparently better able to use it than are artificially fed babies. The mechanisms by which this happens are not known, though other trace minerals may be involved.

Feeding the newborn of one species the milk of another species is not a simple matter. Most formulas for human infants begin with a base of cow's milk. Since there are major differences between the milks of cows and humans, adjustments are made to make them similar. For instance, the protein content of cow's milk is approximately double that of human milk, while the fat and sugar levels are lower. Yet, diluting the cow's milk with water because it is too high in protein (sometimes called "too rich") reduces the fat and sugar levels to below those of human milk.

Up until the recent widespread use of commercial formulas in the 1970s, most artificial infant formulas were made at home out of fresh or canned milk. These home-made formulas called for diluting the cow's milk with water and adding sugar, but usually left the fat content lower than that of human milk—reflective, it seems, of medical concern over high fat content in the diet of adult Americans. For instance, in 1945, Dr. Spock recommended a formula of two parts cow's milk to one part water with granulated sugar added. In recent years he has suggested corn syrup rather than sugar, but otherwise the formula remains the same. Because the vitamin and mineral content of the formula is not the same as that of breast milk, the early addition of iron-rich foods and of orange juice is usually recommended. This approach can be contrasted with the "natural foods" approach of, for example, Adelle Davis,[2] who tried to duplicate human milk as exactly as possible with a more elaborate formula based on goat's milk, which is more humanlike. In the medical and commercial formulas, duplicating human milk does not appear to be the goal; rather, technology is being used to create what "should be" a perfect infant feed. This is particularly clear in the controversy over cholesterol levels in milks.

There are two basic types of commercial formula available, one based on cow's milk and one based on soybeans. The cow's-milk-based commercial formulas use a skimmed milk and substitute vegetable oil for butterfat (the same way margarine is made). Though human milk is very high in cholesterol (20 mg. cholesterol per 10 ml.), the substitution of vegetable oil for butterfat makes commercial formulas quite low in cholesterol. The three most widely used commercial formulas range from 1.5 to 3.3 mg. cholesterol per 100 ml.[3] This is again reflective of concern over adult diet and has not been based on the nutritional needs of infants. Some researchers believe that newborns fed low-cholesterol formulas may have problems with high blood cholesterol later in life, the opposite of what the low-cholesterol formulas are ostensibly trying to achieve.[4] Whether or not the researchers are right, it remains true that the commercial infant formulas are based neither on any long-term controlled studies of infant needs nor on an attempt to duplicate human milk. Technology is assumed to be able not only to substitute for but also to improve upon nature.

The commercial formulas also include some of the missing vitamins (in synthetic form) and minerals, as well as thickeners, such as carrageenin. Carrageenin has been implicated in the development of ulcers and, especially disturbing, fetal damage.[5]

Infant Feeding and Infant Health

Diarrhea,[6] allergies,[7] infections,[8] sudden-infant-death syndrome,[9] and anemia[10] are the most serious possible side effects that have been associated with artificial feeding, those that are most clearly dangerous and life threatening in infancy. Others, such as obesity, may not present problems until much later in life. Breast-fed babies, those who are fed nothing but breast milk, are unlikely to become overweight in infancy, and recent research suggests that overweight in adulthood is based on overproduction of fat cells in infancy.[11] There are several reasons why breast-fed babies do not gain excessively. The most obvious is that they are not encouraged to finish up a bottle or finish a portion. The mother does not know just how much the baby is getting when she nurses and so has no basis for encouraging the baby to take more. In addition, the mother's breasts are producing a finite quantity of milk. The baby cannot take more at a feeding than is there. In bottle feeding, it has been remarked, "all of Borden's dairy" is at the other end of the nipple. Further compounding the problem, commercially made baby foods (strained or pureed "solid" foods as opposed to formulas) used to contain many empty calories in the form of starches and sugars. Through the 1970s Gerber added sugar to 55 percent of its baby foods, Heinz to 65 percent, and Beech-Nut to 66 percent of its baby foods.[12] Changing attitudes toward nutrition in the 1970s caused much of the sugar, along with added salt, to be taken out of the foods. The sugar and salt were added in order to appeal to the adult who was feeding the baby, in much the same way that pet foods added artificial colors to please the animal's owners. As adult attitudes toward sugar and salt have changed, the foods have been adjusted.

A less obvious reason for the lower incidence of obesity in breast-fed babies is the variation in consistency and taste of breast milk from the start to the end of a feeding. A bottle of formula is homogeneous throughout. Milk from the breast is not. At the beginning of the feeding the baby gets the watery fore-milk that is already in the breast ducts. As the baby nurses, the fattier milk, which clings to the cell walls of the breast, is released. The milk at the beginning of the feeding quenches the baby's thirst, and the milk at the end is rich enough to satisfy the baby's appetite. This change in consistency and taste may teach babies appetite regulation.[13]

This is by no means a complete list of all the problems and complications of artificial feeding for infants, but rather an indication of the ways in which breast milk and artificially made formulas differ. Note that most of these differences are not inevitable in the use of artificial formula—as Adelle Davis showed—but are based on considered medical judgment. Rather than starting with the assumption that whatever is in breast milk is what should be in infant feeds, medicine has started from an analysis of presumed infant needs, much of that based on research into adult diet.

Another difference in the use of human milk compared to artificial formulas is that it is possible for an infant to develop an allergic reaction to artificial formulas but not to its mother's milk. Every so often a little article shows up in a newspaper or "women's magazine" saying that infants have had allergic reactions to their mother's milk. When you read the article through, however, you find that what they are saying is that infants can have allergic reactions to something that their mother ate, which passed through the milk. One of the most frequent offenders is cow's milk. Babies can be so highly allergic to cow's milk that even when filtered through their mother's breasts it causes an allergic reaction.

Approximately 10 percent of artificially fed babies do develop allergic reactions to cow's milk, usually very early in life. Eczema, diarrhea, vomiting, and shock may follow.[14] It is common practice among pediatricians dealing with newborns who have diarrhea or other signs of allergy to switch them to soy-based formulas, avoiding all milk products, in addition to treating them with antibiotics and intravenous feedings. Rather than encouraging mothers to begin nursing immediately, doctors have even told women that their sick infants could not "tolerate" breast milk.

It is very difficult for the technologically oriented physician to have any faith in the body, or to in any way relinquish control, as long as there is something to prescribe, some activity or interventionist treatment available. "Prescribing" that a mother take off her shirt and climb into bed with her baby and try to get her milk going is an act of faith in "nature" or "evolution." To send the mother home and admit the baby to the hospital is an act of faith in technology.

Besides the composition of milks and the possibility of allergy, another important difference between human milk and artificial feeds is the immunoglobulins or antibodies that are present in human milk and protect infants against disease. All of the substitute or artificial formulas are missing the immunoglobulins that are in human milk. The immunoglobulins protect the body against infection from viruses, bacteria, and fungi. All babies are born with a limited ability to make their own antibodies. It takes time before they can bring their own antibodies up to levels high enough to protect them from disease.

There are three main immunoglobulins: M, G, and A. Immunoglobulins M (IgM) and G (IgG) circulate. IgM is the larger and more effective of the two, and when infection threatens it is the first immunoglobulin produced. After a short while, however, production shifts to the less effective but smaller IgG. This is important because IgM is too large to cross the placenta in humans, but IgG is passed to the fetus. At birth, before the baby can begin its own production of antibodies, the circulating IgG provides some protection. In those mammals whose placentas do not allow the passage of IgG either, such as the pig and the cow, IgG (along with IgM and IgA) is passed from mother to offspring in the colostrum, the fluid that precedes milk. For those animals, colostrum is an absolute necessity and they die without it. Human infants can survive without it, managing on IgG alone. That is the basic fact on which our ability to develop a life-supporting artificial formula rests.

IgA is an immunoglobulin that is present in all secretions in the gastrointestinal tract and in tears. It is in saliva and is secreted by the stomach and rectal linings. It forms a protective coating on all these moist, open surfaces, which otherwise would allow entrance into the system to bacteria and other foreign cells. IgA, along with IgM and IgG, is in human milk and in human colostrum. It is not present in any formula and is not produced by the infant at birth. The lack of these antibodies explains the repeated findings of higher infection rates, particularly but not only gastrointestinal infections in artificially fed infants.[15] They have IgG but not IgM or IgA.

While artificial-formula feeding may be enabled to meet the nutritional needs of infants, albeit imperfectly, it cannot be made to provide these antibodies. Note that antibodies are not "general," the way antibiotics like penicillin are, but are specific to the pathogens in the maternal environment. The mother produces antibodies specific to the diseases to which she (and her infant) are exposed. When these antibodies are not made available to the infant, problems arise for its health and survival, which, if not dealt with preventively, must be dealt with once the disease has developed. Here we see another example of one technology's being dependent upon another. The technology of artificial feeding depends on the technology of antibiotics in the treatment of disease.

In Third World countries the problem of artificial infant feeding is of course more serious, leading to worldwide protests against the companies that promote artificial formula. The Nestlé corporation is one of the worst offenders, and the target of a boycott sponsored by INFACT. Manufacturers of artificial formulas use such promotional techniques as providing the mothers with free formula for the first week. A week is long enough for the mother's own milk to come in and dry up. The baby is then "hooked" on the formula. The cost of formula for one baby can easily be 40 percent of a family's total income. Instructions and warnings are not usually printed in a language the mother can read, if indeed she can read at all. The formula is usually sold as a powder, and so many people dilute it to stretch it further. The water itself may not be pure, and the means for sterilizing it are often not available. And, of course, the antibiotics so readily available in the United States may not be available at all when these Third World "bottle babies" sicken and eventually die.[16]

Reports in the medical journals make the point that the protective benefits of breast milk are of particular importance in underdeveloped countries. Modern American hygiene and the availability of medical services to overcome infections are claimed to make breast milk less crucial for survival here. Yet we know that infants are exposed to infection even in the hospitals in which they are born.[17] *Williams Obstetrics* reports the development of antibiotic-resistant staphylococci in hospitals and relates this to an increase in the frequency and severity of breast abscesses in mothers who do nurse. The infant becomes infected in the nursery from contact with nursery personnel. The attendants' hands are the major source of contamination for the newborn.[18]

We can sterilize formula, diapers, and all equipment that comes into contact with infants, but we cannot prevent infants from being exposed to infection even under the most careful of hygienic regimens. Depending on medical services to overcome the problem once it has arisen means acknowledging that infants will be sick, hospitalized, and placed on intravenous fluids and antibiotics. When we accept a medical model of interdependent technologies providing alternative solutions to those offered physiologically, that is what we are getting into the bargain. As a solution, it is not acceptable to the parent watching a doctor struggle to start an IV on an infant, that itself is no longer strong enough to struggle. As many critics of American medicine have pointed out, the emphasis is on cure rather than prevention, and there are attendant costs.

Infant Feeding and Maternal Health

If a pregnancy goes to term and the woman decides not to, or is not allowed to nurse her baby, then the biological tie between mother and baby is abruptly severed along with the umbilical cord. The mother has to make her return to the nonpregnant state without the baby, just as the baby has to adjust to the demands of life outside the womb without the aid of the mother. I have discussed some of what that means for the baby. Now let us consider the physical effects of artificial feeding on the mother, and how these are managed by the medical profession, by contrast with the midwifery model's approach.

The growth of the uterus during pregnancy is astounding and very obvious. The involution or shrinking of the uterus after birth is no less astounding for its being less obvious. At the end of labor the uterus is just a couple of inches below the umbilicus and weighs two pounds. Twenty-four hours later it is actually higher, at about the level of the umbilicus, and begins its involution. In less than two weeks it is below the level of the pubic bone and weighs about seven ounces. By six weeks, it is back to its nonpregnant weight of two ounces.

Part of the reduction in size of the uterus is due to the actual absorption of its fibers, but part of it is due to the contraction of the muscle. (The uterus is a muscle and so capable of contracting.) The contractions of labor push the fetus and placenta out, and the contractions after labor close the muscle in on itself, compressing its blood supply. The reduction of the blood supply causes further involution of the uterus. Uterine contractions are not under direct voluntary control, or at least are not generally believed to be; but uterine contractions can be indirectly caused, for example with an orgasm. Nipple stimulation also causes uterine contractions. Midwives use this as a method for speeding up labor that they feel needs some assistance; a borrowed nursing baby is believed to be ideal, but a helpful husband makes a good substitute. This is believed by the midwives to be more "natural" than the use of exogenous hormones, as is the custom of physicians. When the nipple is stimulated by suckling, a complicated chain of messages is set up. Impulses travel through the nervous system to the hypothalamus, which in turn stimulates the pituitary to secrete prolactin. The prolactin causes the alveoli, the milk-producing cells, to secrete milk. Then, within two to three minuts or less, the nipple stimulation causes the pituitary to secrete oxytocin, a hormone that causes smooth muscle to contract. The effect in the breast is the "let-down" of milk, the milk or colostrum rushing into the ducts. The effect on the uterus is that it contracts. The strong contractions of the uterus in response to nipple stimulation can be quite uncomfortable shortly after birth and are commonly called "after-pains." While women who do not nurse will have after-pains also, nursing mothers are especially aware of them while nursing. The contractions caused by nipple stimulation cause the uterus to return to its nonpregnant state quickly, and when the baby suckles immediately after birth, the contractions clamp down on the blood supply to the uterus, and help prevent postpartum hemorrhage, the gravest immediate danger to the mother in the postpartum period.

If a woman does not have nipple stimulation that causes

her to produce her own oxytocin, it may be necessary to give her an injection of oxytocin (or Pitocin) shortly after birth to prevent excessive bleeding. Even for women who are planning on breast feeding, the hospital practice of removing babies from their mothers for six to twelve hours after birth —not allowing them to suckle—necessitates the use of an oxytocin or Pitocin injection.

Not only did the midwives urge, and sometimes require, that the baby be put to breast early as a preventative measure; nipple stimulation was also used therapeutically. Almost all of the midwives referred to suckling as the first response to heavy bleeding and/or retained placenta.

Besides the involution of the uterus, a further change that a woman's body must go through is the loss of fat stored during pregnancy. In the discussion of nutrition and pregnancy (see chapter on pregnancy) it was pointed out that a weight gain over and above that accounted for by the fetus, placenta, and amniotic fluid, and increased blood volume is a physiologically normal part of pregnancy. Attempts to limit the weight gain during pregnancy adversely affect the fetus. Breast feeding uses up about a thousand calories a day, the amount increasing as the baby grows, decreasing with the use of solids or formula. The extra eight to ten pounds a woman usually gains in an unrestricted pregnancy are quickly used up in nursing without any conscious effort on her part to "diet." Women who do not nurse have to lose the weight without the baby's help. Physicians not familiar with prolonged breast feeding have relied on weight-gain limitation during pregnancy to prevent later obesity in the mother, although this puts the fetus at risk.

Breast development during pregnancy has of course no relation to one's plans for breast or artificial feeding. Even without nipple stimulation, almost all women will begin to produce noticeable amounts of milk. For most, the breasts will become at least somewhat engorged. Under normal circumstances—that is, with a nursing baby—the baby's demand determines the milk supply, and over the months, or even years, of weaning, the breasts slowly cease milk production. Since most women begin milk production even without nipple stimulation, not nursing the baby is very much the same as abrupt weaning. It takes some time for the breasts to adjust to the absence of the baby. The most painful part of breast engorgement usually subsides within forty-eight hours, but even nonnursing women can continue leaking milk for weeks, and milk may still be produced in small quantities for months.

It has been fairly standard practice among physicians since the 1930s in the United States to give to women who are not breast feeding hormones, especially estrogens, in order to suppress lactation. Organic and artificial, nonsteroid estrogens have been used, including DES and other stilbestrols whose use has been implicated in cancer, in other circumstances. These estrogens were frequently combined with progestin or testosterones. In addition to the carcinogenic potential, there were immediate side effects of these treatments as well, ranging from unpleasant to life threatening. The estrogens and progestins may interfere with the involution of the uterus and stimulate the growth of the endometrium (lining to the uterus), thus causing uterine bleeding.[19] This is the opposite of the effect of lactation, which suppresses estrogen production, allowing the uterus to return to its nonpregnant size and "rest." Women who do not breast-feed have an abnormally early return of the menstrual cycle and ovulation. Interestingly, in the medical literature, this is usually phrased in the opposite manner, that women who breast-feed have a *delayed* return of ovulation. Once again we see the medical profession's acceptance of artificial feeding as the norm.

The use of estrogens increases the risk of thromboembolic disease (blood clotting, which can be fatal) after birth.[20] Since the 1950s, combinations of estrogens with androgens have been used to suppress lactation. Deladumone, a combination of testosterone and estradiol valerate, was probably the most widely used such combination. While it appears that it was fairly effective in suppressing lactation, there were sometimes the temporary side effects of facial-hair growth and acne,[21] and there may even be a permanent deepening of the voice.[22] Tace, the trade name for chlorotrianisene, a synthetic estrogen, has also been widely used in the United States, though it may be less effective.[23] The effectiveness of Deladumone is enhanced considerably when it is given during labor. Women in labor are still pregnant women, and the practice of giving a powerful estrogen-testosterone preparation to a pregnant woman is adding an unknown risk to the known risks of artificial feeding for the baby. There are no long-term follow-up studies on either maternal or infant side effects. Because of these dangers, most major medical centers have stopped using these drugs in the past few years.

Ideology in Practice

The alternative managements of infant feeding, presented as the "breast or bottle?" choice in many of the how-to books on pregnancy and birth, represent genuine differences in ideology. Even phrasing the issue as a simple choice, like that of using cloth or paper diapers, requires that one see the mother-infant relationship in a particular way. If one sees the mother and baby as an interdependent unit, still part of each other, then the "breast or bottle?" question is almost silly, like asking whether the baby should be maintained in the womb or in an incubator for the last six weeks of pregnancy.

The medical model is very much a part of industrial society and the industrial ideology. Technologies are hooked in to ever widening circles of technologies. Since the ultimate goal is to produce so many live babies, or "successful outcomes," precisely how that goal is achieved hardly matters. In the midwifery model, a nonmechanical or nontechnological orientation, the socio-emotional costs of illness and therapy are more easily taken into consideration. Having a well baby who has never been sick is not the same as having a well baby who has been restored to health in a neonatal intensive-care unit following a gastrointestinal infection. Process and relationship can be considered as important as "product", whether the product is milk or a live baby. The *quality* of the experience itself, as well as its outcome, is of concern to midwives and to people in the home-birth movement. Even if medicine with attendant technologies can produce "satisfactory outcomes," that is, live babies, the *experiences* of doing so may not be satisfactory. At the risk of oversimplification, let us say that in the home-birth model the ends do not justify the means; not all means are equal even if they do achieve the same goals.

Artificial feeding, by both formula and the early introduction of solid foods, is clearly a product of industrialization, which made it not only possible but, given the removal of work from the home, desirable and even necessary. Unfortunately, it has also made artificial feeding fashionable. A major aspect of the ideology of industrialization is the control of nature, the valuing of technology. Breast feeding does not lend itself to mechanistic ways, is not easily subject to mechanical control or measurement. Gesell's classic *Infant and Child in the Culture of Today* placed the blame for the abandonment of breast feeding on mothers, quoting mothers who said, "Why bother?"[24] Yet Gesell's book, like the others of its time, told mothers to weigh babies before and after every single feeding, to record the weight difference and thus know just how much the baby got. That recommendation was not for babies who were not gaining, or to reassure anxious parents, but for normal, healthy babies throughout the duration of nursing. Weighing the baby gave the breast-feeding mother the same knowledge that the bottle-feeding mother had of just how much the baby got. But *why?* If the baby was content and gaining, what was the purpose of recording how many ounces it got at each feeding? Weighing babies, like putting feeding on an arbitrary time schedule, or limiting nursing to the number of minutes it should take to empty a breast—*all* of which recommendations were found in the medical literature of the 1930s through the 1970s—made breast feeding pseudoscientific. It was an interesting example of trying to apply technological expertise to a non-technological process. Thus, the technology-oriented ideology functions even where it is least appropriate. Breast feeding is nontechnological: the baby is hungry, it nurses, and it is full. The baby grows. At about five or six months it starts reaching for the food it sees. After about a year—or two or three—it no longer needs to nurse and it is gradually weaned. There is no place for the directing physician, except to interfere with the process. Understandably, Gessell's study found babies weaned within a few months, a finding typical of the period.

It is that takeover of breast feeding by physicians claiming technological expertise to which La Leche League addressed itself. It is not that physicians ever adopted the principle that women should not nurse their babies. Rather, they took up the more insidious practice of telling women how to nurse their babies and basing that on an inappropriate model. Nursing mothers found it all but impossible to successfully nurse a baby and follow pediatrician's orders; for many it was impossible.

The decline of midwifery and of the extended family left women without anyone to turn to for help in breast feeding and infant care. The profession of medicine was called on to fill this gap, but it filled it in a way appropriate to medical thinking and expertise. Physicians do not study nutrition as part of their training, yet physicians are expected to be the experts on the feeding of infants. Formulas have been prescribed with bananas at four weeks and cereals at six, or the other way around, depending on the biases and whims of the pediatrician, and not on the basis of any scientific evidence.[25] Physicians thought in terms of scheduling feedings not only because of the widespread importance of the clock in industrial societies, but specifically because their contacts with newborns were in hospital nurseries, where feedings are scheduled according to bureaucratic demands. On a schedule of limited four-hour feedings with no night feeding from the day of birth, breast feeding is very difficult to establish. And so the physician has had very little positive experience with it. As one doctor has pointed out in the *Journal of Reproductive Medicine:*

The medical student in his last two years of training is given clinics in obstetrics and pediatrics, but is very rarely shown a normal nursing mother . . . much more time is spent with the preparation of formula and discussion of human vs. artificial food. . . . The prevailing attitude is that the mother is assuming an impossible and insurmountable task.[26]

The midwives, in contrast, see breast feeding as a "natural" phenomenon; the majority of the midwives were unable to give examples of major breast-feeding problems among their home-birth and birthing-center clients. When specifically asked about their role in lactation counseling, they dismissed it with "It just works out" or "irons itself out" or "takes care of itself." A mother may need some help, but nursing is not, from the perspective of these nurse-midwives, a difficult thing to do once she knows how and has social support and, most important, has the baby with her. On this issue, both the nurse-midwives and La Leche League are in agreement, that breast feeding is part of mothering skills and is something that is learned socially and not "prescribed." Yet here is an example of a breast-feeding "prescription" from Dr. Alan P. Guttmacher in a very popular book of the 1960s on pregnancy and birth:

Babies are offered nothing by mouth the first twelve hours. During the remaining twelve hours of the first day they nurse each breast for two or three minutes every four hours. . . . In most instances the child requires no preliminary training or encouragement to take the nipple but begins to suck promptly. Since it gets nothing but a scanty amount of colostrum, it may soon stop and go to sleep. Treat the baby rough; wake it up, fleck the feet by snapping your fingers at its soles. On the second and third days the child suckles for three to five minutes on each breast, and ten minutes on each breast thereafter. The four-hour schedule is continued, the baby being put to both breasts, but alternating the starting breast. As long as the baby gets little milk, it may be offered two ounces of five percent glucose water after each nursing, especially in hot weather.[27]

Several of the nurse-midwives referred to the glucose water, standard in most hospitals, as "baby Coca-Cola." It should be noted here that it is suckling which stimulates milk production; if that were not the case, women would produce large amounts of milk from their first pregnancies throughout the rest of their lives. Without outside scheduling, babies nurse every two to three hours, sometimes for as long as an hour. (Guttmacher's description of a sleepy baby may be typical of the drugged hospital baby of the era.) If suckling is denied, or if the baby is satisfied with other food, breast-milk production drops off accordingly. That is the way weaning works. Guttmacher, however, uses weaning methods from the start:

> If after several days the child does not get enough breast milk to satisfy its needs, discovered by weighing before and after several nursings, the mother's breast milk is supplemented by offering the baby three ounces of formula. If after forty-eight hours of mixed feedings the mother's milk does not increase sufficiently to meet two-thirds of the baby's needs, it is wise to discontinue breast feeding and put the baby on full bottle feedings.[28]

Guttmacher's was the typical medical prescription for breast feeding. The League and the home-birth and birthing-center nurse-midwives take a much more leisurely approach: "Give it time." For specific questions or problems, such as sore nipples, a sleepy baby, or a sleepy mother, many of the nurse-midwives referred the mother either to La Leche League or to what was called an "experienced" midwife—meaning a midwife who herself had been a nursing mother.

In the "official" League history, *The LLLove Story*, [29] two of the founding mothers recalled how they began demedicalizing breast feeding. For example, with regard to when to wean from the breast:

> —"We started giving a lot of thought to weaning and discovered that although the medical textbooks said it should take place no later than nine months; they didn't offer a solid reason why."

—"It gradually dawned on us that we were asking the wrong people. Doctors were men, and why should they know more about it than mothers? Since it wasn't a medical question, their medical education was of no help. That was why no good answer could be found in the medical books. We decided that it would be much more likely to be a woman, a mother, who would know."

Demedicalizing breast feeding makes it part of mothering skills, what LLL calls a "womanly art."

The decline of breast feeding through the 1920s in the United States and the rapid decline in Third World countries cannot be explained on the basis of physician attitudes and ideologies alone. Equally or more important, especially in understanding the exportation of artificial feeding, is the role of commercial interests behind artificial formulas. Here we have a problem not only of the technological orientation of industrial society, and hence of medicine within industrial societies, but also of the capitalist search for new markets. The makers of artificial formulas are in direct competition with breast milk, which of course has no commercial backing and unrecognized market value. Tiny infants grin with healthy glee at the sight of the strained applesauce in the baby-food ads, and the formula companies go so far as to distribute "breast-feeding your baby" pamphlets in the doctor's office and free samples of formula and bottles for the breast-feeding mother to take home from the hospital. Ross laboratories, the makers of Similac, one of the widest-selling artificial infant feeds in the United States, has a pamphlet on breast feeding that has five pages on breast-feeding techniques and seven pages on when and how to give Similac to the breast-fed baby—after a feeding, instead of a feeding, and early enough to get the baby ready for early weaning to Similac. "Similac," we are told, "represents the best in up-to-date scientific nutrition for infants."[30] Because such pamphlets and samples are distributed through doctors and hospitals, they carry with them the weight of professional approval. The message is that the modern, scientific thing to do is to artificially feed the baby, if not directly from birth, then by weaning it within a few weeks.

The midwifery model of breast feeding contrasts to the medical model in every way. It is based on a strong faith in what is "natural," and an emphasis on prevention. Breast feeding is seen as the biologically natural and healthily normal mode of infant feeding. Virtually all home-birth mothers nurse their babies: most of the midwives had never attended a home-birth or birthing-center birth where the baby was not put to the breast. Some actually made it a requirement, as a "safety factor," though that usually referred primarily to the role of suckling in preventing postpartum hemorrhage. In the midwifery model, not only is the baby dependent on the mother, but the mother is perceived as dependent on the baby, with suckling as the physiologically normal last stage of pregnancy.

In sum, the differences between the medical and the home-birth model of breast feeding involves three factors; the underlying physiological model of the relationship between fetus/baby and mother; an ideology of "nature" versus an ideology of interlocking technologies; and an emphasis on prevention versus emphasis on cure.

In the medical model, the mother is host to the fetus; she contains "George's baby" (see chapter on pregnancy), but her interests and those of the fetus are not seen as necessarily harmonious. At birth they are freed from each other and separated quite literally and totally. The baby is sent to a nursery, where specially trained personnel can keep it under observation and care for its needs. Babies need to be kept warm, so baby warmers are used, little incubatorlike boxes.

Babies need nourishment, so artificial formulas are provided. If the babies become sick, antibiotics can be used. Mothers after birth are given hormones to contract the uterus and are sent to recovery rooms where their sleep is not disturbed by their babies.

In the home birth, the fetus is part of the mother, and babyhood is a transitional stage physiologically for both mother and baby. At birth the baby goes directly to its mother's arms. She becomes familiar with what her baby looks like, and along with those who share her life is expected to recognize any problems. The mother's body provides warmth for the baby, and her colostrum and milk provide immunity and nourishment. The suckling provides for the release of hormones in the mother that contract her uterus and prevent hemorrhages. While for the physicians the two are separate problems in medical management, for home-birth advocates and midwives, mother and baby are an inter-dependent pair.

8

Maternal Bonding and
Cultural Binds

others is a biological relationship in a social context, and a social relationship in a biological context. It is hard to say how much of mothering behavior, especially in the first few hours and days after birth, is the result of biology, and how much the result of social learning and social pressures. Those who emphasize the importance of biology in motherhood often refer to animal studies. Many animal mothers, when separated from their newborns immediately after birth, will reject them when they are returned. It is only immediately after the birth that the mothers will accept, or bond to, their young. Similarly, newborns of some species, such as chicks, will bond to their mothers only in the first few hours after hatching, the so-called critical period. If separated during these first critical hours the chick will not display the normal behavior of following behind its mother and staying close to her. On the basis of these and other animal studies, some people suggest that there is a similar critical period for maternal-infant bonding in humans and have attempted to demonstrate this experimentally.

There are indeed some very impressive studies showing the importance of attachment or bonding behavior in the first few hours or days of life. In the original maternal-infant bonding study, reported in the *New England Journal of Medicine,* involving twenty-eight mother-infant pairs, variation in the amount of contact in the first three days of life was shown to affect interaction a month later.[1] Fourteen mothers received what has become standard American hospital treatment. The babies were removed to a separate nursery after the mothers had just a brief glimpse of them in the delivery room and were not returned to the mother for six to twelve hours, and then were allowed only twenty-minute-to-half-hour visits every four hours. The other fourteen mothers were allowed to have their babies for one hour within the first three hours after birth, and then followed the same every-four-horus pattern, except for an extra five-hour visit each afternoon for the three days of hospitalization. The only difference between the two groups was the sixteen hours of "extra" contact permitted the "experimental" group. All babies in both groups were bottle fed, which means that the additional contact had no effect on the amount of milk available.

The mother-child interactions were observed under three separate circumstances by independent researchers a month later. The extended-contact mothers were more reluctant to leave their infants with someone else, usually stood and watched during the pediatric examination, showed greater soothing behavior, and engaged in significantly more eye-to-eye contact and fondling. Differences between the two groups continued to be seen at two years of age.[2] Those who believe in "natural" or "instinctive" maternal behavior would contend that the extended-contact mothers were freer to follow their instincts, while the other mothers had their mother-child relationship disturbed or interrupted, their instinctual patterns blocked by the enforced separation. It is not an unreasonable explanation. An alternative, equally plausible explanation is that mother-child interactions are learned, not instinctual, but that mothers do need the presence of the baby, and the baby that of the mother, to learn how to interact. If the mother is denied her baby except for a few minutes at times based on neither the baby's needs nor her own, learning does not take place, or, even more important, incorrect learning occurs. The baby learns that comforting is unrelated to the need for comfort, and the mother learns that she is superfluous to the child's needs. In either case, the implications for mothering are the same. If there are "maternal instincts," they may be fragile and disturbed by mother-child separation. If the behaviors are learned, they need to be learned in the beginning, before other patterns are learned—by mother or baby—and interfere. We have no reason not to think that this applies to anyone who will be caring for the child—mother, father, siblings, adoptive parents—but as long as all the research is done on mothers, the term "maternal-infant" rather than "adult-infant" bonding will continue to be used. We cannot prove the existence of a distinctively maternal set of responses to infants without doing systematic research on all people who care for infants.

One of the most sophisticated and potentially most influential arguments on the importance of "maternal instincts" in parenting is found in Alice Rossi's article "Biosocial Aspects of Parenting." Rossi bases her argument on some of the studies of maternal-infant bonding and interactions, but unfortunately appears not to recognize their severe limitations. In her strongest statement of the existence of maternal instincts, she points to the following findings:

Mother-infant interaction carries a cluster of characteristics that suggest the presence of unlearned responses. On a strictly physiological level, infant crying stimulates the secretion of oxytocin in the mother, which triggers uterine contractions and nipple erection preparatory to nursing. Without even being aware of it, the overwhelming majority of women cradle their infants in their left arm, regardless of their particular handedness, where the infant can hear and be soothed by the maternal heartbeat familiar from uterine life. Close-up films of women after childbirth show a common sequence of approaches when their nude babies are placed at their side. They touch its fingers and toes with their own fingertips, put the palm of their hand on the baby's trunk, then enclose the infant with their arms, all the while rotating their heads to an *en face* position to achieve full, parallel eye contact, with increasing tension in the mother until her baby's eyes are open and eye contact is made. Even mothers of premature infants peering into incubators at their babies engage in head rotation to achieve *en face* contact.[3]

Let us analyze this point by point. Oxytocin secretion, perceived by the mother in its effect on milk "let-down" and uterine contractions, certainly is stimulated by infant crying. Then, too, it appears to be very easily stimulated in the first days and perhaps weeks after birth. Milk let-down, the rushing of milk into the main milk sinuses under the nipple, or even out of the duct opening to drip or spray from the nipples, can be caused by a number of things, including leaning over, sexual arousal, and emotional arousal; it also occurs without identifiable stimulation. That is experienced by the majority of new mothers as "leaking" of milk, while the uterine contractions caused by the oxytocin are the "after-pains." Gradually, the let-down reflex is less an immediate response and comes to take a minute or so of actual suckling in order for it to be stimulated. That is, it becomes increasingly specific, a good indication of a learned response. So while there is a physiological link, oxytocin release is nonetheless a socially learned response. Mothers are of course responding not to the physical sensations of their infant's crying but to its social meaning. Human beings act toward things on the basis of the socially learned meanings those things have. Just as a pounding-heart, clammy-hand response to a gun aimed at one is a physiological response to a socially learned danger signal, so too are a mother's milk let-down, nipple erection, and uterine cramping in response to her infant's cry a physiological response to the social meaning of the stimulus.

Similarly, women's cradling infants in their left arm is hardly proof of unlearned behaviors. Infants do calm down when they are held on the left side, soothed by the heartbeat. It works. When people do something that works, that achieves a consciously desired end, it may be that they learned, with or without complete awareness, either for themselves or through others, that it works. Because holding an infant on the left soothes it, we do it and we see others do it. It "feels right" because the infant settles in, and it "looks right" because that is how we've seen it done.

A second major criticism is that all of Rossi's statements refer to research on mothers, which tells us something about maternal responsiveness, but certainly nothing about the responsiveness of others. For example, how do men hold babies? Learned or unlearned, is what we are looking at maternal behavior, female behavior, or human behavior?

The study to which Rossi refers, on how mothers greet or first touch their newborns, is a case in point. The physical movements of mothers in touching the newborn were shown to be startlingly similar from one mother to the next:

... When nude full-term infants are brought to their mothers shortly after birth the mothers started a routine pattern of behavior which began with fingertip touching of the infant's extremities and proceeded in four to eight minutes to massaging and encompassing palm contact on the trunk.[4]

But we do not have studies of men's or nonmothers' responses to newborns. In fact, even the studies that we do have of mothers are suspect. The behavior that mothers show in an American hospital birth, where these studies have taken place, may be very different from maternal behavior under other circumstances. In the study Rossi cites, frequently more than an hour had elapsed between the birth and the "greeting." In home births and hospital births in many other cultures, the mother either takes the baby from her body herself or is handed the infant immediately upon its emergence. The hesitant approach from the extremities described in the hospital births is not possible when one is holding a newly born, slick and squirming infant. To say that under one particular, and in fact bizarre, set of social circumstances mothers follow a certain pattern of response tells us neither that the pattern is instinctual nor that it is maternal.

The maternal-infant bonding studies Rossi cites used non-nursing mothers, as explained above, thereby eliminating the basis for physiologically "normal" maternal behavior. (Can there be an "instinctual" greeting sequence that never gets the baby to the breast?) We need studies in which other adults and even children are placed nude in beds under heat lamps, as these new mothers were, and presented with nude one- or two-hour-old babies, before we can begin to talk about "maternal" bonding behavior.

Rossi goes on to cite some of the several studies that have demonstrated the importance of early contact, specifically touching and skin-to-skin contact, between mothers and infants, for the development of maternal responsiveness and interest in later weeks, months, and even years. Again, it is necessary to consider the social situations in which birth takes place. In our society, mothers are removed from their normal social environment and isolated with their infants for these first, crucial days of life. Even the newer, more "permissive" hospitals that allow fathers to witness births have followed the pattern of isolating the babies from anyone but hospital staff and their mothers. (In some few hospitals, and of course in the birthing centers, this is changing.) Only mothers have been allowed physical contact with the infants, while fathers, grandparents, siblings, and all others have been limited to seeing the infant behind a glass wall, if at all. When the mother returns home she is indeed, at least relatively speaking, the expert in the care of the infant. Even the six hours total time spent in contact with the baby (one half hour every four hours for three days with no night visits is standard hospital practice) is still six hours more than anyone else in her family or friendship network has had. We know that denying infant contact hinders the development of "maternal responsiveness," whether by interfering with innate patterns or by preventing learning from taking place. Since we have eliminated paternal or other contact with the baby, we can draw no conclusions about the potential for innate responsiveness of fathers specifically, or of humans generally. Whether these patterns are instinctual or learned, we have no reason to believe that they exist differently for mothers than for nonmothers, or for women than for men.

Rossi calls for studies of child attachment with males who participate in births. Some of those data are being developed. A very important work in this area is a 1974 study on fathers' engrossment.[5] "Engrossment" refers to a sense of absorption, preoccupation, and interest in the infant, and is the phrase that has been adopted by researchers to refer to what in mothers is usually called "bonding." Bonding implies a mutual tie; engrossment, a one-way relationship. The authors consider the father's potential for engrossment in his newborn to be innate, and hypothesize that it is the early contact with the infant that releases this potential for involvement. In their study, fifteen out of thirty fathers were present at the birth and fifteen were not. However, the study took place in a London hospital, and it appears that all of the fathers were allowed early physical contact with their babies. There was some indication that those present for the birth were more highly engrossed than those not present, but the striking thing to emerge from the data is how involved and moved all of the fathers were. The fathers developed a feeling of preoccupation, absorption, and interst in their newborns. They wanted to look at, hold, and touch their babies. The researchers said, "It is as if he has been 'hooked' by something that has transpired in the father-infant relationship."[6]

Engrossment consisted of the following seven characteristics:

1. Visual awareness of the newborn—perceived as attractive, pretty, or beautiful.
2. Tactile awareness of the newborn—manifested by a desire to touch and hold the baby, which was perceived as very pleasurable.
3. Awareness of the distinct features of the newborn.
4. Perception of the newborn as "perfect."
5. A strong attraction to the newborn, which leads the father to a focusing of his attention upon the newborn.
6. Extreme elation, experienced by almost all of the fathers, and often described as a "high" following the birth of the child.

7. An increased sense of self-esteem experienced by the fathers upon seeing their newborn for the first time.

These are of course precisely the same attitudes and feelings we have attributed primarily to mothers in our society.

In another study dealing with father participation in the birth and later father commitment to his infant, Peterson et al. studied forty-six couples from the sixth month of pregnancy through six months postpartum. The sample included thirteen planned home births, twenty-one planned "natural" hospital births, and twelve planned anesthetized hospital births. Fathers were interviewed prenatally; births were observed; fathers were interviewed immediately following the birth to determine their subjective impression of their involvement, and then followed up to determine the father's commitment to his infant. The researchers concluded that the most important variable in the prediction of father commitment to the infant was birth participation.

In other, unpublished data, Mehl and his associates have found father attachment related both to home rather than hospital birth, which may be further indication of father involvement in the birth or may be reflective of "territoriality" needs; and to length of labor. The latter finding may be somewhat surprising. Longer labors are usually more difficult labors for mothers, and it might seem strange that this would be positively related to the father's attachment to the baby. When we observe the labors, or photographs taken during labor, the relationship becomes more understandable. Mehl presents home-birth slides of partially nude fathers and mothers entwined in each other's arms, laboring together.[7] Fathers rub backs, massage legs and perineum, stroke, fondle, and hold their mate. They sit behind her and hold her upright for the birth. The intense physical involvement of the father in a long labor, possibly increasing as the wife weakens with time, explains why the father's response to the newborn might become more like the mother's as the labor is prolonged.

People often assume that if there is a relationship between hormones and behavior, it is the hormones that cause the behavior. But Rossi argues, as most biologists have accepted, that hormone levels may be a dependent variable, caused by social situations. That is, behavior can release hormones. In light of that, note that we have no studies of fathers' or other support persons' hormonal levels during the labors in which they participate, nor of hormonal fluctuations in response to the sight, sound, smell, and feel of newborns.

It is very unusual for a woman in most societies to labor alone without social support from the people who matter to her or to be isolated from them with her new infant. The opportunity for infant bonding is thus available not only to the mother but also to other people who will later share some responsibility for the infant. Rossi states, "As a consequence [of prolonged immaturity of humans] it is more crucial to the survival of humans than to any other mammalian species to provide for prolonged infant care through intense attachment of mother and infant." Actually, studies on animals have shown that nature is flexible as to who gives parenting.[8] While parenting is absolutely necessary for the survival of an infant, that does not mean that it must come from mothers. Even in a strict evolutionary perspective, it would seem useful for the species for birth attendants of the same kinship, most notably the father and siblings, to bond strongly to the infant, thus ensuring its survival in cases of maternal death.

It is certainly true that most societies have used women as primary social parents, for their own biological as well as communal children, and have used women as birth attendants. That is, those who will be responsible for caring for the child are present for its birth and first few hours of life. It has been argued that the emphasis on a relatively isolated nuclear family in our society is more of a middle-class or upper-middle-class ideal than an actuality for most Americans. The childbirth-preparation movement has been a predominantly middle-class phenomenon. Consequently, the concept of "family-centered maternity care" has been used to mean mother-father-baby togetherness. The movement has been to bring fathers (husbands, really) into labor and delivery rooms. If our families are to be organized around mother-father pairs parenting children, then bringing fathers into the birth process should help bring that about. If we would prefer, for example, to strengthen female kinship ties, then grandmothers and aunts should be brought back as birth attendants. In no case does it seem useful for child rearing to isolate mothers from all significant others for birth and the first days of the infant's life, and then further to limit contact between the baby and the mother herself. Whether adult-to-newborn bonding or engrossment (love?) is innate or learned, limiting its potential would seem unwise.

Baby Care

And what of the baby's attachment to and need for its mother? Some studies were done in the late 1950s on love, milk, and infant monkeys. Researchers noted that rhesus monkey infants raised in laboratory cages became deeply attached to the cloth pads in the cages, showing real distress when these were removed for cleaning. "The behavior of the infant monkeys was reminiscent of the human infant's attachment to its blankets, pillows, rag dolls or cuddly teddy bears."[9] What these observations suggested to Harry F. Harlow were some experiments, the outcome of which has important implications for understanding infant-to-adult bonding and the meaning of motherhood.

Infant monkeys were raised alone in cages with two wire dolls, one covered with soft terrycloth and one left bare. Half the monkeys received milk from a breast-level rubber nipple in the wire doll, and half from a similarly placed nipple in the cloth doll. All the infants gained weight and grew normally. All of them spent time cuddling the cloth doll.

Harlow called both of the dolls "surrogate mothers." Of course, calling a wire contraption a "mother" does not make it a mother. An equally plausible alternative would be to call the milk-producing doll "mother," and the non–milk-producing doll "father." That way we could say that each monkey had two surrogate parents, a father and a mother, rather than two surrogate mothers. It is certainly no more arbitrary than Harlow's terminology.

Harlow found that "those that secured their nourishment from the wire mother showed no tendency to spend more time on her than feeding required, contradicting the idea that affection is a response learned in association with the reduction of hunger or thirst." The cloth dolls were a source of reassurance when the infants were frightened, while the wire ones gave no comfort, no matter which one supplied the milk. Using the terminology I suggested, we could say that monkey infants preferred a cloth to a wire parent, regardless of the "sex" of the parent. Or, to put it another way, half of the monkeys preferred their mothers, and half, their fathers.

The question Harlow was asking was "What is it about mothers that infants love?" It is a loaded question. What his experiments demonstrate is that "contact comfort" is more important than breasts or nursing in the development of infant attachment. Harlow did not question the basic assumption that it is *only* mothers that infants will love. A film made of Harlow's experiments, *Motherlove*, implies that not only is the cloth-covered wire a mother, but also that it "loves." Harlow and Charles Collingwood state that some "real" mothers compare unfavorably with the ever available, ever passive cloth doll. Harlow goes so far as to state that the infant monkeys love the "mother" because they *know* she will protect them! (The cloth and wire dolls are totally incapable of motion.)

What Harlow's experiments do show, and *all* that they show, is that first, infant monkeys do not necessarily love the producer of their milk; and second, infant monkeys do form attachments based on contact comfort.

If love in infant humans is like love in infant monkeys, then being a biological mother, including breast feeding, does not have to mean being the sole caretaker, the central person in a baby's life. This contradicts virtually all of the literature on breast feeding and mothering, which has linked breast feeding to full-time, all-encompassing mothering, in which the mother is fully engrossed in the child and the child in the mother; the father encompasses them both with his love and protection. La Leche League, in a 1972 "information sheet," told us that we had to accept "the fact that being a wife and mother is a full-time job in itself and a first class career, worthy of our very best efforts. . . . As for personal fulfillment and retaining identity, what better way is there than to perpetuate ourselves in our children, and our children's children?" Breast feeding, we were informed, is a major part of this because it prevents the mother from ever ignoring her children, even when she is "right in the middle of something BIG, like waxing the kitchen floor or baking a fancy cake." The mother was reassured that although "it's hard to buck the crowd and give up the bowling league or the bridge club because we have a baby at home who needs us more than they do," La Leche League is there to help.

For those whose idea of something BIG has nothing to do with waxing the kitchen floor or baking cakes, whose demands on their time are perceived as being somewhat more pressing than bowling or bridge, this kind of "encouragement" to nurse is probably enough to talk them out of it forever.

If there is such a thing as a "maternal instinct," it most assuredly has nothing to do with waxing floors or baking cakes. It is interesting to reflect that at just that time when breast feeding was at the lowest rate it ever has registered in any group in history, when so few women were nursing their babies that it was necessary for those who were doing so to form a "club" to encourage and help each other, at that same time our society was at the height of the "feminine mystique."[10] Women stayed home and made mothering a "full-time job" and "first-class career," taking care of children, waxing floors, baking cakes, and sterilizing formula. The few women who did try to breast-feed were so overpowered by "doctor's rules" that success at breast feeding was a major accomplishment.

Some women may find it helpful to remember that breast feeding is a natural behavior shared by all mammals. It can be comforting to lie in bed and nurse a baby and feel like a mama cat with her kittens. And sometimes it can be nice to have sex like a cat—mindless, thoughtless, wordless, and careless. But people are not cats. We don't let our babies wander off when they're weaned and forget about them, and we don't choose a mate because we are in heat. We have values, beliefs, language, thoughts. We have a culture. Breast feeding, like birth, sex, death, and the other biological facts of life, takes its meaning from the culture that defines it. In our culture we have made both too much and too little of breast feeding. We have ignored its physiological importance for both mother and baby, thinking that technology could do the same thing better, faster, and more efficiently. At the same time we have taken for granted and subsequently over-emphasized its importance in adult-newborn bonding, and the symbolic implications of breasts for child care. The irony is that we have allowed ourselves to be limited to the idea of family centered on mothers as the "natural" caretakers of infants and young children, while allowing anything natural in the relationship to be overrun by hospital regulations, pediatricians' orders, and the baby-food-formula industry.

PART III

Beyond Obstetrics:
Midwives in Transition

9

Midwives at Work

What is it like to work as a nurse-midwife doing home or birth-center births? The demands on these women's time, especially if they are doing home births, are extraordinary. They're "on call" constantly, having to be there when their clients need them. And, whether they work at home or in a birth center, they know that to many people—including some of their colleagues and many of those in charge of their licensing—what they are doing is marginal and questionable. Their clients are dependent on nurse-midwives, so they have to be there for them; but in another sense, they need the clients to support them and what they are doing, to give them the reasons to go on. They take on as much responsibility for human life as any professional worker in this society ever does, and all the while believe that responsibility belongs with the birthing woman, that it is her right to take over responsibility for her body, her baby, and her birth. It is not an easy life, and at the end of each interview I felt both guilty and relieved to go home to my typewriter, climb back into the "ivory tower," and have the freedom to think about the issues and the decisions that the midwives were faced with, without having to make those decisions each day myself.

Two Midwives[1]

While there is no more a "typical" midwife than there is a typical anyone else, Karen is representative of many nurse-midwives who do home births. She went into nursing as a safe and classic career for a woman, but found herself increasingly dissatisfied with the lack of autonomy, the restrictions always imposed on her. She tried working as a "well-baby" nurse in a public-health clinic but in her late twenties decided on midwifery as the best way to meet her needs to control her own work. She went through a master's-degree program at a fine university, where all of her training was in hospitals on clinic patients. Her subsequent jobs were hospital based as well. But she did help out a classmate who wanted a home birth, and later chose home birth for herself. After her son's birth she was not ready to resume a full-time hospital job and agreed to do some home births, first for a few friends and then branching out as other people heard about her and called on her. Having her own baby and a husband in law school, she found that three or four births a month were all she could handle.

One of the mothers Karen attended informally apprenticed herself to Karen, going out on births with her and helping out. Having an assistant, just a calm pair of hands, was something Karen found reassuring. On the other hand, Karen never was able to arrange suitable, dependable backup with an obstetrician in the area—a problem shared by most of her colleagues. One doctor agreed to be a backup, only to find that when the two wanted to bring a newborn into the hospital for observation and testing for jaundice, the hospital refused to accept the baby. Another doctor also agreed to back up, but when Karen brought a client in because she needed medication to stimulate an overly long labor, the doctor did what Karen and the mother felt was a totally unnecessary cesarean section. Clients tried to find their own backup doctor, someone near where they lived, who would agree to meet them at the hospital if medical services were needed. For second births, some women were able to talk the obstetrician they had used for the first birth into providing backup. Others went through prenatal care with a doctor and never told him that they had no intention of going into the hospital unless a problem arose. That of course meant paying for duplicate services, and dissembling all through the pregnancy. And in the few cases—perhaps one in ten births—where the hospital trip was needed, the local hospital was not always receptive and did not always provide the best of care. The lack of good backup services was one of the reasons Karen eventually left the area, moving to a state that would allow her hospital-admitting privileges, so that she could bring a client into the hospital and know that medical services would be there.

Violet is a nurse-midwife who represents a different career pattern. She is in her mid forties, with teenage children. She was trained in the West Indies, where nursing training includes home-based midwifery. She and her husband emigrated to the United States, where she worked as a nurse, and he worked as a truck driver. Her children were born here, in standard obstetrical fashion, before midwifery services were available in the U.S. . Violet did not enjoy the surgical-nursing jobs she had, and jumped at the chance to take a three-month "refresher" course, designed to certify foreign-trained midwives as American certified nurse-midwives. She then worked in obstetric clinics at large inner-city hospitals for many years, but always remembered how much nicer home births had been in her own country. When the opportunity arose, she joined the birth-center staff, and felt more at home there than she ever had in hospitals. Violet also felt that she could never handle the "hassles" someone in Karen's position has to put up with: the lack of backup, the constant on-call, the low and irregular income. Work life at the birth center is more routinized than home-birth practices can be.

The Organization of Work

The birth-center nurse-midwives I interviewed are salaried employees of the association that owns and operates the birth center. They work in shifts, which often means long and irregular hours but also means that they have scheduled time off. Clients usually have the opportunity to meet all of the nurse-midwives in the course of their prenatal care and are attended by whoever is on duty at the center when they go into labor. There are two nurse-midwives in-house at all times, one actively responsible for phoned questions as well as for incoming laboring women, and the other on-call as needed. In addition, there are assistants to the nurse-midwives. Physicians are not in-house, but backup arrangements are made with a nearby hospital to accept birth-center transfers. The birth-center nurse-midwives, like the home-birth nurse-midwives, do not have hospital privileges. Pediatricians come to the birth center to check the babies at their mothers' sides in the less than twelve hours after birth before the family goes home.

The midwives working at the birth center are not all of a

mind, not in total agreement about the way birth should be "managed." They expressed their differences as being more "physically oriented" in contrast to being more "emotion- ally" or "psychologically" oriented. I would phrase it in terms of the two models: some are closer to the medical, and some, to the midwifery model. There was a high degree of consen- sus as to which midwives were oriented in which ways. The midwives all saw themselves essentially as the others saw them, and indeed as I would order them along a medical-to- midwifery continuum.

The more medically oriented nurse-midwives saw the more midwifery-oriented nurse-midwives as being less cau- tious and not as "safe." (That was usually in reference to a timetable issue, and will be discussed later.) But it worked both ways: the more midwifery-oriented nurse-midwives also saw the more medically oriented as less cautious and not as safe. For example, one strongly midwifery-oriented nurse- midwife expressed concern over certain other birth-center midwives' feeling "too secure" because of the institution:

> Not using drugs, not any of that, they're very safe that way, but on the emotional and psychological aspects, making sure the parents are truly prepared, responsible—it should be treated like a home birth.

The birth center is near a hospital, but so too are most urban homes. Most of the midwives in the center felt that birth at the center was in no way "safer" than a home birth and offered no "medical" advantages. (It also carried a greater risk of infection than home births.) The most strongly medically oriented midwife disagreed. She said that the birth center was "definitely safer" than home. When I asked what made it safer, she referred to the infant-resuscitation equip- ment. Because I know that the equipment to which she referred is highly portable, and because I have seen such equipment at home births, I asked her to be more specific. She thought, and came up with the "baby warmer" as the thing that makes the birth center safer than home for births. The baby warmer is not a life-saving piece of equipment. Oven-warmed blankets are used at home if extra warming (beyond human contact) is needed or wanted. It seems that it is the social power of an institution, a place set aside for births, which makes people (clients as well as midwives) feel "safe."

It is not only the possible sense of physical safety at births that protects the birth-center nurse-midwives but also their own integration into a supportive community. Whatever their differences, they stand together as a well-known pilot project backed by an esteemed institution. Because of shifting work schedules, they get to see each other at work. They may be somewhat critical of each other's approaches, but they did seem to feel a sense of solidarity and interdependence. To a question about other birth-center midwives and home-birth practitioners, a birth-center midwife answered:

> I know most of the people because we all know each other. That's how we got where we are today, by keeping a close network and having good communications.

She did not, in fact, know most of the home-birth practitioners, but she *felt* integrated into a community. A home-birth nurse-midwife, in contrast, who in fact *did* know almost all of the other nurse-midwives, said:

> The kind of support for myself as a midwife is so weak, there's no one else I can talk to about these issues. We're not organized into a group, nobody's organized in terms of a philosophy. Just support each other in terms of making the delivery if someone's sick.

In one way or another, each home-birth midwife has expressed to me this feeling of lack of solidarity and lack of community. One expressed her need for support:

> Working by myself is a real frightening experience in that because you can't possibly be doing ten to fifteen home births in a month—it's absolutely impossible for one person to do—but in order to maintain the kind of stimulation and the kind of thing so that you're learning from your experience as well, you need to be working with another couple of people, so that by talking with them and explaining what's happening to you, happened to them, those kinds of descriptive things, you learn from one another, and it isn't such a vacuum.

That nurse-midwife was doing home births only part-time, and working in a teaching hospital full-time. Another nurse-midwife who was working full-time at home births after years of hospital experience said:

> The transition from hospital to home-birth midwifery is anxiety provoking for the midwife. *You're by yourself.* You mature radically as a woman and as a professional.

On several occasions the home-birth nurse-midwives called meetings to "try and set up a support network for home births." The first meetings had more clients than practitioners. Subsequent meetings were called for nurse-midwives only (and for me, as resident sociologist). Each meeting generated excitement and interest, and then would not be repeated for quite a while. No ongoing group was ever formed. During the time I was doing the interviews, each nurse-midwife was extremely interested in what others were doing, something I could ethically divulge in only the most general terms. But they did not just call each other up to ask directly.

Why should there be this frustrated desire for community and yet no organized or sustained effort to form such a community? It is most definitely not a question of economic competition: no midwife lacked for clients, and many felt overburdened. Feeling overburdened may itself be part of the answer. These nurse-midwives are unusually busy people. Some have children, some have full-time hospital jobs, and some have both, in addition to their home-birth practices. It may be that their time commitments are a major factor in their failure to develop a more active group life. There is also a factor that Dorothy and Richard Wertz suggested led to the overthrow of midwifery in America in the nineteenth century, namely that midwives felt their allegiance to the local community of women which they serve[2] as their clients, rather than to each other. The focus is very definitely on each client and each birth. "A family has only so many births, and they should be tops, you know, they should just be tremendous experiences." Home-birth midwives invest a great deal of emotional energy in their clients, which may bring about some kinds of work satisfaction, but does in the long run leave them alone, as most clients move on to other parts of their lives: "You've got to be ready to give of yourself and not expect too much back."

Most of the home-birth nurse-midwives saw their work more as a series of favors than as a business or profession. They charged fees of only $300 to $500 or even less—fees so low that they could not have supported themselves on the home births alone—and they did not always collect those fees. Only one home-birth nurse-midwife, Ann, had a clear sense of her practice as a business and a profession. Ann is the one who said that the transition from hospital to home-birth midwifery matured one as a woman and as a professional. She had moved from standard nurse-midwifery training and hospital jobs to doing home births full-time, and had supported herself on a salary comparable to or better than that available in hospital nurse-midwifery for several years. She had organized a home-birth practice that included the use of a telephone receptionist, a nutritionist, regularly scheduled orientation meetings for new clients, and five other nurse-midwives. There was a fixed flat fee for services, which included prenatal care, a nutritionist's evaluation, the birth, and postpartum visits. The fee was comparable to that of the birth center (approximately $500 at the time). Ann said that the client must provide her own "support people"—people to provide the intense emotional support necessary for labor. She would provide midwifery expertise and technical competence.

Some other midwives expressed their ambivalence about such "cut and dried" arrangements. For example:

Ann becomes a kind of business. Horrible dichotomy. You don't want to think of birth and that whole scene as a business. She's very businesslike and it's very smart and she's doing very well . . . I think it could be masked in this whole thing of, hmm, she's really committed and that proves her commitment almost, whereas I'm just sure that everybody should have a home birth that wants one and that sort of thing, but I'm not really willing to figure out an efficient way of providing that to people and being committed to that belief.

Most of the other home-birth nurse-midwives, including those that were part of Ann's group, said that they would not take on just any client in a purely business arrangement:

—"Both husband and wife have to feel comfortable with the midwife." (Q: Always couples?) "The people involved. Try to make it clear in early contacts that their emotional state is important and that it is a criterion for risking out. Sometimes I turn people away because I don't like them, and that is not negotiable. I won't go to someone's house if I can't form a relationship with them."

—"And for myself it always comes back to am I willing, committed to a home birth with these people?—feeling them out as far as personalities, and whether or not we are going to jibe . . . I don't think you can be so businesslike that you can't recognize that as a component in a satisfactory outcome."

—"We don't make any commitment until we've all met and we've really talked and spent some hours together, and if we all feel it's gonna feel good together, work out, then we go ahead."

As Ann pointed out to me, that left her with everybody else's rejects, something of which the other midwives were aware. As one laughingly said about difficult-to-get-along-with clients: "Oh, well, I can always send them to Ann."

Birth-center nurse-midwives did not have to have the same sense of personal commitment to each client, and have no individual contracts with clients. Home-birth midwifery involves a real commitment from the midwife for at least two reasons. One is the problem of work autonomy, which I discussed in the chapter on nurse-midwifery. If a birth does not work out and the woman is hospitalized, the nurse-midwife has drawn attention to herself. For many of the nurse-midwives, that was threatening. The other aspect is that home-birth midwifery is extraordinarily demanding. Each nurse-midwife, even those in the joint practice, had her own individual clients. Two of the nurse-midwives had "beepers," but all the others had to stay near their phones whenever a woman was near term. As one nurse-midwife pointed out, if she just went shopping for a couple of hours, she had to worry that a client might need her and not be able to find her. And once she is there, a birth can take quite a long time and of course is never scheduled. Those employed in hospitals miss work or have to arrive at work after an all-day or all-night birth. Several nurse-midwives talked about organizing a practice into "shifts" where a nurse-midwife would be on call only part of the time, but were ambivalent about that too. As one of them said of a one-to-one relationship, where each midwife has her own clients:

> Seems where you'd get the most satisfaction and your client would get the most satisfaction, but then again that's the same kind of demand—when they're ready to deliver, you're it.

The birth-center nurse-midwives do not have to have that kind of personal responsibility. One said, "If I had to be responsible seven days a week, twenty-four hours a day, I'd lose interest; I would get harassed."

It is the tie to the individual clients that gives home-birth nurse-midwives their work satisfaction, but it is very much a tie that binds.

What makes the stresses and strains of the life of a midwife worthwhile for her are the births themselves. Nurse-midwives doing home and birth-center births feel that they are doing more than providing a service, an alternative to the hospital. They see themselves as helping women get what they want out of a basic life experience. All of the nurse-midwives I interviewed, those working in birth centers and those doing home births, felt that there was a genuine difference in the quality of the experience for women birthing outside of the hospital, and that this *mattered*. It is not just a question of one better day, the hours of labor themselves, but of how women feel about themselves as people able to control their lives, and how they can feel about themselves as mothers.

So where is the magic? What is the difference between the kind of conscious, minimally medicated, prepared childbirth that I described in Chapter 6, and the home birth? What goes on at a home birth?

Home Birth

Mothers are usually in telephone contact with their midwife in the days before birth. For modern urban midwives (compared to village or tribal midwives) the telephone is of crucial importance. Phones are very common in our society, but one of the nurse-midwives said that she had once attended a woman without a phone, and would never agree to do it again. Labor does not usually have a clear-cut beginning. The women are therefore unsure about whether their labor has begun, and will call the midwife to describe sensations and ask for confirmation, especially for first births. The midwives I interviewed did not want to go to the woman's home, or have her arrive at the birth center, at the first sign of labor. Going too early makes the labor seem too long. They preferred to wait until labor was "well established," "just about 4cms.," "starting active labor." They wanted to *know* as soon as the mother felt "something was going on," and then keep in close telephone contact. Several nurse-midwives mentioned that talking on the phone to the mother through several contractions gave them a lot of information about "where she is in her labor."

When the midwife arrives she introduces herself to anyone she does not know—prospective grandparents, friends of the parents, and such—though some of these people may have come to prenatal visits. Some of the nurse-midwives said they liked to be met at the door by the laboring woman. One said, "No woman lies down in labor—no one's sick so they don't go to bed." But labor and birth usually do take place in the woman's bedroom, and many women are in bed for much of labor. They are not in any way "attached" to the bed, however, as with a hospital labor bed, where getting out of bed would involve moving IV poles and more and more frequently unhooking the fetal monitor. Women get up regularly to go to the bathroom. An enema is uncommon in a home birth, but diarrhea is a frequent part of early labor for undrugged women who have free access to a bathroom. Women are encouraged to empty their bladders frequently. They may be eating lightly, especially during the long early labor, and drink water, teas, and juices throughout labor. Women in hospitals are usually allowed no food or drink once admitted to the labor room, in anticipation of the use of anesthesia, even for planned "natural" births. This necessitates the use of intravenous fluids. One of the birth-center nurse-midwives said that at an education meeting for current nurse-midwifery students, somebody asked about nausea and vomiting in labor, a fairly common hospital occurrence, which she and others have attributed to the lack of protein and an empty stomach. "It's amazing, working here—you don't realize and then it draws you up short when someone asks a question and you compare between the hospital and here and you think, 'Ooh, yeah, that's right.'"

All of the nurse-midwives perceived laboring women as requiring a great deal of emotional support, particularly as labor progresses. The role of "support person" is most usually taken on by the mother's mate, but it may be her sister, her own mother, or a friend. I have seen birth slides of a woman's brother supporting her in labor and have heard midwives talk about the mother's father, the husband's mother, or some other family member stepping in for all or part of the labor as the "support person." The role of support person usually involves close physical contact, holding, stroking, petting, doing abdominal effleurage (light fingertip massage), washing the woman, giving her sips of juice, applying back pressure, and so on and on through the long hours of labor. The support person may "breathe through" contractions with the laboring woman, doing the breathing patterns of prepared childbirth either in the mother's ear or while making eye contact, so that she joins the support person's breathing with her own and does not lose the rhythm. The difference between hospital and home for the support person seems to be largely a matter of intimacy and intensity. In a labor room the mother is confined to bed, and the father kept out of bed; equipment may stand between them psychologically if not physically (fathers fear dislodging the monitor or IV), and strangers have access to the room. These things interfere with intense and intimate involvement. In a home birth the supportive relationship may evolve into a kind of lovemaking.

Nurse-midwives will do vaginal exams during labor, but not usually on a clocked schedule. They will, on a more regular basis, listen for fetal heart tones. According to these nurse-midwives, the ideal role of the midwife in labor is to keep a check on the physical changes, and not to interfere with the interpersonal relations.

—"Sometimes it means the nurse-midwife bowing out of the scene for a little bit and leaving the couple to themselves because there are times when I as a stranger interfere with their interaction."

A number of nurse-midwives expressed their role in labor as "supporting the support person," providing reassurance to the woman and her support people that labor is progressing normally, and occasionally offering advice on how to give support. People are often not fully prepared for just how painful labor can be, or how needful the laboring woman may become. The midwife provides reassurance that her condition, however distressing, is normal, and suggests positive ways of coping:

—"I try to get the main support person involved in doing the birth because it's really their birth and not mine, and I try to show him constructive ways he can do it. Sometimes husbands are hesitant and they hang back a bit and I say, 'Gosh, wouldn't you like to just give her a back rub?' —something practical he can do with his hands, or, you know, so he can participate, not be so helpless."

—"If she has a support person, to actually encourage that person to do a good bit of support, almost to support the support person in that sense, and to give them a feeling that I am observing the labor and they can concentrate on working with the contractions."

—"There are often a number of little jobs to break up depending on who's there, and that kind of keeps the energy controlled."

When working in the hospital with women who have no support person with them the role of the nurse-midwife is to provide emotional support, and it is often said to be one of the most gratifying aspects of midwifery. As a midwife working with pregnant teenagers told me: "I just feel so great if I can take some kid and get her through her labor so she knows *she* did it." In the home births and birth-center births, the nurse-midwives take on that role only as a last resort. One midwife described sitting and "gritting my teeth" in the next room as she heard the woman call her husband repeatedly, and he at first did not answer and then kept putting her off with "I'll be in soon." "I finally had to go in and support her myself," she said. Another nurse-midwife described a similar situation:

> He was just busy running all around, getting water, getting the thermometer, getting the this, the that, turning the lights down, so I had to go in and give emotional support to the mother.

These are the only circumstances in which I have heard nurse-midwives speak disparagingly of their clients ("the jerk"). Any other behavior seemed acceptable. They spoke of stoic, tearful, screaming, calm responses of laboring women almost as if these were "stylistic" differences and without value. Similarly, support people might range from calm to frantic, but as long as they were responsive to the laboring woman, the midwives spoke acceptingly of their behavior.

There are of course no changes in room (labor room to delivery room) for the second stage of labor in either birth center or home births, but there is usually a marked change in the ambience. The end of active labor (transition), as the woman reaches full dilatation, is usually quite painful for the mother and difficult for the support person. The pushing stage is usually exciting, climactic. The mother may be semisitting at the edge of or on a bed, braced by her support person. Less commonly, she may be squatting, lying on her side, on a chair, or on her hands and knees, depending on her comfort and the suggestions of the midwife. The mother is in no way physically restrained. This is the point where the midwife's hand skills are in evidence, as she helps the mother ease the baby out without tearing. If it does appear that the mother is going to tear (frequently as a result of a previous episiotomy scar) the nurse-midwife will do an episiotomy.

During the birth one notices the juxtaposition of lay mid-wifery with hospital-based obstetrics. Some nurse-midwives use olive-oil massages; some, herbal teas. At a birth I observed there were two pots on a bedside table. One held sterilized cord clamps, surgical scissors, and other impressive-looking instruments. The other held ginger-root tea for hot compresses. The midwife said, "It's supposed to help the skin stretch. It smells good, anyway."

The mother's need for emotional support at the time of the birth is seen as especially intense, and the father's plans to catch the baby frequently do not work out:

—"The fathers usually stay up near the mother's head. Usually by the time the head is crowning, I have the woman delivering in bed—I will deliver in another position, but this does seem fairly comfortable for them and I know I have good head control. I've given them the option that if the father wants to deliver the baby that'll be fine, that maybe he'd let me deliver the head and he could deliver the body because I have the greatest luck getting the head out without a tear, or I can put his hands over mine. Most women at that time don't want him to leave her head, and that feels nice."

—"There's such a long distance between the face and the perineum . . . It's such a long way for the father to be away from her. You really need someone right at your ear."

—"Towards the end of the birth process, that's the time when she wants that man closest to her . . . when that baby's coming out she wants to hold him, and I haven't yet had a husband who's been allowed to leave the head and get down to the tail to catch the baby, because she just physically hangs on to him. She gets her emotional support that way."

Several midwives mentioned encouraging the mother to reach down and feel the baby's head emerging. Some said it helped the woman to push more effectively.

> I can remember one mother, the head was up a little, so I told her put your finger in, and she had the baby shortly thereafter. How many times we held people up from delivering with our being overly prudish—and what germs does the mother have that the baby isn't going to be exposed to anyway?

Three nurse-midwives specifically referred to Nancy Mills's speech at the first NAPSAC meeting. Mills is a lay midwife from California who had attended over 600 births. She said:

> The thing that I am doing now at home birth is having ladies sit up and initially touch the baby's head when it is crowning. It has taken a long time for me to get to a place where I feel comfortable doing it myself. It's amazing the resistance I get at the elbow when I try to pull a woman's arm down and get her to touch the head of that baby. But you ought to see her face when she does it . . . One woman who had her hand on that head as it emerged said to me the next day, 'You know, I felt one with myself. I felt I was giving birth to myself and my baby . . .' I think that the level of satisfaction for women to participate in their births is just amazing.[3]

After the baby emerges, into either the mother's hands or the midwife's, the mother draws the baby up to her.

> There are at least thirty seconds of both mother and baby looking at each other and going, "Who are you?" Then

everybody usually starts climbing all over the baby and we usually back off at that point, just back off a bit and keep an eye on the placenta, what's going on.

The ability to "back off" is raised almost to an art by some midwives. One said that she never lets herself call out, "It's a boy," or "It's a girl," because "all her life a woman will remember the sound of those words, and she should hear them in a voice she loves."

After a few minutes the midwife will either cut the cord herself, or may help the father or, less commonly, the mother or someone else to do so. The baby will be wrapped in warm blankets and given back to the mother to put to the breast. Many parents had plans for the "Leboyer birth," the technique developed by the French obstetrician to help babies recover from the supposedly terrible experience of birth. The baby is born without the bright operating-room lights, into a quiet room, and then given a warm bath, a ritualistic rebirthing. Home births, of course, do not have operating-room lights. The bath may or may not take place as planned:

> We've had plans for many more Leboyer baths than ever have taken place because the couple sees that the baby is very happy, you know, content, and much more interested in breast feeding than in bathing, and just forego that.

Suckling usually stimulates uterine contractions, and the mother will hand the baby to someone else while she expels the placenta. After checking the placenta and showing it to the mother if she is interested in seeing it, as most women are, the midwife will check the mother for tears and for excessive bleeding. An episiotomy or tear will be repaired under local anesthetic. If all is well, the mother might get up and bathe or shower, while other people dress the baby and weigh it. Some midwives make a point of leaving the parents and the baby together by themselves very soon after birth.

Where there are older children in the family, they may be there for all or part of the labor, may be there for the birth alone, or may not be brought in until after the birth, as the mother wishes. One midwife expressed her concern about the mother's being inhibited by her child's presence: "She has to be able to let go, be herself; this is a time for *her.*" Several mentioned the importance of having a special person there for the children, to reassure and interpret events for them.

Most nurse-midwives said they stay for three to six hours after the birth, depending on the needs of the family and the condition of the mother and baby. Many families celebrate the birth with the traditional glass of champagne; others, with organic apple juice. People are frequently ready for a meal, and a party atmosphere may prevail. At other births, the family may just want to sleep.

The schedule of postpartum visits varied among midwives, but all described some contact within the first few days, again referring to the importance of the telephone, a visit about a week later, and then again six to eight weeks later.

10

Radicalization:
Going through Changes

A British-trained midwife, after working in an American hospital, reflected on the transition from home to hospital births:

> I knew I was being turned about . . . she was getting dehydrated and instead of getting her something to drink, I put up an IV, thinking this was good management, you know, thinking that this was a great thing. And the next thing I take her blood pressure and it's up, really sky-high . . . So she now has two IV solutions . . . Then of course the contractions stopped, right, and we put up an IV on the other hand. So we now have the monitor attached to the lady, one arm has two IV bottles and the other has one. The woman was in agony, you know, when I could've just given her apple juice, walked her around, and talked to her. And that was the first time I really realized what was happening.

An American-trained midwife talked about the transition from hospital to home births:

> Over there the maternity floor is on the eighth floor, and I heard this poor woman from where she had come in in the sub-sub-basement admitting unit, all the way up on the elevator, in such distress, and my thought was, my word, these Spanish people really have a frightful concept of labor. She was noisy and out of control, it was just nightmarish, and I felt, "I hope I don't have to take care of too many Puerto Rican women in my career." Well, the first home birth I went out on was a Puerto Rican family, and I almost dropped my teeth, because there was the mother, when we arrived, very close to pushing, and she was lying peacefully propped up on her bed with her cousin speaking soft Spanish in her ear. She was eating a banana between contractions. I was sort of an observer, and the senior student actually received the baby, and assisted the midwife. But it was like watching a silent movie. I came away and I thought, what are we doing to people in hospitals to put them into this frantic distress I had observed?

Giving birth at home changes things. It reshapes the experience of birthing women and their families. It lessens the monopoly that hospitals have had on childbirth in this country. And it deeply affects the nurse-midwives.

For a nurse-midwife with standard hospital-based training, doing home births is a radicalizing experience. It makes her think hard about her work and its meaning. In this new setting she has to question many of the taken-for-granted assumptions of the medical setting and the medical model. And she finds herself constructing a new model, a new way of explaining what she sees. This is the process of *reconceptualization,* taking something you've confronted maybe a hundred times, and suddenly seeing it anew, seeing it as something else entirely.

There is a simple experiment that shows this process at work.[1] People were asked to identify a set of playing cards flashed on a screen. Most were standard playing cards, but some were made anomalous, for example, a red six of spades, a black four of hearts. The subjects were able to correctly identify "normal" cards. However, they not only failed to identify the anomalous cards correctly, but without any apparent hesitation or puzzlement "normalized" them. For example, a black heart would be identified as a regular red heart, or seen as a spade. When they were allowed to look at the cards longer, however, the subjects began to hesitate. They displayed more and more hesitation until they switched over and began to perceive the cards correctly, identifying a black heart as a black heart, a red spade as a red spade.

For the nurse-midwife making the transition from hospital to home births, many anomalies will present themselves. The nausea that she was taught was part of labor may not be there. She may begin to see that in the hospital this discomfort was caused by not letting the woman eat or drink anything during labor. The amount of time something takes, such as expelling the placenta, may begin to look, in this new setting, very different from the way it did in the hospital delivery room. At first she will try to apply the medical model in the new setting, attempting to utilize the knowledge gained in the hospital to what she is seeing in the home. That won't always work for her. When she is faced with an anomaly in the medical model that she cannot ignore or "normalize," she has a radicalizing experience: she rejects at least part of the medical model. She may share that experience with other nurse-midwives, and many such stories are told. Hearing the resolutions achieved by others supports and furthers her own radicalization. Certain themes develop in these stories; one common theme is that of women controlling their own labors and births by an act of will.

Autonomy and Control

The majority of the nurse-midwives I interviewed had their original training and experience in American hospitals. Training in nurse-midwifery does differ from training in obstetrics, yet both are hospital based. In the hospital it is the obstetrician's version of reality that has legitimacy. There may be, as suggested earlier, some inherent contradictions in the role of the nurse-midwife, but once midwifery moved into the hospital as nurse-midwifery, the medical ideas and beliefs surrounding labor and delivery prevailed. One midwife described the medicalization of midwifery, as she experienced it in her own home births, eighteen and sixteen years earlier. She was attended in the first birth by midwifery colleagues who had been trained doing home births. She described the reactions of her hospital-trained colleagues to her second home birth:

Well, when the second birth was due two years later, the nurse-midwives who were going to be the main call group were those who had graduated from [hospital] and they were the first ones really to come through the large medical-center program. And I displayed my wares again, the same homespun equipment, and they were politely acknowledging what I had, and then one said, "Well, where do you plan to have the oxygen tank?" and "Where will you get intravenous?" and "Suppose you need some anesthesia," and on and on and on, and *it was a completely different concept* . . . there had been such a change in just two years.

The idea that obstetric paraphernalia are absolutely essential indicates a shift in the center of action from the mother, who is, after all, giving birth, to the attendant, who is the manipulator of the equipment. That is, if one *needs* an IV in order to give birth, then the person who attaches the IV is necessary. When the attendants and their equipment are perceived as necessary, then manipulating the equipment appears to bring about the birth.

A male sociologist described to me his wife's hospital birth, for which he was in the delivery room, as "choreographed like a dance." There were so many people, all so busy, and all interacting in familiar, even ritualized ways. All the work they were doing seemed to him very intricate and complicated, yet beautifully coordinated. His wife, he said, lay in the center of it as they worked. Thus, the presence of the staff and equipment shifts the locus of the action—that is, the perception of who is actually *doing the work*—from the mother to the attendants. At the same time, of course, the social status and power inherent in the ability to create a new human being is shifted from the mother to the attendants as well. She just lies there; they work.

Anything that appears to shift control back to the mother becomes a challenge to the medical model. In other words, it becomes an anomaly. The prepared-childbirth movement has come close to doing just this, notably by defining the mother's conscious and active pushing efforts as bringing the baby down the birth canal. But that movement has stopped just at the point of presenting a real challenge, by assigning the directions for these expulsive efforts to the doctor. Women can push, but they need to be told when, to be "given permission."[2] ("You can push now, Marion.") The mother is instructed not to push until she's told it's all right, and conversely, must push when she is told to, whatever her own urges are telling her. Her work and her efforts are thus viewed as *helping the doctor* to deliver the baby. Control of the situation remains with the doctor.

The medical model has accepted one way of seeing the mother as controlling labor, and that is to see her "unconscious" as interfering with her body. It is a way of explaining the complications of labor by referring to "psychosomatic" factors.[3] This approach blames the woman herself for some complications of pregnancy or childbirth, and is frequently based on retrospective studies, those which start with the presence of a problem and look back in time to find its cause.[4] Studies of women with severe nausea during pregnancy thus find that they are more ambivalent toward pregnancy than are women who are not nauseated,[5] and that women who have had three or more consecutive spontaneous abortions show an impairment of the ability to plan and anticipate and greater proneness to guilt feeling than women with no history of spontaneous abortions.[6] It is as if these studies were designed to prove that the attitudes *cause* the physical condition, such as nausea or tendency to miscarry.

Certainly there is reason to believe that mind and body work together. But we have no *prospective* studies, that is, studies *starting* with the woman's attitudes and beliefs, and then showing physical responses such as nausea or spontaneous abortions following from certain attitudes. Such studies might show something very different: that any woman, whatever her attitude, can, for example, become nauseated when pregnant. And, more important, they might show that being nauseated *causes* her to feel ambivalent toward her pregnancy. So, while there is, in the discussions of psychosomatic factors in obstetrics, a connection made between mind and body, it is only to show that the woman's neurosis can impair her bodily functions. If only she would accept her pregnancy, the reasoning goes, she would stop vomiting. Or if only she would come to feel in control of her life, able to plan ahead, she would maintain a pregnancy.

The stories that are told by the nurse-midwives I interviewed and observed are about a different kind of control, a more conscious and positive control. The most common stories are about going into labor, or into active labor. As one of the nurse-midwives herself pointed out, "It's an area you can't document that well—it's more or less anecdotal." She then told me about a woman she had attended who had begun labor on a Sunday, "petered out," then came to the birth center in labor on Tuesday. Once again she began to "slow down to nothing." They talked, and she learned that the couple's son had been sick for four days. The husband called home, and came back to report that the child was okay and eating. Labor picked up and the baby was born in a couple of hours.

In the medical model, labor does not stop and start. A stopped labor is either "false labor," and therefore never really started, or, if it is labor, then slowing down is seen as a symptom of a pathological condition that requires treatment. When the nurse-midwife told me this story of a stopped labor, she said that she had seen such things (labor stopping and starting) but not "understood" the phenomenon until she heard Ina May (the lay-midwife author of *Spiritual Midwifery*)[7] describing how she had dealt with a similar situation. Ina May had asked a woman whose labor was stopping what was worrying her. Once the problem was resolved she "felt free" to go on in her labor. In this instance, the nurse-midwife was very aware of turning from the medical model to the alternative view of women laboring when they are comfortable doing so.

Other nurse-midwives told similar stories, including one who described her own labor as slowing down at four centimeters (early labor) until her two-year-old was brought to her. After seeing that the child was being taken care of and happy, she quickly went on to full dilatation. Some nurse-midwives also pointed out that women who were not really comfortable with a home or birth-center birth, but felt safer in a hospital, would not make progress in labor until they were hospitalized. "One way a woman can cope with not wanting to deliver in a certain place is by not doing it, so that labor progress can stop." And from another nurse-midwife, "There has to be a willingness to let it happen." A birth-center nurse-midwife who had been at the center since its first days said that they used to have more women who "failed to progress," whose labors slowed down to a halt for no apparent reason. But as the midwives themselves got more comfortable working outside of the hospital, the mothers too became more comfortable in the new setting; the rate of halted labors, failure to progress, fell off sharply. Now, she said, when a labor slows down they can usually find a specific reason, such as the baby's being turned in an awkward position, or, very rarely, being too large for the mother's pelvis. When that happens, the mother will transfer to the hospital for medical assistance—a forceps delivery, or a cesarean section if necessary. But the slowing down for no physical reason, the woman's just stopping her labor because she doesn't want to be there, has mostly disappeared. When labor slows to a halt in the hospital, it is either diagnosed by the medical staff as "false labor" or treated, usually with drugs, as a pathologic condition.

It is not only entering labor and its active phase that the nurse-midwives are now seeing as being under the mother's control. One nurse-midwife described a situation in which she came to see the third stage of labor, the expulsion of the placenta, as requiring the mother's attention and effort. The mother had given birth, and after the first brief flurry of excitement, still holding the baby, she began to make phone calls. She called her family, her friends. The nurse-midwife stood by, growing more and more anxious as time passed and the placenta did not. She finally asked the woman to give the baby to someone else and get off the phone, that there was still work to be done. The mother complied, and within a few minutes her contractions started and she expelled the placenta. This too is the kind of situation that will not be seen in the hospital. Not only is the possibility of social distractions much more severely limited, but, more significant, the obstetrician sees his job as removing the baby and the placenta, and he proceeds directly from one to the other. If the woman wants to celebrate, acknowledge, or share her motherhood, that has to wait until the surgical procedure has been completed. It is still standard procedure in most hospitals simply to hold the baby up in front of the mother for a moment before passing it on to the pediatric staff. A woman's initial extrauterine contact with her baby may be delayed for hours, sometimes as much as a day, even for normal births. Other social contact, with the possible exception of her husband, must wait until she has returned from the recovery room. In the hospital, the birth is, first and foremost, a surgical procedure.

One story I was told by several nurse-midwives on different occasions referred always, to the best of my knowledge, to the same birth. A nurse-midwife found herself at a birth without an assistant and running into trouble. The baby needed suctioning and assistance, and the mother was bleeding too heavily. Instead of smiling at the mother and saying it would all be okay, she told the mother, "The baby needs help and you're bleeding too much. I'll take care of the baby. You try and stop bleeding." And the mother did. Very clearly this would never have occurred in a hospital, where the bleeding would have been medically treated.

Thus, a radicalizing experience for one midwife is shared and so moves that midwife and her peers toward an alternative ideology. What's more, it also opens the door for more such experiences, as midwives try to reproduce these phenomena in their own work. It becomes common practice, for example, to try to find out what might be bothering a woman whose labor is slowing down, or to ask for the mother's conscious assistance in expelling the placenta or in controlling her bleeding.

Seeing the mother as having *more* control is part of the story. The other side is that the birth attendant at home may be seen as having *less* control than in the hospital. For example, one of the contributions many nurse-midwives feel that a good midwife can make to a birth is, ideally, getting the baby out "over an intact perineum," or at least with very minimal damage to the mother, and avoiding the surgical incision (episiotomy) that has become routine in American obstetrics. On a delivery table the woman is so positioned that the birth attendant has complete access to her perineum and the forthcoming baby. But since the use of stirrups makes tearing likely,[8] "control" is exercised by the attendant performing an episiotomy. In a home birth, or any non–delivery-table birth, the woman will usually position herself so that the midwife can have "good head control," can support her perineum and use oils, massage, or a variety of techniques to control the damage done to it. One nurse-midwife described to me a home birth in which the mother was squatting and the nurse-midwife felt that she could not control the perineum:

> I don't know how much control we really do have . . . She ripped a little bit, but not any more than the people you have "quote" control over—so, y'know, I don't really think I contributed anything more in any other situation where I think I have control.

Without the institutional supports that encourage the practitioner to think (s)he is in control, control may come to be seen as an illusion; and the soundness of the medical model, so firmly based on the practitioner's *doing* the birth, is shaken for the nurse-midwife. Eventually she may move away from the medical model completely. One nurse-midwife who was fully involved in home birth and had essentially completed the transition expressed her view of control in labor:

> Every woman gives birth to her own baby, and no midwife delivers any baby. Every contraction and every push, the woman controls.

Timetables

Timetables are basic to the medical management of birth. They provide a way of structuring and a justification for controlling what is happening. By setting up ideas of what "on time" means—whether for due dates or length of a particular stage of labor—medicine also sets up the occasions for medical intervention to bring women back on schedule. There are timetables for each stage and phase of the pregnancy-birth process.

Pregnancy

To be pregnant implies something other than simply containing a conceptus, the product of conception. Approximately 30 percent of all conceptions are lost with the menstrual period, so that many women are "pregnant" for a few days without knowing it at all. That is in fact the principle behind one of the forms of birth control, the intrauterine device. The IUD is generally believed not to interfere with the majority of sperm-egg unions, but to prevent the fertilized ovum from implanting in the uterus. If pregnancy meant containing a conceptus, then the answer to the question "Have you ever been pregnant?" might be "Yes, probably thirty or more times," for a woman using an IUD for "contraception."

A woman who is menstruating considers that menstrual period as a sign of her nonpregnant state. Yet if two weeks later she conceives, a physician will date her pregnancy from the first day of her last menstrual period. The very date on which she knows she is not pregnant becomes, retroactively, the first day of pregnancy. It is not usually possible to become "officially" pregnant before the sixth week, the earliest time to get a positive result on the standardly available pregnancy tests. Furthermore, the pregnancy is always approximately two weeks older than the fetus whose existence presumably determines the pregnancy. A full-term pregnancy is forty weeks; a full-term fetus, thirty-eight. This professional definition is not particularly well suited to the needs or perceptions of women themselves. For example, the seven to twelve weeks considered optimal for an early abortion include those first six weeks, two of which are prior to conception.

In pregnancy the medical profession not only validates the woman's claim to pregnancy; it creates its own unique version of that condition. This in turn legitimizes the profession's control over "diagnosis." A woman may "suspect" early pregnancy, but medical evaluation is needed for verification. Even the "at-home" pregnancy tests instruct the woman to have medical verification of the test results.

When women construct pregnancy timetables, they refer to a variety of different "checkpoints": conception, missed period, "showing," "feeling life," or quickening are the starting points that are important, rather than the "LMP," last menstrual period. The medical definition of pregnancy as dating from the last menstrual period is now widely accepted, even within the home-birth movement. Midwives and nurse-midwives may be more trusting of a woman's reports of known conception times, however, and will not automatically disregard the woman's reports, as doctors will.[9] But quickening, once considered by early midwives to be crucial, is largely rejected in favor of more "objective" measures. Quickening is subjective: it is when the woman *feels* life.

Decision Making and Timetables

In the medical model a full-term pregnancy is forty weeks. There is a two-week allowance made on either side for "normal" births. Any baby born earlier than thirty-eight weeks is "premature"; after forty-two weeks, "postmature." The nurse-midwives accept this definition of prematurity. If a woman goes into labor much before the beginning of the thirty-eighth week the nurse-midwives will send her to the hospital, where the premature fetus can get medical services. (This is not to imply that the nurse-midwives are in agreement with the medical *management* of prematurity, only that they share the same set of definitions.) The nurse-midwives I interviewed had few clients go into labor prematurely. Undoubtedly selection plays a part—the "screening" process—as may, too, the better nutrition. Postmaturity, however, has become something of an issue.

The medical treatment for postmaturity is to induce labor, either by rupturing the membranes or by administering hormones to start labor contractions, or both. Both of these practices are viewed as "interventionist" and "risky" by midwives. Physicians appear to be relatively comfortable with inducing labor purely for convenience, even without any "medical" justification.[10] Induction for postmaturity is certainly not something that appears to bother doctors, and is a standard procedure.

Induced labors are very much more difficult for the mother and the baby. Contractions are longer, more frequent, and more intense. The contractions close down the baby's oxygen supply. The mother may require medication to cope with the more difficult labor, thus further compromising the baby. In addition, once the induction is attempted, doctors will go on to delivery shortly thereafter, by cesarean section if necessary. The nurse-midwives' clients do not want to face hospitalization and induction and are therefore motivated to negotiate for time and to find "safe" and "natural" techniques for starting labor. Nipple stimulation causes uterine contractions, and some nurse-midwives suggest that to women who are going past term. Sexual intercourse in a comfortable position or masturbation are also suggested to stimulate labor, as castor oil and enemas may also be.

The problem of postmaturity seems to come up relatively often, leading some lay midwives and home-birth advocates to suggest a reevaluation of the length of pregnancy. They point out that the medical determination of the length of gestation is based on observations of women under medical care. Many of these women have been systematically malnourished by medically ordered weight-gain limitations. Teenage women in particular are known to have a high level of premature births, and are also known to be particularly malnourished in pregnancy because of the needs of their own growing bodies as well as their poor eating habits. The argument offered is that very well nourished women are capable of maintaining a pregnancy longer than are poorly or borderline nourished women. Thus, the phenomenon of so many women going past term can now be viewed as an indication of even better health, instead of as the pathological condition of "postmaturity."

Going Into Labor

The traditional medical model of labor is best represented by "Friedman's curve," a "graphicostatistical analysis" of labor, introduced by Emanuel A. Friedman in seven separate articles between 1954 and 1959 in the major American obstetrical journal.[11] "Graphicostatistical analysis" is a pompous name for a relatively simple idea. Friedman observed labors and computed the average length of time they took. He broke labor into separate "phases," and found the average length of each phase. He did this separately for primiparas (first births) and for multiparas (women with previous births). He computed the averages, and the statistical limits—a measure of the amount of variation. Take the example of height. If we computed heights for women, we would measure many women, get an average, and also be able to say how likely it was for someone to be much taller or much shorter than average. A woman of over six feet is a statistical abnormality. What Friedman did was to make a connection between *statistical* normality and *physiological* normality. He uses the language of statistics, with its specific technical meanings, and jumps to conclusions about physiology:

It is clear that cases where the phase-durations fall outside of these [statistical] limits are probably abnormal in some way. . . . We can see now how, with very little effort, we have been able to define average labor and to describe with proper degrees of certainty the limits of normal.[12]

Once the false and misleading connection is made between statistical abnormality and physiological abnormality, the door is opened for medical treatment. Thus, *statistically abnormal labors are medically treated.* The medical treatments are the same as those for induction of labor: rupture of membranes, the administration of hormones, and cesarean section. Using this logic, we would say that a woman of six feet one inch was not only unusually tall, but that we should treat her medically for her "height condition." For many years medicine held very closely to these "limits of normal" for labor; many doctors are still being trained with the idea that all labors should follow the statistical norm.

How does this work in practice? The first phase of labor Friedman identified was the *latent* phase. This he said began with the onset of regular uterine contractions and lasted to the beginning of the *active* phase, when cervical dilation is most rapid. But how can one know when contractions are "regular"? There is no way to examine a particular contraction and identify it as "regular." It can only be determined retroactively, after contractions have been *regularly* occurring for a while. This brings us to the confusion over "false labor." The only difference between "false labor" and "true labor" is in what happens next: true labor pains produce a demonstrable degree of effacement (thinning of the cervix) and some dilatation of the cervix, whereas the effect of false labor pains on the cervix is minimal.[13] The difference is then one of degree: how *much* effacement and dilatation, and how *quickly.*

The concept of "false labor" serves as a buffer for the medical model of "true labor." Labors that display an unusually long "latent phase" or labors that simply stop can be diagnosed as "false labors." Doctors can continue to believe that labor does not stop and start, even after they have seen it, because they can retroactively diagnose the labor as "false." Friedman pointed out that the latent phase may occasionally be longer than the time limits, yet the active phase be completely normal. He explained these "unusual cases" by saying that part of the latent phase must really have been "false labor." That way his tables of what is statistically normal still work out. These are of course techniques that are used to prevent anomalies from being seen, to "normalize" the events one observes so that they conform to the medical model.

In the midwifery model, strict time limits are abandoned: each labor is held to be unique. Statistical norms may be interesting, but they are not of value for the management of any given labor. When the nurse-midwives have a woman at home or in the birth center, there is a very strong incentive to keep her out of the hospital, both for the client's benefit and the midwife's. Arbitrary time limits are "negotiated" and the midwife looks only for *progress,* some continual change in the direction of birthing. ("I am comfortable as long as I find there's progress." "We look for progress.") Yet a more medically oriented nurse-midwife expressed her ambivalence about the two models: "They don't have to look like a Friedman graph walking around, but I think they should make some kind of reasonable progress." She was unable to define "reasonable" progress, but the emphasis was on "reasonable" to distinguish it from "unreasonable" waiting.

A more midwifery-oriented nurse-midwife expressed her concern in terms of the laboring woman's subjective experience:

There is no absolute limit—it would depend on what part of the labor was the longest and how she was handling that —was she tired? Could she handle that?

Another nurse-midwife described her technique for dealing with long labors:

> Even though she was slow, she kept moving. I have learned to discriminate now, and if it's long I let them do it at home on their own and I try to listen carefully, and when I get there it's towards the end of labor. This girl was going all Saturday and all Sunday, so that's forty-eight hours worth of labor. It wasn't forceful labor, but she was uncomfortable for two days. So if I'd gone and stayed there the first time, I'd have been there a whole long time; then, when you get there you have to do something.

"Doing something" is the cornerstone of medical management. Every labor that takes "too long" and cannot be stimulated by hormones or by breaking the membranes will go on to the next level of medical intervention, the cesarean section. Breaking the membranes is an induction technique that is particularly interesting in this regard. The sac in which the baby and the amniotic fluid are enclosed is easily ruptured once the cervix is partially opened. Sometimes that happens by itself early on in labor, and "the waters breaking" may even be the first sign of labor. But once broken, the membranes are no longer a barrier between the baby and the outside world. Physicians believe that if too many hours pass after the membranes have been ruptured, naturally or artificially, a cesarean section is necessary in order to prevent infection. For women who are exposed to the disease-causing microorganisms in the hospital, especially through repeated vaginal examinations to check for dilatation, infection is a genuine risk. Yet because in the hospital medical personnel always proceed from one intervention to the next, there is no place for feedback: that is, one does not get to see what happens when a woman does stay in the first stage for a long time, without her membranes being ruptured. Instead there are three times as many cesarean sections for "first-stage arrest" among women laboring in the hospital, compared to those who planned a home birth.[14]

While one might think that women laboring in hospitals would have longer labors because of the stress of the hospital situation compared to that of home births, the opposite is true. Hospital labors are shorter than home-birth labors, and, it would appear, are getting shorter all the time.

Length of labor is not a basic, unchanging biological fact, but is subject to social and medical control. The fourteenth edition of *Williams Obstetrics,* in the early 1970s, was still reporting data gathered in 1948 for length of labor. Presumably the authors believed that length of labor is physiologically determined and saw no need to get more current data. But there are big differences between what *Williams* reports as length of labor in 1948, and what Mehl's study of 1,046 matched planned home and hospital births found, and what the 1980 edition of *Williams* reports.[15]

Mehl found that the average length of the first stage of labor, from onset to complete dilatation, for first births was 14.5 hours for home-birth women and 10.4 hours for hospital women. In 1948 the average length of the first stage for first births was 12.5 hours. For multiparas (women having second and later births), Mehl found that first-stage home births take 7.7 hours, and hospital births, 6.6 hours. *Williams* 1948 data reported 7.3 hours. It seems that 1948 hospital births were comparable to present-day home births, and hospital births now are shorter than in 1948, suggesting an increase in "interventionist obstetrics," as home-birth advocates claim. The most current *Williams* reports even shorter labors than Mehl found: 8 hours for first births and only 5 hours for later births. These data are summed up in Table 1.

TABLE 1

Length of First Stage of Labor, in Hours

Birth	Home 1970s	Williams Hospital 1948	Hospital 1970s	Williams Hospital 1980
First	14.5	12.5	10.4	8
Subsequent	7.7/8.5*	7.3**	6.6/5.9*	5**

*2nd births/3rd births
**2nd and all subsequent births

Second Stage: Delivery

The medical literature defines the second stage of labor, the delivery, as the period from complete dilatation of the cervix to the birth of the fetus. According to *Williams,* in 1948 this second stage took an average of 80 minutes for first births, and an average of 30 minutes for all subsequent births. As with the first stage, contemporary home births are comparable to the 1948 hospital births: for first births delivery averaged 94.7 minutes, and for second and third births, 48.7–21.7 minutes. Contemporary medical procedures shorten second stage in the hospital to 63.9 minutes for first births and 19–15.9 minutes for second and third births. And in 1980 *Williams* states that the average is 50 minutes for first births and 20 minutes for subsequent births.

The modern medical management of labor and delivery is geared to hastening the process along. In delivery, this is done most obviously by the use of forceps and fundal pressure (pressing on the top of the uterus) to pull a fetus, rather than waiting for it to be born. Friedman presented averages

TABLE 2

Length of Second Stage of Labor, in minutes

Birth	Home 1970s	Williams Hospital 1948	Hospital 1970s	Williams Hospital 1980
First	94.7	80	63.9	50
Subsequent	48.7/21.7*	30**	19/15.9*	20**

*2nd births/3rd births
**2nd and all subsequent births

for the second stage of 54 minutes for first births and 18 minutes for all subsequent births. His "limits of normal" were two and a half hours for first births, and 48 minutes for subsequent births. Contemporary hospitals usually hold even stricter limits of normal, and allow only two hours for first births and one hour for later births at maximum. Time limits vary somewhat within American hospitals, but one will not get to see a three-hour, and certainly not a six-hour, second stage in most hospital training or practice. "Prolonged" second stage will be medically managed so as to effect immediate delivery. In Mehl's study, low or outlet forceps, used when the scalp is visible, were fifty-four times more common; and mid-forceps (used when the head is engaged but not yet visible), twenty-one times more common for prolonged second stage and/or protracted descent in the hospital than in home births. This does not include the *elective* use of forceps (without "medical indication"), a procedure that was used in none of the home births and 10 percent of the hospital births (4 percent low forceps and 6 percent mid-forceps). Note that any birth which began at home but was hospitalized for any reason, including protracted descent or prolonged second stage, was included in home-birth statistics.

Midwives and their clients are even more highly motivated to avoid hospitalization for prolonged second stage than for prolonged first stage. There is a sense of having come too far—through the most difficult and trying stage of labor—to switch to a hospital. Once the mother is fully dilated she is so close to birth that one hesitates to start moving her, knowing she could end up birthing on the way to the hospital. The mother is usually not in pain during second stage, and very anxious not to be moved.

In a standard hospital birth, the mother is moved to a delivery table at or near the end of cervical dilatation. She is strapped into leg stirrups and heavily draped. The physician is scrubbed and gowned. The anesthetist is at the ready. It is difficult to imagine that scene continuing for three, four, or more hours. The position of the mother alone makes such a thing impossible. In a home birth the mother is usually feeling much better as dilation is completed. Her birth attendant has been with her for hours. There may be less of a sense of urgency and immediacy about getting the birth done. There is also the emphasis on the individual and unique nature of each labor, so that each must be judged and managed on its own terms. "Progress" again becomes the most important criterion:

—"Second stage, I think, could be longer than the conventional two hours some hospitals think, or one hour even, and that would depend on the pattern of the labor."
—"If there was some definite progress, however slow, whether the baby was posterior or anterior, size of baby, if it all was going well, baby's heart beat reflecting no stress whatsoever, I think you could be in second stage well over three hours, maybe four."

That nurse-midwife went on to give an example of a six-hour second stage with no complications.

In the medical model second stage begins with complete cervical dilatation. Cervical dilatation is an "objective" measure, determined by the birth attendant rather than the mother. That means that the birth attendant defines second stage and so controls the time of formal entry into second stage. One of the ways nurse-midwives quickly learn to "buy time" for their clients is in when and how they measure cervical dilatation:

> If she's honestly fully dilated I do count it as second stage. If she has a rim of cervix left I don't, or any cervix at all, the slightest minuscule cervix left, I don't count it, because I don't think it's fair. A lot of what I do is to look good on paper.

"Looking good on paper" is a serious concern. Nurse-midwives expressed their concern about leaving themselves out on a legal limb if they do, for example, allow second stage to go for more than the one- or two-hour hospital limit, and then want to hospitalize the woman. One told of allowing a woman to be in second stage for three hours, and then hospitalizing her for lack of progress. The mother, in her confusion and exhaustion, told the hospital staff she had been in second stage for five hours. The nurse-midwife risks losing her backup at that hospital. Nurse-midwives talked about the problems of writing down on the woman's chart the start of second stage:

> —"If I'm doing it for my own use, I start counting when the woman begins to push and push in a directed manner, really bearing down. I have to lie sometimes. I mean, I'm prepared to lie if we ever have to go to the hospital, because there might be an hour or so between full dilatation

and when she begins pushing and I don't see—as long as the heart tones are fine and there is some progress being made—but like I don't think in this city—you'd be very careful to take them to the hospital after five hours of pushing. They [hospital staff] would go crazy."

—"All my second stages I write down under two hours: by hospital standards two hours is the upper limit of normal but I don't have two-hour second stages, except that one girl that I happened to examine. If I had not examined her, I probably would not have had more than an hour and a half written down because it was only an hour and a half that she was voluntarily pushing herself."

Not looking for what you do not want to find is a technique used by many of the nurse-midwives. They are careful about not examining a woman if she might be fully dilated, for fear of starting up the clock they work under:

I try to hold off on checking if she doesn't have the urge to push, but if she has the urge to push, I have to go in and check.

Some nurse-midwives have taken this a step further, and redefined second stage itself. Rather than saying it starts with full dilatation—the "objective," medical measure—they measure second stage by the subjective measure of the woman's urge to push. Most women begin to feel a definite urge to push and begin bearing down at just about the time of full dilatation. But not all women have this experience. For some, labor contractions cease after full dilatation. These are the "second-stage arrests," which medicine treats by the use of forceps or cesarean section. Some nurse-midwives now think "second-stage arrest" may just be a naturally occurring rest period at the end of labor, instead of a problem requiring medical intervention. Some women, they claim, have a rest period after becoming fully dilated but *before they begin* second stage. In the medical model, once labor starts, it cannot stop and start again and still be "normal." If it stops, that calls for medical intervention. But a nurse-midwife can call the "hour or so between full dilatation and when she starts pushing" as *not* second stage. This is more than just buying time for clients: this is developing an alternative set of definitions, changing the way she sees the birth process.

Midwives who did not know each other, who did not work together, came to this same conclusion:

—"My second-stage measurement is when they show signs of being in second stage. That'd be the pushing or the rectum bulging or stuff like that. . . . I usually have short second stages [laughter]. Y'know, if you let nature do it, there's not a hassle."

—"I would not, and this is really a fine point, encourage a mother to start pushing just because she feels fully dilated to me. I think I tend to wait till the mother gets a natural urge to push. . . . The baby's been in there for nine months."

It may be that buying time is the first concern. In looking for ways to avoid starting the time clock, nurse-midwives first realize that they can simply not examine. It makes sense not to look for what you don't want to find. They then have the experience of "not looking" for an hour, and seeing the mother stir herself out of a rest and begin to have a strong urge to push. The first few times, that hour is an anxiety-provoking experience. Most of the nurse-midwives were able to tell anecdotes of "the first time I let——go for——time," and of their own nervousness. The experience of breaking the timetable norms and having a successful outcome is a radicalizing experience. They then talk not only about techniques for buying time and looking good on paper, but about a whole new version of the event. This opportunity for feedback simply does not exist in the hospital. In its tight control of the situation, medicine prevents anomalies from arising. A woman who has an "arrested" second stage will not be permitted to simply nap, and therefore the diagnosis remains unchallenged. Forceps and/or hormonal stimulants effect the delivery. The resultant birth injuries are perceived as inevitable, as if without the forceps the baby would never have gotten out alive.

Third Stage: Afterbirth

Third stage is the period between the delivery of the baby and the expulsion of the placenta. In hospitals the third stage is expedited as quickly as possible, and takes five minutes or less. A combination of fundal massage and pressure and gentle traction on the cord are used routinely. *Williams Obstetrics* says that if the placenta has not separated within three to five minutes of the birth of the baby, manual removal of the placenta should probably be carried out.[16] In Mehl's data, the average length of third stage for home births was twenty minutes.

For the nurse-midwives the third stage sometimes presented problems. It occasionally happens that the placenta does not simply slip out, even in the somewhat longer time period they may have learned to accept. Their usual techniques—suckling, squatting, walking—may not show immediate results:

—"I don't feel so bad if there's no bleeding. Difficult if it doesn't come, and it's even trickier when there's no hem-

orrhage, because if there's hemorrhage then there's a definite action you can take, but when it's retained and it isn't
coming it's a real question—is it just a bell-shaped curve?
and that kind of thing. . . . In the hospital if it isn't coming
right away you just go in and pull it out."

—"I talked with my grandmother. She's still alive,
she's ninety, she did plenty of deliveries, and she says that
if the placenta doesn't come out you just let the mother
walk around for a day and have her breast-feed and it'll
fall out. And I believe her. Here I would have an hour
because I am concerned about what appears on the
chart."

Like the ninety-year-old grandmother, a very midwifery-
oriented nurse-midwife with a great deal of home-birth experience said:

> If there was no bleeding, and she was doing fine, I think
> several hours, you know, or more, could elapse. No prob-
> lem.

Why the Rush?: Institutional Demands and the Birth Process

There are stated medical reasons for rushing the second and
third stages of labor. A prolonged third stage is believed to
cause excessive bleeding. The second stage is rushed to spare
the baby and the mother, because birth is seen as traumatic
for both. Even in 1980, *Williams* still refers to using the
baby's head as a "battering ram." The clean, controlled,
medically wielded forceps are trusted more than the
mother's body and her efforts. There is another factor as well.
Williams states:

The vast majority of forceps operations performed in this country are elective low-forceps. One reason is that all methods of drug-induced analgesia and especially conduction analgesia and anesthesia often interfere with the woman's voluntary expulsive efforts, in which circumstances low-forceps delivery becomes the most reasonable procedure.[17]

Williams goes on to affirm that this does not constitute an indictment of the procedures for analgesia, but merely requires the proper use of forceps. The lithotomy position also contributes to the need for forceps because the baby must be pushed upwards. This is the phenomenon that home-birth and midwifery advocates refer to as the "snowballing effect" of obstetrical intervention:

> Like a snowball rolling downhill, as one unphysiologic practice is employed, for one reason or another, another frequently becomes necessary to counteract some of the disadvantages, large or small, inherent in the previous procedures.[18]

Besides the medical reasons given, there are also institutional demands for speeding up birth. In Rosengren and DeVault's study of time and space in an obstetric hospital, the authors discussed the importance of timing and tempo in the hospital management of birth.[19] Tempo relates to the number of deliveries taking place in a given period of time. Physiological tempo will be kept at a pace appropriate to functional tempo, the needs of the institution. If there were too many births, the anesthetist slowed them down—an unphysiologic and dangerous but time-efficient practice. An unusually prolonged delivery will also upset the tempo; there is even competition among obstetrical residents to maintain optimal tempos. A resident said:

> Our [the residents'] average length of delivery is about 50 minutes, and the Pros' [the private doctors'] is about 40 minutes.[20]

That presumably includes delivery of baby and placenta, and probably episiotomy repair as well. Rosengren and DeVault said:

> This "correct" tempo becomes a matter of status competition, and a measure of professional adeptness. The use of forceps is also a means by which the tempo is maintained in the delivery room, and they are so often used that the procedure is regarded as normal.[21]

Rosengren and DeVault, with no out-of-hospital births as a basis for comparison, apparently did not even think of the management of the third stage as serving institutional needs. Once the baby is quickly and efficiently removed, the staff will certainly not wait twenty minutes or more for the spontaneous expulsion of the placenta. One could watch innumerable hospital births and never learn that the placenta can emerge spontaneously.

In the home and to a lesser extent in birth-center births the motivations for maintaining institutional tempo are not present. Each birth is a unique event, and birth attendants do not move from one laboring woman to the next. Births do not have to be meshed with each other to form an overriding hospital schedule. Functioning without these demands, nurse-midwives are presented with situations that are anomalous to the medical model, such as labor stopping and starting, second stage not following immediately on first, or a woman taking four hours to push out a baby with no problems. Without obstetrical interventions, things that were defined as "pathologies" may be seen to right themselves, and so the very idea of what is pathological and what is normal is challenged.

Hospitals so routinize the various obstetrical interventions that alternatives are unthinkable. A woman attached to an IV and a fetal monitor cannot very well be told to go out for a walk or to a movie if her contractions are slow and not forceful. A woman strapped to a delivery table cannot take a nap if she does not feel ready to push. She cannot even get up and move around to find a better position in which to push. The entire situation reinforces the medical model. Once a laboring woman is hospitalized, she will have a medically constructed birth.

In a home birth, and possibly to a lesser extent in a birth-center birth, the routine and perceived consensus are taken away. In a woman's home a birth is, whatever else it may be, a unique life event. Each nurse-midwife stressed the individuality of each out-of-hospital birth, that each birth was a part of each mother and family. They described tight-knit extended-kin situations, devoutly religious births, partylike births, intimate and sexual births—an infinite variety. The variety of social contexts seems to overshadow the baby-out-of-vagina sameness. Medical "management" has to occur within the context of the birth as a personal life event. The mother as *patient* must coexist with or take second place to the mother as *mother,* or wife, daughter, sister.

Stripped of institutional supports, the nurse-midwives perceive the functions of timetables. They are a way of managing women in labor, a way of controlling the situation in a medically appropriate manner.

Epilogue

In Sum: A Comparison of the Two Models

Perhaps the most important factor in the way maternity care is provided is the way the fetus-mother relationship is viewed. In the medical model, this relationship is seen as that of a parasite and host. The fetus, in the medical model, is a foreign intruder in the mother's body. The basis for this way of seeing it can be found in the ideology of patriarchal society, in which women are the carriers of men's children. Thus pregnancy is defined in terms of the man, and the desire to be pregnant is seen as the desire to have *his* child. This idea affects the management of infertility and, even more clearly, the management of genetic diseases. The social couple is treated as a biological unit, with the woman bearing the brunt of the treatment. This is best exemplified in the medical management of Rh incompatibilities, where grave risks are taken with both the mother and the baby in order to ensure that the child is the product of the genetic union of those two particular parents.

The implications of this single idea—the fetus as the child of the man in the woman—can be seen throughout the organization of maternity care in medicine. The medical management of pregnancy can best be understood in terms of the separation of mother and fetus, their needs seen as being at odds with each other. Pregnancy, in the medical formulation, is a stress on the mother: the goal of medical management is to keep her as normal as possible throughout the stress. One important implication of this is that prenatal care involves teaching the mother to accept a relationship with her infant in which she must make continual personal sacrifices in the interest of her child's well-being. She is taught that the baby is her adversary, but that as the stronger, she, the mother, must give in and allow the baby's needs to dominate. She is told, for example, that she (the mother) needs medication for her pregnancy-caused (i.e., baby-caused) nausea, but that medication may be dangerous for her baby.

In the developing midwifery model, in contrast, which rises from a woman-centered, rather than a patriarchal, ideology, the fetus and mother are an organic whole, the fetus being part of the mother's body. Nausea in the midwifery model is a sign of a protein deficiency, the effects of which will be felt by the mother-and-fetus unit. The needs of the mother and the fetus are the same: meeting the needs of one meets the needs of the other.

These viewpoints carry over directly to the care of the mother and baby after birth. In the medical model, the needs of the mother and baby are again at odds, with the mother requiring rest and a rapid return to normal (nonpregnant) state, and the baby needing care and nourishment. By contrast, in the midwifery model the mother *needs* her baby just as the baby needs the mother: lactation is the last stage of pregnancy and is important for both of them.

The medical belief in an adversary relationship between the mother and the baby is also found in the medical management of birth itself. The baby must be stopped from ripping its mother apart, and the surgical scissors are considered to be more gentle than the baby's head. At the same time, the mother must be stopped from crushing her baby, and the obstetrical forceps are seen as being more gentle than the mother's vagina.

In the midwifery model, again in contrast to the medical model, childbirth is viewed from the perspective of the woman, as a normal and healthy *activity*. The mother works to bring forth her baby, and whatever helps the mother in her work is believed to help the baby. As in pregnancy and in postpartum care, the needs of the two are interrelated and interdependent.

Just as the role of the mother vis-à-vis her baby is seen in very different ways in the two models, so too is the role of the mother in relation to her birth attendants. The way that this relationship is viewed has to do with the responsibility and autonomy of the birthing woman. In the medical model, the woman is a patient presenting herself for needed medical services. Responsibility and decision making pass to the doctor. In the midwifery model, responsibility remains with the mother. In maternity care, as with other health care, we see the *medicalization* of decision making, including moral and ethical decisions. These decisions become routinized, and their moral/ethical component is no longer seen.

This is best represented by the situations in which the preferred medical management of one, either mother or child, compromises the health of the other. For example, maternal pain-relief medication will invariably compromise the infant to some extent, even if slight. The decision to use pain medication is usually not presented or dealt with as a moral decision, either in the medical literature or in the interaction between doctor and patient, but rather as a medical decision, with the physician determining the best balance of the needs of the two. A similar situation exists when the preferred management of a condition of the fetus damages the mother, such as the use of cesarean section for fetal distress. The cesarean section is major surgery, with all its attendant risks to the mother. A vaginal birth of a distressed infant is of no greater risk to the mother than any other vaginal birth. Here too the decision is seen as a *medical* decision rather than a moral or ethical one, and it is for doctors to decide when and whether to perform a cesarean section for fetal distress. In other situations in which taking a chance with the health of one person might possibly, though not certainly, benefit another person, the question would almost surely be phrased as a moral/ethical problem. The issue is even more complicated when the personhood of the one being benefited is at question.

In the midwifery model, personal responsibility is a major concern, and midwives expect parents to take responsibility for their pregnancies and births. However, the legal limitations placed on the midwives in turn limit the responsibility of the parents. Midwives are at most allowed only to "manage" normal births. If there is any sign of pathology on the part of either the mother or fetus, the case is turned over to a physician.

One consequence of this is that decision making that involves pathology remains with doctors, and it is in this area that the most interesting and the most complex moral decisions are to be made. The second and related consequence is that there is very limited midwifery theory about pathology. We do not know how midwives would treat pathology, nor can we know, as long as they are limited in these ways.

It remains therefore an intriguing but essentially unanswerable question as to how midwives would or would not use the currently available technology. One can only wonder what forceps would look like if midwives had the chance to use and develop them, what techniques would be developed for dealing with any of the assortment of pathologies, real or medically defined, from which they are currently cut off. I have heard some interesting proposals. One nurse-midwife said she had read of a technique for managing cephalo-pelvic disproportion, or CPD (baby too large for the pelvis), which involved breaking the pelvic bone and then allowing the baby to be born vaginally. To my involuntary grimace, she replied, "Is it really any worse than cutting through the skin and muscle of the abdomen, cutting open the uterus, and taking the baby out that way?" Her thinking was that broken bones in young women heal well and quickly and that the worst complication in a later birth would be the bone breaking spontaneously, as compared to the very serious complication of a ruptured uterus, which may occur after a cesarean section in later births. It may be a terrible idea, or it may be, as she thought, less traumatic and less dangerous for the mother and fetus alike. But even with a willing mother, the midwife cannot experiment in her clinical practice. Neither the mother nor the midwife can assume the responsibility (unless the mother wants to do it to herself) for an alternative management. If the midwife diagnoses CPD, she must turn the case over to a physician.

For this reason we do not know how midwives would resolve the management of complications and pathology from a purely technical standpoint: what kinds of instruments and procedures they would develop. Nor do we know how midwives would resolve the moral questions in their work, though what I have been able to show about the midwifery model indicates that decisions would not be made *for* birthing women but *by* birthing women. For example, the medical profession has of late made it standard practice to try and save every baby born, and we have seen in recent years the proliferation of neonatal intensive-care units. Some home-birth advocates claim that an advantage of a home birth is that *parents* can make the decision not to use every ("heroic") measure to save every baby. They cite the cases of parents whose children are saved by the miracles of modern medicine, only to require life-long institutional care. On the other hand, Ina May, in *Spiritual Midwifery*, tells of an anencephalic baby, a baby with absolutely no chance for survival, which was denied food and comfort in the hospital. Ina May and the baby's parents, her clients, brought the baby home so that it could die in peace, to be able to love and care for it during its short life.

Possibly because midwives are not trained with the idea that their work is a struggle against death, it is possible for them to take a more balanced view of the death of a baby. Again the element of faith comes in, and there appears to be a religious or philosophical acceptance of death as a part of life. This is something that I have observed in the home-birth movement and among midwives, and was found in Hazell's study of home-birth parents.[1] What this would mean for maternity care if midwives were in a position of control, we can only guess.

The practical questions, the ethical and moral questions—all are unanswered in the midwifery model, and will remain unanswered as long as midwives are cut off from the experience of working with the full range of maternity care, including pathology.

The Midwife as a Health Worker

Let us consider how the skills of the midwife might best be used. First, it is important to make a distinction between medical services and health services. Medical services are supplied by physicians and others in medical settings using medical models. Besides childbirth, there are other life events for which medical services are used, over which medical services may indeed also hold a virtual monopoly, and in which medical services may be no more appropriate. The situations that come to mind are the conditions of wellness, healthy and normal conditions, which involve changes in the body. Examples are well-baby care, geriatric care, and gynecologic care.

What are the problems with medically managing health? Ironically, one might say that the problems are both over-treatment and undertreatment. Overtreatment is the most obvious problem, the one that has been documented here for the birth cycle. Once an event or process is medicalized, it is open to medical treatment, with a certain amount of iatro-genic (doctor-caused) damage seemingly inevitable. This has been demonstrated in, among other places, the pediatric overuse of both antibiotics and tonsillectomies.

But what of undertreatment? One of the consequences of defining a physiologically normal process as pathologic is that one subsequently loses the ability to make discriminations of real pathology. If the entire process, be it menstrual cycle, birth, infancy, or old age, is viewed as a "complication," then there is no way of envisioning a complication of the process. How could medicine take dysmenorrhea, for example, as a serious problem, however incapacitating it may be for the individual woman, as long as *all* menstruation was viewed as incapacitating? Or how can older people have their illnesses treated seriously when old age itself is viewed as a disease? It is a frequently heard complaint among the elderly that their symptoms are dismissed with a reference to their age, and not taken seriously, even when, after examination, treatment may be found to be perfectly possible.

Perhaps what we are missing is the management of health-care concerns from a nonmedical perspective. Health workers, not physicians and medical workers, could provide assistance and education with health/body needs and questions, from a perspective similar to that of the midwifery model: nontechnological, nonauthoritarian, nonsexist, and nonagist. People would be able to maintain control over their bodies and their lives, using genuine *health* workers for their teaching skills and their experience with health.

How would that translate into practical terms, using maternity care as an example? Since I reject the idea that pregnancy and childbirth are diseaselike states, I would envision midwives as the appropriate profession for maternity services. I would simply, in my pipe dream, do away with obstetrics. The current policy of distinguishing low-risk care from high-risk, assigning midwives to low-risk care and obstetricians to high-risk care, is, in my view, inherently irrational. I can see no logic in there being specialists in the abnormalities of a normal condition. Without continuously dealing with the normal, physicians, like the barber-surgeons of old, would lack perspective in conceptualizing and managing conditions of pathology. And midwifery has much to offer to childbearing women who are not well, healthy, or normal.

How, then, would I have pathology managed? Midwives would have the state mandate to practice their profession. Where there are medical/pathological complications, the midwife would seek the appropriate consultation for those complications, without the midwife's "losing the case." That is the arrangement that has been worked out *within* medicine. What prevents it from being extended outside of medicine is professional dominance, not rationality or expertise. For example, an internist may manage the case of a diabetic patient. The internist will send the patient to an ophthalmologist for glaucoma testing and treatment. The opthalmologist will work with this particular complication and not take over the management of the diabetes. Similarly, if as a result of the diabetes the patient develops a gangrenous leg requiring amputation, the internist will send the patient to a surgeon. The surgeon will remove the leg but not take over the management of the diabetes.

So it could work for the midwife, gerontological worker, well-baby nurse, women's-health worker, and others. If a midwife, for example, had a woman whose baby was lying transverse (sideways rather than head or breech down), in a position in which it could not be born vaginally, she—or rather *they*, midwife and client—could call in a surgeon to do a cesarean section. (There are some obvious advantages to having the person who does the surgery not have total control over the decision to operate.) The midwife would continue to be the professional, working directly with and for the woman and her baby. Her expertise with normal birth and babies would help her in understanding the special problems facing this mother and baby, as well as how much of their condition and experience was common to all mothers and babies, and how much unique to the surgical experience. In the same way, if a woman had diabetes, the midwife would work with an internist specializing in diabetes. The midwife would be the expert in pregnancy, able to help the woman and the physician understand what in her condition was normal to pregnancy, while the internist would be the expert on diabetes and its management. Or if a woman had heart disease, the midwife would work with a cardiologist.

The midwife, or other health worker, would not connect only into the medical system. Medical needs are only a small part of the life needs that people have, related to these transitional periods. She (or he) would make referrals to and work with nutritionists and social-service workers, for instance.

The training that these health workers I envision would have would have to take place, for the most part, away from medical settings. It must be centered around the settings of the clients' lives—their homes, places of work, communities. As the nurse-midwives have shown me, it is working outside of medical settings that makes demedicalization possible.

Making Change:
The Importance of the Birthplace

What I have shown is that the setting in which people practice is both a reflection of and a cause of the beliefs held by practitioners. Birth moved into hospitals in large part because doctors believed it was a surgical event. And, in turn, after one has seen a birth in the setting of the hospital, it is difficult for one to imagine it as anything but a surgical event.

This relationship between setting and the way we see or conceptualize what is happening has several important implications. On one level, the setting controls what can be seen, and thus serves to maintain the model. This was made especially clear in the medical management of birth, in which medicine controls the birthplace in accord with its ideology, and thus reinforces the medical model of birth for practitioners. The institutions of medicine prevent anomalies in the model from showing up. This is done most effectively, as I have discussed earlier, by defining all anomalies as pathological, and treating them. Friedman's curve is the example par excellence of this management of anomalies. (Friedman's curve is the timetable developed for "normal" labor and delivery, discussed in Chapter 10.) All deviations from the established statistical norms in the birth timetable are defined as physiological abnormalities requiring medical treatment. The treatment brings the statistical abnormality back into the normal timetable, so that, for example, a healthy second stage cannot take four hours. It will be terminated by the second hour. The hospital birth represents the epitome of medical management's preventing anomalies from developing, and that is because within the tightly controlled setting there is a coherence of model and institutional control.

On another level, the relation between settings and beliefs has important implications for reform and social change. The medical management of pregnancy and of infant care and the postpartum period are less perfectly hooked to setting: pregnant women and new mothers and babies spend most of their time away from medically controlled settings. That may be why change is more readily seen in the management of pregnancy and infant care than it is in the management of birth. For example, if medicine controlled the settings of pregnancy as it controls the settings of birth, then one would not have seen healthy women bearing healthy babies and gaining thirty or more pounds. Weight gain would have been limited as physicians believed it should be, and those data which showed that medicine was wrong in its evaluation of weight gain would never have been generated. The profession of medicine may be just as wrong in its evaluation of birthing timetables, but those data will not be generated in hospitals run according to those timetables.

The difference in control of settings similarly explains why La Leche League had much the easier time of creating change than did the natural-childbirth movement. League literature continues to acknowledge that breast feeding may be very difficult in the hospital, particularly if rooming-in is not available. However, the period of hospitalization is short, and then the setting is one that is created by the mother and family, in the context of the subculture and the larger society. The League moved to change that setting by offering peer support, thus normalizing and positively valuing breast feeding.

An awareness of the importance of settings in determining

beliefs about birth should lead those who are interested in change to focus on setting rather than on the amorphous "attitudes." The natural-childbirth movement worked to change attitudes of both birthing women and birth attendants with remarkably little success as long as the setting remained unchanged. The current movement has made some change in setting, and it will be interesting to see what, if any, meaningful changes in practice ensue. For example, in response to the proliferation of home births and birthing centers, hospitals are starting to offer "birth rooms." Women demanding the use of the birth rooms, which combine labor and delivery in one room, doing away with the delivery-room setting, bring in physicians who are in no way committed to the underlying philosophy. These physicians, brought into the birth rooms by their patients, try to use the same philosophy, the same timetables, in essence the same management, in the new setting as they have always used. However, it is well within the range of possibility that the birth rooms, although relatively modest changes in one sense, will provide some of the radicalizing experiences for the physicians in the hospital that home births provided for the nurse-midwives I interviewed. For example, the new labor-delivery beds used in some of the birthing rooms have much lower stirrups, or none at all. As more women object to the routine episiotomy, physicians who do not know how to deliver a baby over an intact perineum are attempting it. In the old delivery-table position, that is, in the old medical setting, tears were all but inevitable, reinforcing the medical model of birth and of the necessity for the episiotomy. On the new bed, or the delivery chair, even an inexperienced doctor, one who has always relied on episiotomies, will see some successful births over intact perineums. This may lead the doctor to rethink the necessity of the episiotomy. It may even open the door for further reevaluation of the model.

That is the most optimistic conclusion I can draw from my research: that maybe, by accident, things will get better. Careful planning is bringing us regionalization of maternity care, the sorting and matching of women and hospitals in risk categories; more and fancier technology; and a well-thought-out attempt to coopt midwives and the home-birth movement. Maybe they will just put flowered sheets on the beds, hang a plant on the IV pole, and go on about business as usual. But maybe it will backfire. Maybe the attempt to coopt those seeking alternatives will end by creating change in the medical institutions, as doctors and nurses work in the new settings. Maybe obstetrics will go through some changes too.

A Personal Postscript

It's been seven years and a lot of research since Danny was born on a rocking chair in my bedroom. And now I've just had a second baby.

I entered this pregnancy knowing a lot more than I did last time. Choosing a midwife was a pleasure—I could actually *choose,* picking, among those competent women I now know, the one who would best meet my needs. I chose one who was doing home births on a regular basis, so that I would not be imposing on friendship. And I chose a midwife who was originally trained doing home births, someone who was genuinely at home, at home. She and Hesch and I, and sometimes Danny, spent hours together talking—about Danny's birth, about our feelings about this pregnancy, about our hopes and expectations for the coming birth.

Finding a backup obstetrician was not much easier this time than finding a doctor was last time. I could find no one at any of the hospitals near where I live. In case of a genuine emergency we would be at the mercy of emergency-room services. It's one argument against having a July baby, as mine both were—all the new interns and residents start in July.

We did finally find a physician not too far away. She had, during her residency, worked with my midwife, and was willing to have both my husband and my midwife come in with me if we had a problem. Hesch and I went to meet her once. That visit, with a warm, caring, and open-minded young woman, spoke worlds to me about the differences that still exist between the two models. For example, whereas my midwife took great care to discuss what I was eating and to make sure I was properly nourishing myself, the doctor simply cautioned me about weight gain (I'd put on twenty pounds at thirty-four weeks), and warned me about a "very large" baby. Afterward, feeling vaguely anxious, I realized that such a comment must create anxiety if a woman has any doubts at all about her ability to push a baby through—and what pregnant woman doesn't feel like the man who built a boat in his basement and can't figure out how to get it out?

But the highlight of the visit was when she tried to listen to the baby's heartbeat. She began by taking out an ultrasound device, which I rejected. I was not willing to expose the baby to ultrasound just to hear the heartbeat, when a stethoscope works just as well. The doctor was gone for a good ten minutes, presumably trying to find one. The stethoscope used to hear a fetal heart has an extra piece, which goes from the forehead of the listener to the mother's abdomen. She never put the headpiece on. She also had a hard time finding the heartbeat. It was a big baby, at thirty-four weeks, and kicking. She asked if my midwife had trouble, too, and I restrained myself from saying that the midwife was used to the "old-fashioned" equipment. What I realized was that if the newly trained people know how to find a heartbeat only with ultrasound, then they may be right about needing to use fetal monitors. In all, I was doubly reassured about the wisdom of birthing at home with a midwife, and, in the case of a problem, being able to bring my midwife into the hospital.

My due date was July 11, but since I'd been a week early last time, I rather expected I would be early again. My sister and brother, living over 200 miles away, in Boston, asked me to aim for the July Fourth weekend. I fully expected to do so. The night of July 2 I almost chickened out—said I didn't feel ready, we'd all have to wait. Then I got one of those bursts of energy some women use to "nest," clean the floors and such. Me—I worked on the references for this book.

I had some bloody show, a good sign of impending labor, the afternoon of the third. One of my sisters was in town for the month, and she vacuumed the bedroom, changed the linen and such, while I puttered around. I called Hesch and the midwife, and put them on "standby." Hesch came home from work, and by late afternoon family started arriving.

The contractions I was having were no stronger than ones I had had on and off for weeks, a normal part of late pregnancy. We timed them around seven in the evening, and found them to be a minute long, and five or so minutes apart, but so mild I could really ignore them. I expected this labor to be like the last one, even though I knew each one can be different. I was afraid of the long hours of endless contractions without pause, but until that started, I wouldn't feel that it was really happening.

Hesch and I tried napping, to conserve energy for later. He fell asleep, but I heard the family downstairs. Why should they have a party without me? I went down to the kitchen.

All evening and into the night the family arrived. I have three sisters and a brother; Hesch has a sister and two brothers. It adds up. We watched "M*A*S*H" reruns on television at 11:00, and then I lay down with Danny and read him to sleep. Again I thought of napping, but again was enticed back to the party.

It really was a party. We sat around joking, telling stories, being silly. I got uncomfortable after a while and started using basic breathing techniques to deal with the contractions. Every few minutes things would sort of hush, and all eyes went up to the clock over my head. I had reread all of *Spiritual Midwifery* to psych myself up for this, and tried to think of "rushes" rather than contractions. They are right. There is a lot else going on besides the pain in the belly. I felt my nose and teeth going numb, rather as from drinking too much wine. I also saw the colors in the kitchen getting brighter and stronger. I'm not into mystical things, or thinking about auras, but yes, labor is a kind of high if you flow with it, and a room full of loving people does produce energy, or gives you strength. There are parts to enjoy, side by side with the painful parts.

By 3:30 I really hurt with each contraction and sent up Hesch's brother to wake him. Having him near was important. I was in no rush to go upstairs. It felt to me that then I would begin laboring in earnest, and quite frankly I was not looking forward to it. I kept thinking that the contractions were going to get a lot longer, the breaks eventually disappearing as they had last time. So I stalled—didn't go up to my bedroom, didn't call the midwife, just tried to put it off a bit.

Around 4:30 I figured that if I was ever going to get upstairs under my own power, now was the time. We sent quilts downstairs for everyone to camp out on the floor on, and Hesch and I secluded ourselves in our bedroom. Away from everyone else, I no longer felt like bothering with the breathing exercises. I didn't have to be polite, or put on a show. Hesch just reminded me to take a deep breath as each contraction ended, and that was good. It helped me to let go of it, to relax.

We watched it getting light. I tried walking around, sitting, walking again. I was incredibly sleepy. I sat in my rocking chair and dozed but found myself arching my back out of the chair with contractions. That was not comfortable. So I lay on my side on the bed, and Hesch cuddled behind me, rubbing my back and just being there. We had brilliant bits of dialogue that night. I said, "I don't feel well," and Hesch asked me what was the matter. And I actually said, "I don't know." Clever stuff like that.

Around six we decided we probably should call the midwife soon—we'd just wait till seven, a decent hour to call. I was still having contractions of only a minute, with breaks of three or four minutes, sometimes more. And my waters had not even broken yet. Oh, I had lots of time to go yet, I could tell.

Then all hell broke loose in my body. I had a really rough contraction and felt a clicking sensation inside. I got scared, and Hesch ran to call the midwife. But I called him right back for the next contraction—I felt as if I was exploding. And I guess I did. My waters burst. Now, I figured, we really had better call the midwife. She listened to Hesch, heard me in the background trying not to push, and was on her way.

The contraction lasted in waves, but the pain was gone. I felt the head coming down. I called for my mother and sisters to come up, and for somebody to wake Danny. We'd carefully prepared him to be at the birth, and now he was sleeping right through it.

I blew and blew to avoid pushing till Danny came in, but I felt the head move into my hand, coming forward and then receding. Hesch checked that the cord was not around the baby's neck. The third time the head came on through. My sister, awed, whispered, "Oh, Barbara, it's perfect." Hesch supported the head, urged me to push when I was ready, and caught our baby. I sat right up and took it, held it upside down over my hand, and stroked its back. It made soft noises and was all pink. Danny came in. I realized I hadn't checked as to whether it was a boy or a girl and turned it over, no, turned *her* over. I had a baby girl, a daughter, Leah. My sisters cheered. I just held her and looked and looked, and hugged Hesch, and Danny, and anyone else who came near.

Then I started to feel as if I could really use a midwife. We had nothing ready. I ended up sitting on a big casserole waiting for the placenta, sending people scurrying around to —don't laugh—boil water for shoelaces and a scissor to cut the cord. The midwife arrived just then: Leah at 6:45, the midwife at 7:15. The placenta took a little while to show up, maybe an hour after the baby. The midwife cleaned us up and checked us out. All perfect. Perfect baby, no damage to me, all just perfect.

The whole family came in for a birthday party then, Danny carrying the chocolate cake we had put in the freezer, and blowing out the candle for Leah. A great party—the champagne, the laughter, the joy, the pure, perfect joy of it all.

Notes & Index

Notes

CHAPTER 1

1. René Dubos, *Man, Medicine, and Environment* (New York: New American Library, 1968), p. 76.

2. Ina May Gaskin and the Farm Midwives, *Spiritual Midwifery* (Summertown, Tenn.: Book Publishing Company, 1975), p. 323.

3. Ibid., p. 346.

4. Edward C. Hughes, ed., *Obstetric-Gynecologic Terminology* (Philadelphia: Davis, 1972).

5. Ivan Illich, *Medical Nemesis: The Expropriation of Health* (New York: Bantam Books, 1976).

6. Elliott A. Krause, *Power and Illness: The Political Sociology of Health and Medical Care* (New York: Elsevier, 1977), pp. 117–18.

7. Estelle Ramey, "Men's Cycles: They Have Them Too, You Know," *Ms.*, August 1972, pp. 8–14.

8. Milton Abramson and John R. Torghele, "Weight, Temperature Change, and Psychosomatic Symptomatology in Relation to the Menstrual Cycle," *American Journal of Obstetrics and Gynecology* 81 (1961): 223.

9. Sheldon Segal, "Contraceptive Research: A Male Chauvinist Plot?" *Family Planning Perspectives* 4, no. 3 (1972): 21–25.

10. Miriam Siegler and Humphry Osmond, *Models of Madness, Models of Medicine* (New York: Harper & Row, Colophon Books, 1976), p. x.

11. Janet Carlisle Bogdan, "Nineteenth-Century Childbirth: The Politics of Reality" (Paper presented to the Seventy-first Annual Meeting of the American Sociological Association, 1976).

12. Dorothy C. Wertz, "Childbirth as Controlled Workspace: From Midwifery to Obstetrics" (Paper presented to the Seventy-first Annual Meeting of the American Sociological Association, 1976).

13. Eliot Freidson, *Profession of Medicine: A Study of the Sociology of Applied Knowledge* (New York: Dodd, Mead, 1970), p. 168.

14. Frances Kobrin, "The American Midwife Controversy: A Crisis in Professionalization," *Bulletin of the History of Medicine* 40 (1966): 350–63.

15. Jean Donnison, *Midwives and Medical Men: A History of Inter-Professional Rivalries and Women's Rights* (New York: Schocken, 1977), p. 120.

16. Barbara Katz Rothman, "Home Birth: A Radio Documentary," WBAI–FM, New York, 1975. Distributed by the Pacifica Network.

17. Lewis E. Mehl et al., "Complications of Home Birth," *Birth and the Family Journal* 2 (1975–76): 123–31.

18. Statistics regarding the hospital deliveries were collected by chart review at two hospitals in Madison, Wisconsin, a largely upper-middle-class community with a median income of $16,000 per annum. Both were private community hospitals, both university affiliated, both performing approximately 2,000 deliveries yearly, one with a regional neonatal intensive-care unit and the other with a regional maternal intensive-care unit and a developing regional neonatal intensive-care unit. Both were staffed by neonatologists and university pediatric and obstetrical faculty and residents as well as private physicians. One hospital's obstetrical services were also staffed by university family-practice residents. The great majority of deliveries studied were of private patients with resident involvement at the discretion of the patient's physician. Virtually all women had childbirth classes, from both home and hospital groups. Lewis E. Mehl, "Research on Childbirth Alternatives: What Can It Tell Us About Hospital Practice?" in Lee Stewart and David Stewart, eds., *21st Century Obstetrics Now!* (Chapel Hill: NAPSAC, 1977).

19. Marcia Millman, *The Unkindest Cut: Life in the Backrooms of Medicine* (New York: Morrow, 1977), p. 245.

20. Albert D. Haverkamp "Evaluation of Continuous Fetal Heart Rate Monitoring in High Risk Pregnancy," *American Journal of Obstetrics and Gynecology* 125 (1976): 310–21.

CHAPTER 2

1. Vern Bullough, *The Development of Medicine as a Profession: The Contribution of the Medieval University to Modern Medicine* (New York: Karger, 1966), p. 102.

2. For a History of American midwifery, see Jane B. Donegan, *Women and Men Midwives: Medicine, Morality, and Misogyny in Early America* (Westport, Conn.: Greenwood Press, 1978). Also see, for British and European midwifery, Jean Donnison, *Midwives and Medical Men: A History of Inter-Professional Rivalries and Women's Rights* (New York: Schocken, 1977).

3. Ibid., p. 31.

4. Ibid., p. 33.

5. Ibid., p. 34.

6. Donegan, *Women and Men Midwives*.

7. Donnison, *Midwives and Medical Men*, p. 49.

8. Ibid., p. 185.

9. Frances Kobrin, "The American Midwife Controversy: A Crisis in Professionalization," *Bulletin of the History of Medicine* 40 (1966): 158.

10. Thomas Dawkes, cited in Donnison, *Midwives and Medical Men*, p. 24.

11. Datha Clapper Brack, "Displaced: The Midwife by the Male Physician," *Women and Health* 1 (1976): 18–24.

12. Barbara Ehrenreich and Deirdre English, *Witches, Midwives, and Nurses: A History of Women Healers* (Old Westbury, N.Y.: Feminist Press, 1973).

13. Brack, "Displaced."

14. Joseph B. DeLee, "The Prophylactic Forceps Operation," *American Journal of Obstetrics and Gynecology* 1 (1920): 32–44.

15. Doris Haire, *The Cultural Warping of Childbirth* (Seattle: International Childbirth Education Association, 1972).

16. Carol Brendsel, Gail Peterson, and Lewis Mehl, "Episiotomy: Facts, Fiction, Figures, and Alternatives," in Lee Stewart and David Stewart, ed., *Compulsory Hospitalization: Freedom of Choice in Childbirth?* (Marble Hill, Mo.: NAPSAC, 1979).

17. DeLee, "Prophylactic Forceps."

18. Alan Guttmacher, *Pregnancy and Birth: A Book for Expectant Parents* (New York: New American Library, 1962).

19. Nancy Stoller Shaw, *Forced Labor: Maternity Care in the United States* (New York: Pergamon, 1974).

20. Ibid., p. 75.

21. Ibid., p. 73, emphasis in original.

22. Ibid., p. 74.

23. Talcott Parsons, *Essays in Sociological Theory*, rev. ed. (New York: Free Press, 1964).

24. Brack, "Displaced."

25. Ibid.

26. Ruth Watson Lubic, "Myths about Nurse-Midwives," *American Journal of Nursing* 75 (1975): 268–69.

27. Louis M. Hellman and Francis B. O'Brien, "Nurse-Midwifery: An Experiment in Maternity Care," *American Journal of Obstetrics and Gynecology* 24 (1964): 343–48.

28. Suzanne Arms, *Immaculate Deception: A New Look at Women and Childbirth in America* (Boston: Houghton Mifflin, 1975).

29. Hellman and O'Brien, "Nurse-Midwifery."

30. "Return of the Midwife," *Newsweek*, March 31, 1969, p. 107.

31. Barbara Brennan and Joan Rattner Heilman, *The Complete Book of Midwifery* (New York: Dutton, 1977), p. 17.

32. Ibid., p. xi.

33. Arms, *Immaculate Deception*, p. 155.

34. Ibid., p. 157.

35. Margaret Myles, *Textbook for Midwives*, 8th ed. (New York: Churchill Livingstone, 1975), p. xxx.

36. Ibid., p. xxv.

37. Ehrenreich and English, *Witches, Midwives, and Nurses.*

38. Elliott Krause, *Power and Illness: The Political Sociology of Health and Medical Care* (New York: Elsevier, 1977), p. 53.

CHAPTER 3

1. Dorothy C. Wertz and Richard Wertz, *Lying-In: A History of Childbirth in America* (New York: Free Press, 1977), p. 195.

2. William R. Rosengren and Spencer DeVault, "The Sociology of Time and Space in an Obstetrical Hospital," in Eliot Freidson, ed., *The Hospital in Modern Society* (New York: Free Press, 1963), pp. 284–85.

3. Judith Lorber, "Good Patients and Problem Patients: Conformity and Deviance in a General Hospital," *Journal of Health and Social Behavior* 16 (1975): 220.

4. Grantly Dick-Read, *Childbirth without Fear: The Principles and Practice of Natural Childbirth* (New York: Harper, 1944), p. 2.

5. Ibid.

6. Ibid., pp. 5–6.

7. Ibid., p. 19.

8. Ibid., p. 7.

9. Ibid., p. 155.

10. Wertz and Wertz, *Lying-In*, p. 192.

11. Ibid., p. 193.

12. Deborah Tanzer and Jean Libman Block, *Why Natural Childbirth?: A Psychologist's Report on the Benefits to Mothers, Fathers, and Babies* (New York: Schocken, 1972). p. 30.

13. Elisabeth Bing and Marjorie Karmel, *A Practical Training Course for the Psychoprophylactic Method of Painless Childbirth* (New York: ASPO, 1961).

14. Pierre Vellay, "The Psycho-Prophylactic Method: Its Evolution, Present Situation, and Prospects," in International Childbirth Education Association, *Report of the Fourth Biennial Convention* (Milwaukee, 1966), pp. 45–55.

15. Bing and Karmel, *Practical Training Course*, p. 33.

16. Irwin Chabon, *Awake and Aware: Participation in Childbirth through Psychoprophylaxis.* (New York: Delacorte, 1966).

17. Lorber, "Good Patients and Problem Patients."

18. Boston Women's Health Book Collective, *Our Bodies, Ourselves* (New York: Simon and Schuster, 1973).

19. Norma Swenson, "Comparison between Prepared Childbirth Movement and the Home Birth Movement," *Proceedings for the 1975 Conference on Women and Health*, p. 42.

20. Ina May Gaskin and the Farm Midwives, *Spiritual Midwifery* (Summertown, Tenn.: Book Publishing Company, 1975).

21. Marjie Hathaway and Jay Hathaway, *Children at Birth* (Privately printed, 1976).

22. Marion Sousa, *Childbirth at Home* (Englewood Cliffs: Prentice-Hall, 1976).

23. Ibid., p. xxi.

24. Ibid., p. 8.

25. Robert A. Bradley, *Husband-Coached Childbirth* (New York: Harper & Row, 1975).

26. Karen E. Paige and Jeffrey M. Paige, "The Politics of Birth Practices: A Strategic Analysis," *American Sociological Review* 38 (1973): 664.

27. Judith Lorber, "Lysistrata Revisited: The Politics of Reproduction" (Paper presented to the New York Metropolitan Chapter of Sociologists for Women in Society, 1978).

28. E. T. Silva, "Participatory Birthing as Male Role Enrichment" (Unpublished paper, 1977).

29. Tanzer and Block, *Why Natural Childbirth?*

30. Frédérick Leboyer, *Birth without Violence* (New York: Knopf, 1975).

31. Charlotte Ward and Fred Ward, *The Home Birth Book* (Washington, D.C.: INSCAPE, 1976), p. 93.

32. Ibid., p. 107.

33. Marion Thompson, "Family Bonding: Why Families Should Be Together at Birth and Why We Chose Home Birth," in Lee Stewart and David Stewart, eds., *21st Century Obstetrics Now!* (Chapel Hill: NAPSAC, 1977).

34. Kaye Lowman, *The LLLove Story* (Franklin Park, Ill.: La Leche League International, 1977), p. 11.

35. C. Wright Mills, *The Sociological Imagination* (New York: Oxford University Press, 1959).

36. Benjamin Spock, *The Common Sense Book of Baby and Child Care* (New York: Duell, Sloan and Pearce, 1946), p. 2.

37. Ibid., p. 27.

38. Ibid., p. 30.

39. Ibid., p. 28.

40. Ibid., p. 29.

41. Beech Nut Company, *Happy Mealtimes for Babies* (1953), p. 7.

42. Susan Doering, "Coping with Childbirth: Its Effect on Maternal-Infant Bonding" (Paper presented to the American Foundation for Maternal and Child Health, 1977).

43. Judith Randal, "The Patient Woman," *Progressive*, December 1980, p. 18.

44. Lowman, *The LLLove Story*, p. 27.

45. Ibid., p. 28.

46. Elizabeth Nihell, quoted in Jean Donnison, *Midwives and Medical Men: A History of Inter-Professional Rivalries and Women's Rights* (New York: Schocken, 1977), p. 36.

47. Maryann Napoli, "The Women's Health Movement" (Paper presented to the New York Metropolitan Chapter of Sociologists for Women in Society, 1977).

CHAPTER 4

1. Melvin R. Cohen, "Female Infertility: Not Always a Dilemma," in *Clinician* (n.p.: Searle and Company, 1974), pp. 52–62.

2. *Gould Medical Dictionary*, 3rd ed. (New York: McGraw-Hill, 1972).

3. Gerald Leach, *The Biocrats* (New York: McGraw-Hill, 1970).

4. Sharon Strassfeld and Michael Strassfeld, *The Second Jewish Catalog* (Philadelphia: Jewish Publication Society of America, 1976).

5. Amitai Etzioni, *Genetic Fix* (New York: Harper & Row, Colophon Books, 1973).

6. Leach, *The Biocrats*.

7. Elizabeth Horman, *Relactation: A Guide to Breastfeeding the Adopted Baby* (privately published, 1971).

8. Etzioni, *Genetic Fix*.

9. Judith Lorber, "Lysistrata Revisited: The Politics of Reproduction" (Paper presented to the New York Metropolitan Chapter of Sociologists for Women in Society, 1978).

10. Ibid.

11. Leach, *The Biocrats*.

12. CIBA Foundation Symposium, *Law and Ethics of A.I.D. and Embryo Transfer* (New York and Amsterdam: Elsevier, 1973).

13. "Symposium: Infertility," *Contemporary Ob/Gyn* 4 (1974): 111–48.

14. Jay Gold, "Therapy of Infertility: Male and Female," in Jay Gold, ed., *Gynecological Endocrinology* (New York: Harper & Row, 1975), p. 545.

15. Sheldon Segal, "Contraceptive Research: A Male Chauvinist Plot?" *Family Planning Perspectives* 4, no. 3 (1972): 21–25.

CHAPTER 5

1. Donald McKay, "Alternative Points of View," in Duncan E. Reid and C. D. Christian, eds., *Controversy in Obstetrics and Gynecology*, vol. 2 (Philadelphia: Saunders, 1974).

2. Jack A. Pritchard and Paul C. McDonald, eds., *Williams Obstetrics*, 16th ed. (New York: Appleton-Century-Crofts, 1980), p. 303.

3. Edward C. Hughes, ed., *Obstetric-Gynecologic Terminology* (Philadelphia: Davis, 1972).

4. Virginia Apgar and Joan Beck, *Is My Baby All Right?* (New York: Trident, 1973).

5. Louis M. Hellman and Jack A. Pritchard, eds., *Williams Obstetrics,* 14th ed. (New York: Appleton-Century-Crofts, 1971), p. 1069.

6. Ibid., p. 344.

7. Daniel H. Winship, "Gastrointestinal Diseases," in Gerald N. Burrow and Thomas F. Ferris, eds., *Medical Complications during Pregnancy* (Philadelphia: Saunders, 1975).

8. Edward J. Quilligan, "Prenatal Care," in Seymour L. Romney et al., eds. *Gynecology and Obstetrics: The Health Care of Women* (New York: McGraw-Hill, 1975).

9. Pritchard and McDonald, eds., *Williams Obstetrics,* p. 324.

10. B. Schenkel and H. Vorherr, "Non-Prescription Drugs during Pregnancy: Potential Teratogenic and Toxic Effects upon Embryo and Fetus," *Journal of Reproductive Medicine* 12 (1974): 27–45.

11. Lester Dessez Hazell, *Commonsense Childbirth* (New York: Berkley, 1976).

12. Adelle Davis, *Let's Have Healthy Children* (New York: New American Library, 1972).

13. Ina May Gaskin and the Farm Midwives, *Spiritual Midwifery* (Summertown, Tenn.: Book Publishing Company, 1975), p. 291.

14. Frank E. Hytten and Tom Lind, *Diagnostic Indices in Pregnancy* (Summit, N.J.: CIBA-GEIGY, 1973).

15. Ibid.

16. National Research Council, Committee on Maternal Nutrition, *Maternal Nutrition and the Course of Pregnancy* (Washington: National Academy of Sciences, 1970).

17. Ibid.

18. P. F. Giles et al., "The Effect of Prescribing Folic Acid during Pregnancy on Birth Weight and the Duration of Pregnancy," *Medical Journal of Australia* 2 (1971): 17–21.

19. For a more complete explanation, see Gail Sforza Brewer, *What Every Pregnant Woman Should Know: The Truth about Diet and Drugs in Pregnancy* (New York: Random House, 1977).

20. For example, see Grant et al., "The Metabolic Clearance Rate of Dehydroisoandrosterone Sulfate," *American Journal of Obstetrics and Gynecology* 123 (1975): 159–63.

21. Milton Terris and E. M. Gold, "Epidemiological Study of Prematurity," *American Journal of Obstetrics and Gynecology* 103 (1969): 371–79; and Lawrence Berger and Mervyn Susser, "Low Birth Weight and Prenatal Nutrition," *Pediatrics* (1973): 948–66.

22. E. A. McKinney, "A Study of Selected Psycho-Social and Physical Factors and Their Relationship to Weight and/or Gestational Age at Birth" (Ph.D. Diss., University of Pittsburgh, 1974).

23. Kenneth R. Niswander and Myron Gordon, *The Women and Their Pregnancies* (Philadelphia: Saunders, 1972).

24. National Research Council, *Maternal Nutrition.*

25. Alan Guttmacher, *Pregnancy and Birth* (New York: New American Library, 1962), p. 91.

26. Judith Singer et al., "Relationship of Weight Gain during Pregnancy to Birth Weight and Infant Growth and Development in the First Year of Life," *Obstetrics and Gynecology* 31 (1968): 417.

27. Harry Stein, "Maternal Protein Deprivation and Small for Gestational Age Babies," *Archives of Diseases of Childhood* 50 (1975): 146.

28. National Research Council, *Maternal Nutrition.*

29. Walter M. Hern, "Is Pregnancy Really Normal?" *Family Planning Perspectives* 3, no. 1 (1971): 5–10.

30. Guttmacher, *Pregnancy and Birth,* p. 74.

31. Milton Terris and Marvin Glasser, "A Life Table Analysis of the Relation of Prenatal Care to Prematurity," *American Journal of Public Health* 64 (1974): 869–75.

32. Nancy Mills, "The Lay Midwife," in David Stewart and Lee Stewart, eds., *Safe Alternatives in Childbirth* (Chapel Hill: NAPSAC, 1976), p. 131.

33. David Stewart and Lee Stewart, eds., *21st Century Obstetrics Now!* (Chapel Hill: NAPSAC, 1977).

34. Ibid.

CHAPTER 6

1. Marcia Millman, *The Unkindest Cut: Life in the Backrooms of Medicine* (New York: Morrow, 1977).

2. Joseph B. DeLee, "The Prophylactic Forceps Operation," *American Journal of Obstetrics and Gynecology* 1 (1920): 32.

3. Nancy Stoller Shaw, *Forced Labor: Maternity Care in the United States* (New York: Pergamon, 1974), p. 84.

4. Julius Roth, *Timetables: Structuring the Passage of Time in Hospital Treatment and Other Careers* (Indianapolis: Bobbs-Merrill, 1963).

5. Erving Goffman, *Asylums: Essays on the Social Situation of Mental Patients and Other Inmates* (Garden City, N.Y.: Doubleday, 1961).

6. Judith Lorber, "Deviance as Performance: The Case of Illness," *Social Problems* 14 (1967): 302–10.

7. Shaw, *Forced Labor*, p. 62.

8. Ibid., p. 64.

9. R. Clay Burchell, "Predelivery Removal of Pubic Hair," *Obstetrics and Gynecology* 24 (1964): 272–73.

10. George Annas, *The Rights of Hospital Patients: The Basic ACLU Guide to a Hospital Patient's Rights* (New York: Discus, 1975), p. 147.

11. Ibid., p. 80.

12. Margaret Myles, *Textbook for Midwives*, 8th ed. (New York: Churchill Livingstone, 1975).

13. Thomas Szasz and M. H. Hollender, "A Contribution to the Philosophy of Medicine: The Basic Models of the Doctor-Patient Relationship," *AMA Archives of Internal Medicine* 97 (1956): 585.

14. Elisabeth Bing and Marjorie Karmel, *A Practical Training Course for the Psychoprophylactic Method of Childbirth* (New York: ASPO, 1961), p. 33.

15. "The Story of Eric" (ASPO films, 1973).

16. Nancy Mills, "The Lay Midwife," in David Stewart and Lee Stewart, eds., *Safe Alternatives in Childbirth* (Chapel Hill: NAPSAC, 1976), p. 134.

17. Ibid.

18. Freemont Women's Clinic, "A Working Lay-Midwife Home Birth Program in Seattle Washington: A Collective Approach," in David Stewart and Lee Stewart, eds., *21st Century Obstetrics Now!* (Chapel Hill: NAPSAC, 1977), p. 514.

19. Thya Mertz, "A Working Lay Midwife Home Birth Center in Madison, Wisconsin," in ibid., p. 545.

20. Shaw, *Forced Labor*, p. 87.

CHAPTER 7

1. See, for example, Hugh Josephs, "Iron Absorption in Human Physiology," *Blood* 13 (1958): 1–54; Citizen's Committee on Infant Nutrition, *White*

Paper on Infant Feeding Practices (Washington, D.C.: Center for Science in the Public Interest, 1974); S. G. Srikantia et al., "Anemia and Immune Response," *Lancet*, June 19, 1976, pp. 1307–9; Edmund Eastham, "The Advantages of Breastfeeding," *Journal of Continuing Education in Family Medicine* (1977): 17–26.

2. Adelle Davis, *Let's Have Healthy Children* (New York: New American Library, 1972).

3. Citizen's Committee on Infant Nutrition, *Infant Feeding Practices.*

4. Raymond Reiser and Zvi Sidelman, "Control of Serum Cholesterol Homeostasis by Cholesterol in the Milk of the Suckling Rat," *Journal of Nutrition* 102 (1972): 1009.

5. Jacqueline Verrett and Jean Carper, *Eating May Be Hazardous to Your Health* (Garden City, N.Y.: Anchor Books, 1975), pp. 36, 63.

6. A. G. Ironside et al., "A Survey of Infantile Gastroenteritis," *British Medical Journal* 2 (1970): 20; M. Behar, "The Role of Feeding and Nutrition in the Pathogeny and Prevention of Diarrheic Processes," *Bulletin of the Pan American Health Organization* 9 (1975): 1–9.

7. John W. Gerrard, "Breastfeeding: Second Thoughts," *Pediatrics* 54 (1974): 757–64.

8. L. A. Hanson and J. Winberg, "Breast Milk and Defense against Infection in the Newborn," *Archives of the Diseases of Childhood* 47 (1972): 945; Gerrard, "Breastfeeding," p. 757; Paul Gyorgy, "Biochemical Aspects of Breastmilk," *American Journal of Clinical Nutrition* 24 (1971): 970–75; J. D. Baum, "Nutritional Value of Human Milk," *Obstetrics and Gynecology* 37 (1971): 126–30; Jean F. Kenny et al., "Bacterial and Viral Coproantibodies in Breastfed Babies," *Pediatrics* 39 (1967): 201–11; M. Robinson, "Infant Morbidity and Mortality: A Study of 3266 Infants," *Lancet* 260 (1960): 788.

9. M. Gunther, "The Neonate's Immunity Gap: Breastfeeding and Cot Death," *Lancet*, February 22, 1975, pp. 441–42; idem, "Preventing Sudden Infant Death," *Science News* 112 (1977): 167.

10. Josephs, "Iron Absorption"; Eastham, "Advantages of Breastfeeding."

11. E. E. Eid, "Follow-up Study of Physical Growth of Children Who Had Excessive Weight Gain in the First Six Months of Life," *British Medical Journal* 1 (1970): 74.

12. Citizen's Committee on Infant Nutrition, *Infant Feeding Practices.*

13. Barbara Hall, "Changing Composition of Human Milk and the Early Development of Appetite Control," *Lancet*, April 5, 1975, pp. 779–81.

14. Derrick B. Jelliffe and E. F. Patrice Jelliffe, "Introduction" to the sympo-

sium "The Uniqueness of Human Milk," *American Journal of Clinical Nutrition* 24 (1971): 968–69.

15. See above, note 8.

16. For more information on the sale of infant formula in Third World countries, write INFACT, Minneapolis, MN.

17. G. Hemming et al., "Nosocomial Infection in a Newborn Intensive Care Unit," *New England Journal of Medicine* 294 (1976): 1310–16.

18. Louis M. Hellman and Jack A. Pritchard, eds., *Williams Obstetrics*, 14th ed. (New York: Appleton-Century-Crofts, 1971).

19. Helmuth Vorherr, *The Breast: Morphology, Physiology, and Lactation.* (New York: Academic Press, 1974).

20. V. R. Tindall, "Factors Influencing Puerperal Thromboembolism," *Journal of Obstetrics and Gynecology of the British Commonwealth* 75 (1968): 1324–27; A. C. Turnbull, "Puerperal Thromboembolism and the Suppression of Lactation," ibid., pp. 1321–23.

21. Tom P. Barden, "Perinatal Care," in Seymour L. Romney et al., eds., *Gynecology and Obstetrics: The Health Care of Women* (New York: McGraw-Hill, 1975).

22. Vorherr, *Breast.*

23. Barden, "Perinatal Care."

24. Arnold Gesell, Frances Ilg, and Louise Ames, *Infant and Child in the Culture of Today: The Guidance of Development in Home and Nursery School* (New York and London: Harper, 1943).

25. Robin Weir and William Feldman, "A Study of Infant Feeding Practices," *Birth and the Family Journal* 2 (1975): 63–64.

26. Richard M. Applebaum, "The Obstetrician's Approach to the Breasts and Breastfeeding," *Journal of Reproductive Medicine* 14 (1975): 98–116.

27. Alan Guttmacher, *Pregnancy and Birth.* (New York: New American Library, 1962), p. 251.

28. Ibid.

29. Kaye Lowman, *The LLLove Story* (Franklin Park, Ill.: La Leche League International, 1977).

30. Ross Laboratories, *Breastfeeding Your Baby* (c. 1974).

CHAPTER 8

1. Marshall Klaus et al., "Maternal Attachment—Importance of the First Postpartum Days," *New England Journal of Medicine* 286 (1972): 460–63.

2. N. M. Ringler et al., "Mother-to-Child Speech at Two Years—Effects of Early Postnatal Contact," *Journal of Pediatrics* 86 (1975): 141–44.

3. Alice Rossi, "Biosocial Perspectives on Parenting," *Daedalus* 106 (spring 1977): 1–32.

4. Klaus et al., "Maternal Attachment."

5. Martin Greenberg and Norman Morris, "Engrossment: The Newborn's Impact upon the Father," *American Journal of Orthopsychiatry* 44 (1974): 520–31.

6. Ibid., p. 525.

7. Gail H. Peterson, Lewis E. Mehl, and P. Herbert Leiderman, "Some Determinants of Parental Attachment" (Paper presented to the Seventy-second Annual Meeting of the American Sociological Association, 1977).

8. Ibid.

9. Harry F. Harlow, "Love in Infant Monkeys," in William T. Greenough, ed., *The Nature and Nurture of Behavior: Readings from Scientific American* (San Francisco: Freeman, 1973).

10. Betty Friedan, *The Feminine Mystique* (New York: Dell, 1963).

CHAPTER 9

1. Midwives' names and certain superficial characteristics have been changed to protect confidentiality.

2. Dorothy C. Wertz and Richard Wertz, *Lying-In: A History of Childbirth in America* (New York: Free Press, 1977), p. 47.

3. Nancy Mills, "The Lay Midwife," in David Stewart and Lee Stewart, eds., *Safe Alternatives in Childbirth* (Chapel Hill: NAPSAC, 1976), p. 137.

CHAPTER 10

1. The experiment by Bruner and Postman is discussed in Thomas S. Kuhn, *The Structure of Scientific Revolutions,* 2nd ed. (Chicago: University of Chicago Press, 1970).

2. See, for example, Arthur Colman and Libby Colman, *Pregnancy: The Psychological Experience* (New York: Herder and Herder, 1971).

3. For a review of this literature, see Robert L. McDonald, "The Role

of Emotional Factors in Obstetric Complications," in Judith Bardwick, ed. *Readings on the Psychology of Women* (New York: Harper & Row, 1972).

4. Jean Lennane and John Lennane, "Alleged Psychogenic Disorders in Women: A Possible Manifestation of Sexual Prejudice," *New England Journal of Medicine* 288 (1973): 289–92.

5. McDonald, "Emotional Factors."

6. Elaine R. Grim, "Psychological Investigation of Habitual Abortion," in Judith Bardwick, ed., *Readings on the Psychology of Women.*

7. Ina May Gaskin and the Farm Midwives, *Spiritual Midwifery* (Summertown, Tenn.: Book Publishing Company, 1975).

8. Doris Haire, *The Cultural Warping of Childbirth* (Seattle: International Childbirth Education Association, 1972).

9. See Rita Seiden Miller, "The Social Construction and Reconstruction of Physiological Events: Acquiring the Pregnant Identity," in Denzin, ed. *Studies in Symbolic Interaction* (JAI Press, 1977).

10. Ronald R. Rindfuss, "Convenience and the Occurrence of Births: Induction of Labor in the United States and Canada" (Paper presented to the Seventy-second Annual Meeting of the American Sociological Association, 1977).

11. For an overview of Friedman's work, see Emanuel Friedman, "Graphic Analysis of Labor," *Bulletin of the American College of Nurse-Midwifery* (1959): 94–105.

12. Ibid., p. 97.

13. Louis M. Hellman and Jack A. Pritchard, eds., *Williams Obstetrics,* 14th ed. (New York: Appleton-Century-Crofts, 1971).

14. Lewis Mehl, "Research on Childbirth Alternatives: What Can It Tell Us about Hospital Practice?" in David Stewart and Lee Stewart, eds., *21st Century Obstetrics Now!* (Chapel Hill: NAPSAC, 1977).

15. Mehl, "Childbirth Alternatives"; Hellman and Pritchard, eds., *Williams Obstetrics;* and Jack A. Pritchard and Paul C. McDonald, eds., *Williams Obstetrics,* 16th ed. (New York: Appleton-Century-Crofts, 1980).

16. Ibid., p. 425.

17. Pritchard and McDonald, eds., *Williams Obstetrics.*

18. Ibid., p. 1044.

19. William R. Rosengren and Spencer DeVault, "The Sociology of Time and Space in an Obstetrical Hospital," in Eliot Freidson, ed., *The Hospital in Modern Society* (New York: Free Press, 1963).

20. Ibid., p. 282.
21. Ibid.

EPILOGUE

1. Lester Hazell, *Birth Goes Home* (Seattle: Catalyst Publishing, 1974

Index

Index

Index

Index

Index

Index

Index

Index

Index